MICHAEL G. FINLAYSON

Historians, Puritanism, and the English Revolution: the Religious Factor in English Politics before and after the Interregnum

UNIVERSITY OF TORONTO PRESS

Toronto Buffalo London

© University of Toronto Press 1983
Toronto Buffalo London
Printed in Canada
ISBN 0-8020-5600-8
Reprinted in paperback 1985

CANADIAN CATALOGUING IN PUBLICATION DATA

Finlayson, Michael George, 1938-
Historians, Puritanism and the English Revolution
Includes bibliographical references and index.
ISBN 0-8020-5600-8

1. Great Britain – History – Charles I, 1625-1649.
2. Great Britain – History – Restoration, 1660-1688.
3. Great Britain – History – Puritan Revolution,
1642-1660 – Historiography. I. Title.
DA445.F56   942.06   C83-098265-5

To Ann, for whom ...

Contents

Preface

Ever since I was an undergraduate student at the University of Melbourne my academic interests have centred on two subjects – the 'Puritan Revolution' and the character of the historian's discipline. This book, whose gestation period has been longer than I care to contemplate, represents my attempt to bring these subjects into focus. The reader should be aware from the outset that what follows is a conventional work in neither history nor historiography. It is not a traditional historical monograph because a major part of its concern is to trace the development of two concepts which have, for the past hundred years or so, been fundamental to historians of seventeenth-century England – 'Puritanism' and 'revolution.' In suggesting that historical knowledge, like scientific knowledge, is dependent upon paradigms which are themselves subject to historical explanation, the influence of Thomas Kuhn will be apparent even to the casual reader. Yet the book is not a study in historiography either, because in the end I try to deal with 'what actually happened' and to suggest a way of handling the problem of religious factors in England's political history between 1620 and 1690 that leaves fewer loose ends than presently exist.

In the course of thinking about, and then writing the book I have accumulated debts which, if fully enumerated, would exhaust the publisher's patience. I can simply acknowledge my outstanding obligations and rely on the charity of my minor creditors. The influence of the Melbourne School of History where I studied, and, for a while, taught, is clear to anyone familiar with it. There I was encouraged both to write and to reflect on what I was writing. To the University of Toronto, the home of A.S.P. Woodhouse, and to my colleagues in the Department of History, I also owe an enormous debt, for support, stimulation, and time.

Other institutions which have received me as a visitor have also helped. I am grateful to the program committee of the William Andrews Clark Memorial

Library at the University of California, Los Angeles, where I spent a fruitful summer as Clark Library post-doctoral Fellow under the genial direction of Stephen Baxter. Members of the two seventeenth-century English seminars at the Institute of Historical Research, London, heard portions of chapters and made stimulating suggestions as did Dr William Lamont's seminar at the University of Sussex. I am grateful also to Dr Lotte Mulligan for her hospitality while I was a visiting Fellow at La Trobe University in Melbourne. I would also like to thank the Master and Fellows of Corpus Christi College, Cambridge, for electing me a Visiting Scholar in 1982, when the book was finally completed. Participation in Dr Morrill's seminar in Cambridge also helped me resolve a few last-minute problems. A leave fellowship from the Canada Council and other research grants from the Social Sciences and Humanities Research Council and from the University of Toronto were indispensable. Finally, this book has been published with the help of a grant from the Social Science Federation of Canada, using funds provided by the Social Sciences and Humanities Research Council of Canada, and a grant from the Andrew W. Mellon Foundation to the University of Toronto Press.

Then there are the people to whom I owe so much: my parents, one of whom did not live quite long enough to see this concrete result of all his sacrifices, provided constant support, as did others in my widely dispersed, yet closely knit family; my friend, John Beattie, and my former supervisor, Bill Nelson, both read parts of the manuscript and made helpful comments, though they should not be blamed for any of it; Chris McKenzie typed most of the book from an almost indecipherable manuscript; Carol Robb typed the index when my patience was at a low ebb; Tom and Jenny McDonnell provided crucial support, comparable to a research grant, especially in their Highgate living room; the editorial staff at the University of Toronto Press, especially Rosemary Shipton, have been generous and highly efficient. My final and greatest debt, however, is to Ann, to whom the book is dedicated.

Throughout this book quotations have been modernized for both spelling and punctuation. Dates are old style, with the exception of the calendar year which is taken to begin on 1 January.

HISTORIANS, PURITANISM, AND

THE ENGLISH REVOLUTION

1

Introduction

Does the world really need another book about the Puritans? This is a question that might well be asked before readers embark on the present study. In the last forty or fifty years so many titles on this general subject have poured from the presses in both England and America – as well as elsewhere – that one may well ask what more need be said about Puritans and about Puritanism. And it cannot be denied that among them have been works of scholarship that will long be models of the historian's craft. William Haller, Marshall Knappen, Patrick Collinson, Christopher Hill, Paul Seaver, George Yule, and J. Sears McGee, to name only a few, have all written about Puritan ideas, attitudes, and forms of organization in ways that have greatly added both to our stock of knowledge and to our understanding of this complex phenomenon.[1]

What follows is, however, another book that deals with Puritanism, one which stems from an acute sense of dissatisfaction with the existing state of scholarship on the subject. For despite the profusion of learned works there is a good deal of confusion, a disturbingly large number of unanswered questions, and even a few that are not asked.

The first of these problems relates to the connection between 'Puritans' and 'Puritanism,' and to the extremely elusive character of the latter term. There is no doubt that the term 'Puritan' was used frequently, albeit variously, by contemporaries between 1560 and 1660 to refer to individuals, often but not always clergymen, who were known to be critics of the church.[2] It is possible to compile a list of such persons that begins with some of the returned Marian exiles in the 1560s, such as Thomas Sampson, and includes Thomas Cartwright, members of the Dedham classis, scholar-preachers such as William Perkins and Laurence Chaderton, as well as some members of Elizabethan Parliaments and a few Elizabethan courtiers, such as the Earl of Leicester. In the seventeenth century the list includes Jacobean preachers such as John Preston and Richard

Sibbes, a few of their patrons such as Fulke Greville or Lord Saye and Sele, and an extraordinarily diverse assortment from the Caroline period including Sir Henry Vane, Jr, Hugh Peter, Stephen Marshall, Richard Baxter, John Pym, Oliver Cromwell, John Milton, and Praise-God Barebone. In compiling such a list, we encounter some difficulties when we come to distinguish between those whom contemporaries labelled 'Puritan' and those so labelled by subsequent historians. If we simply accept the contemporary usage of 'Puritan' we would end up with a list so long and so diverse that modern scholars would find it less than useful, for 'Puritan' was, as is well known, a term of opprobrium with social, political, religious, and theological implications. Rather like 'communist' in our own times, 'Puritan' served many purposes and was used with remarkable absence of precision.[3]

Clearly there are problems in our use of the term 'Puritan.' First we must distinguish between those whom contemporaries labelled 'Puritan' and those whom later historians have so designated, for the two groups are far from identical. This problem is aggravated by the fact that to most contemporaries 'Puritan' was derisory and was rarely a label that was voluntarily accepted by individuals. Second, even when we discard the blatantly political usages of 'Puritan' and focus upon those individuals between 1560 and 1660 who seem to have had a particular and demonstrable concern for religious reform, the range is extreme. Was there really a core of doctrinal belief to which the Vestiarians, John Field, Sir Thomas Barrington, and Denzil Holles all subscribed, and which distinguished that group from 'Anglicans' such as Richard Hooker, William Laud, or Edward Hyde? If there was, then how do we identify it? If there was not, then historians are obliged to exercise caution in their general treatment of the Puritans over a century and, it goes without saying, in their consideration of Puritanism. It is quite valid to refer to Puritans throughout this period of English history; contemporary usage of the term clearly legitimizes our use of it. Yet it also seems obvious that, when we refer to Puritans over three generations, we must recognize that, notwithstanding the fact that the label was constant, its connotations may not have been. A Puritan in the 1570s was a far cry from one eighty years later.

If the problems associated with the word 'Puritan' seem great, however, they fade into insignificance when compared with those that follow our use of the term 'Puritanism.'[4] While there were many contemporary references to Puritanism, it is only in the last 100 years or so that the term has been employed chiefly as a source of explanation. Occasionally, contemporaries referred to Puritanism as a strictly theological and ecclesiological concept, but it was not until the nineteenth-century popularization of a panoply of 'isms' that Puritanism came into its own. Only then, for instance, did Puritanism come to be viewed as an autonomous force in pre-Civil War England, permeating large parts of society and capable of carrying the burden of explanation of important aspects of the course of English history. Even before S.R. Gardiner converted the study of seventeenth-century English history into an academic discipline, historians paid considerable attention to the way religious belief impinged upon the political developments which culminated in the English Civil War, though they focused their narrative not on the ubiquitous Puritanism, a word rarely used in historical narratives, but upon the individual or collective action of the Puritans. Since Gardiner first coined the expression 'Puritan Revolution,' however, scholars have increasingly resorted to the abstraction 'Puritanism' both to characterize and to explain. For example, A.S.P. Woodhouse saw 'Puritanism' as the overriding explanation for the emergence of liberal aspirations in the 1640s. From his point of view, both John Milton and the Levellers could be explained by their 'Puritanism.' From a very different stance, Michael Walzer shares Woodhouse's reliance upon 'Puritanism' as a means of explanation. For Walzer, it was 'Puritanism' which informed the distinctively modern, politically radical, approach to politics that brought about the 'Revolution of the Saints' and, incidentally, which provided a paradigm for revolutionary politics.[5] Moreover, as Walzer attests, the effects of 'Puritanism' have not been confined solely to English politics in the 1640s and 1650s. 'Puritanism' has been called upon to explain not only aspects of England's Civil War but also 'capitalism,' 'modernization,' and 'democracy,' to name only three modern phenomena.[6]

Lawrence Stone's usage of 'Puritanism' typifies that of dozens of historians who have written over the past hundred years and a brief analysis will illustrate why it is so awkward. In his somewhat schematic survey of the pre-Civil War period Stone referred to Puritanism as the 'most far-reaching' of the 'intellectual currents' in the early seventeenth century that were necessary to fuel the 'true revolution' of the 1640s. He went on to define Puritanism as 'a generalized conviction of the need for independent judgment based on conscience and bible reading,' and to refer to the 'spread of Puritanism among the lower middle class' as related to 'the unusual size of England's prime industrial activity.'[7]

What Stone has done in this example is similar to the approach of many other historians. He has inferred from the activities of many 'Puritans' over a number of years the existence of the abstraction 'Puritanism.' Having created the concept, he has proceeded to analyse it as if it possessed the properties of a phenomenon in the natural world. In this particular instance Stone has bestowed on Puritanism the qualities of a current of water that is capable both of flowing and being harnessed to generate energy, and also of spreading through an identifiable sector of society.

As a rhetorical device, the reification of the abstraction 'Puritanism' and the subsequent treatment of the concept as though it were a real thing (its metaphorical treatment) represent part of the conventional historians' stock-in-trade. 'Puritanism' may justly be regarded as a shorthand way of referring to the various activities of large numbers of Puritans; to analyse it as if it were an organism or some other phenomenon in the natural world may be defended as a particularly illuminating way of portraying the activities of individual Puritans or events. Metaphor is, after all, intrinsic to language and the metaphorical treatment of Puritanism may be viewed simply as a particularly persuasive kind of metaphor. Metaphors can be dangerously deceptive, however.[8] And the more persuasive the metaphor, the more inclined we are to overlook the nature of the literary device. The more we write about the strands of Puritanism, its roots and branches, or its balloon-like rise, the more likely we are to forget that what is in fact being analyzed are the discrete acts of thousands of individual Puritans. The notion of Puritanism as a tide washing over the East Anglian countryside, for example, is compelling, but, simultaneously, misleading.[9]

We know, for instance, that there were many different kinds of Puritans holding radically different beliefs and coming from widely different social strata between 1560 and 1660. To attribute to them all a common doctrinal core of any substance is a risky simplification of a complex past.[10] To create the thing, then, is bad enough. To bestow upon this entity, 'Puritanism,' an independent existence with the distinguishing characteristics of biological or other natural phenomena is yet more misleading. Such fabrication does not illuminate the past but obscures it.

The difficulty can be illustrated by reference to the conventional way in which historians have treated the political origins of the English Civil War since the late nineteenth century. Almost invariably they have insisted that the political history of England between 1560 and 1660 may not be understood without reference to Puritanism. In assigning to Puritanism such a profoundly important role, they have suggested that opposition to the court in the 1620s and 1630s, and to the king in the 1640s, was essentially Puritan. Yet when we look closely at the laymen who were most heavily engaged in resisting first the court, and later the king, 'Puritan' does not seem to characterize the beliefs of more than a few of them. When Mary Keeler came to write short biographies of every member of the Long Parliament between 1640 and 1642 she was able to refer to the 'Puritanism' of the pro-Parliamentarian group, yet she was able to identify only a handful as Puritans.[11] So, too, with David Underdown. Like Keeler, he regards 'Puritanism' as an essential part of his explanation of events in the 1640s, yet, for want of evidence, he can say nothing about the religious beliefs of almost half the 471 members in 1648. In addition, there were another 178 members whom he labelled as 'Presbyterian,' which, two months before the execution of the king, appears to have meant little more than a commitment to a national church. He seems, then, to have been describing more their political than their theological or religious views. Thus, while referring freely to the 'Puritanism' of the parliamentarians in the 1640s, Underdown was in fact able to provide specific information concerning the religious persuasion of only a tiny minority.[12]

If 'Puritanism' is conceived as a grand majestic force flowing through a century of England's history, it seems an appropriately weighty, albeit partial, explanation for the 'revolution' of the 1640s. However, when one tries to come closer to details, to see just where all of the Puritans are in 1640, the content of 'Puritanism' evaporates. It sounds persuasive to talk about the 'Puritanism' of parliamentarians between 1620 and 1642 and to suggest that this was the most important intellectual current informing their political position. When one looks at the individuals closely, however, to see in what sense they might be described as 'Puritan,' the concept does not seem as helpful.

There is another problem raised by the ubiquity of 'Puritanism' in most historians' explanations of the Civil War. If 'Puritanism' is so very important to our understanding of English political society between 1560 and 1660, why then is it not also important after 1660? What happens to 'Puritanism?' It is an obvious feature of post-Civil War historiography that 'Puritanism' is scarcely mentioned. Whereas in almost every explanation of political events before 1642, 'Puritanism' is an indispensable factor, after 1660 it is trivial. Nor is this merely because 'Puritanism' becomes 'Dissent.' Much more important than the change in nomenclature is the profoundly different way in which Restoration historians perceive religious phenomena impinging upon secular politics. Before around 1650, it is generally agreed, one cannot hope to understand political developments without reference to the all-pervasive influence of Puritanism. Yet historians who deal with this same society a mere decade later rarely feel obliged to give the religious factor more than passing attention.

It is possible that the reason why historians of Restoration England pay relatively little attention to 'Puritanism' is that the phenomenon had declined in importance. If true, the process by which this decline occurred requires explanation. If Puritanism was indeed such a potent force in English society in the first half of the seventeenth century and was of minor importance in the second half, then how did this happen? What precisely was the character of this process of deconversion that thousands of gentry families must have experienced between the 1650s and the 1660s? It is the obverse of this problem – the restoration of 'Anglicanism' rather than the collapse of Puritanism – that was disturbing John S. Morrill when he wrote recently of the 'puzzle that if Anglicanism collapsed so utterly in the 1640s and 1650s, how was it that it emerged so quickly, confidently and joyfully in most parishes in 1660-2?'[13]

The question of deconversion is raised not with a view to suggesting that it might be answered but to show that it is really rather absurd. There was no dramatic process of secularization within the ranks of political society in the period immediately before and after May 1660. We are left, then, with only two alternatives. Either Puritanism was much more important to Restoration Englishmen than historians are inclined to suggest, or it was less important to the generation of English gentry which constituted political society in the years leading up to civil war than is generally thought.

A principal purpose of this study is to suggest that Puritanism was of less importance to the most influential members of political society before 1641 than historians have generally believed. Furthermore, it goes on to posit another way of handling the problem of religion in seventeenth-century English politics that is not so dependent upon the elusive, and ultimately indefinable, abstraction 'Puritanism.'

It is worthwhile at this point to emphasize that although the study moves freely through the political history of England before and after the Civil War and deals with broad concepts like 'revolution' and 'Puritanism,' its focus is narrow. It is specifically concerned with the way in which religious forces have been seen, and might be seen, as impinging upon political developments in England before and after the Civil War. The concern is not to analyse the character of Puritanism any more than it is to provide an ultimate explanation of political change in seventeenth-century England. Nor is this another study of the origins or nature of the English Civil War. Insofar as there is a narrative, it leaps from 1641 to 1666 because its purpose is to consider the way in which historians, whose attention is focused essentially upon the political changes in Stuart England, have conceived of 'Puritanism' as carrying more or less of the burden of explanation of their narrative, and to suggest an alternative approach. The complexities of the 1642-60 period, when Puritans – often socially outside the normal political mainstream – may well have had an unmistakeable impact on political developments, are deliberately and necessarily omitted.[14] The concern here is with historians' explanations of the political origins of the Civil War between 1621 and 1641, and with their accounts of a comparable period later in the century with a view to isolating their approach to the problem of religion and its impact on politics.

The assumption that Puritanism was a fundamentally important force in English society before 1640 but was relatively insignificant after 1660 is simply one example of the way in which seventeenth-century English historiography has in modern times developed almost schizophrenic tendencies. The point at which religious phenomena are seen as impinging upon politics illustrates just one of the many ways in which the mind-set of the scholar of the earlier period is fundamentally different from that of his colleague whose focus in on the Restoration and its aftermath.

This brings us to the second problem that this book attempts to explore: that for reasons that are not absolutely straightforward, the Civil War is perceived to be a chasm in seventeenth-century English historical studies, one which is rarely bridged. This gulf can be illustrated in two ways. Most simply, relatively few historians attempt to span the century. Certainly, those early modern historians whose focus is at all political rarely try to cross this great divide. For most, other than writers of textbooks, the Interregnum represents either the beginning or the end of their work. John Morrill has recently referred to 'the 1660 barrier' as 'as rigid a historiographical divide for all but economic historians as 1485 was for generations of historians up to the 1950s.'[15] The reason for this inflexibility is neither hard to grasp nor surprising. There are at the present time probably more historians working on problems in seventeenth-century English history than in all the years between 1700 and the Second World War. Inevitably, there is a degree of specialization which has fostered a reluctance to deal with too many decades and the Interregnum seems like an obvious place to start or to stop.

There is, however, another reason which contributes to this reluctance to span the gap between 1640 and 1660 and which is also reinforced by it. It can, I think, be fairly said that most historians of seventeenth-century England who have written since the mid-nineteenth century have accepted the proposition that events between 1640 and 1660 constituted a 'revolution.'[16] What has inevitably followed from this judgment has been the assumption that, in those areas of greatest interest to individual historians, English society after 1660 was fundamentally different from English society before 1640. Thus, for instance, Christopher Hill can say that 'in trade, colonial and foreign policy the end of the Middle Ages in England came in 1650-1.' Historians whose interests are much more conventionally political and constitutional than Hill's, G.E. Aylmer for instance, are just as convinced that after 1660 the distribution of power was fundamentally and irrevocably altered. J.G.A. Pocock has recently summarized this dominant historiographical convention, writing that the restored (post 1660) world 'is so unlike the old that historians are required to begin interpreting it anew, with new ideas and assumptions.'[17]

What is particularly striking about this assumption is that it contrasts sharply with the Restoration experience. For despite the fact that elements of the modern sense of 'revolution' can be perceived in the writings of one or two contemporaries like Marchmont Nedham and James Howell, few if any viewed the events of 1660 as anything other than a 'restoration.' Even Howell could confidently predict that, in the midst of 'the calamities of the time,' these zealots 'do but dance in a circle all this while, for the Government will turn at last to the same point it was before viz. to Monarchy and this King will be restored.'[18] And this indeed was how 1660 was interpreted by virtually all writers at the time.

Those few like Lucy Hutchinson who continued to identify with the 'Good Old Cause' felt that the cause was lost and that they themselves were betrayed; the overwhelming majority were persuaded that an attempt to turn the world upside down had been narrowly averted. In neither case did men or women believe that their world had necessarily been permanently or significantly altered.[19]

Here it may be objected that the contrast between the contemporary perception of the Restoration and historians' analyses is only to be expected. Amongst other things, it is the historian's function to place contemporary perception of itself into a longer perspective. Yet one must still wonder, if the political world of John Pym and John Eliot between 1620 and 1642 was so different from that of Shaftesbury and Danby in the 1670s and 1680s, why was this fact not clear to the latter? Why did parliamentarians in the latter period think they were doing battle with many of the same enemies who had laid siege to their fathers a generation or two before? Here we confront the second central problem with which this study is concerned. How can we reconcile contemporaries' assumptions that continuity characterized the seventeenth century with the assumption that has informed the analysis of most historians for over a hundred years that revolutionary discontinuity provides the most appropriate paradigm?

At this point the problem of 'Puritanism' merges with the problem of continuity. I have suggested that the present convention amongst historians to view 'Puritanism' as a crucial element in the political and social history of pre-Civil War England, but a relatively unimportant one a few years later, creates more problems than it solves. By creating an abstraction which is susceptible to highly metaphorical treatment, historians have attributed to a broad sector of English political society a greater preoccupation with religious matters than is warranted by the evidence.[20] Furthermore, by making 'Puritanism' such a fundamentally important element in England before 1660, and then dismissing it after 1660, historians oblige us to ask what happened to 'Puritanism,' to which question there is no very sensible answer. Finally, it is apparent that there may well be a connection between the assumption of discontinuity as the governing model in terms of which seventeenth-century English political history is seen and the other assumption that 'Puritanism' was at first of crucial importance and then became a negligible factor. Perhaps by expecting continuity throughout the whole period we may understand better how contemporaries interpreted their recent history and, at the same time, grasp more clearly the way in which religious phenomena impinged on political behaviour before and after the so-called 'revolution.'

The study that follows is in two parts. The first part, which is historiographical, focuses on the way in which two concepts, 'Puritanism' and 'revolution,' have been employed as explanatory and organizing devices by those who have written about seventeenth-century English political history over the past three hundred years or so. These chapters are not intended to provide an exhaustive survey of everything that has been written on the subject over three centuries partly because this daunting task has been successfully attempted by several scholars in recent years.[21] Instead, by considering the work of a few such highly influential historians as the Earl of Clarendon, David Hume, and S.R. Gardiner, I will focus on the way these two concepts developed and came to assume their current function around the middle of the nineteenth century. Following the general adoption by historians of 'Puritanism' as the label for the religion of the parliamentary side and of 'revolution' as the label for what happened between 1640 and 1660 – the two concepts most obviously come together in Gardiner's 'Puritan Revolution' – historians came to approach England's political history in the seventeenth century in a new and schematic way.

The second part of the study is historical. After looking at three of the four 'tremors' and the early part of the 'one major earthquake' that together constitute Lawrence Stone's 'seismic rift' in English politics between 1621 and 1721,[22] the study suggests an alternative way of perceiving the role religion played in them. Here the self-imposed limits of the study need to be made explicit. This is not primarily a book about Puritanism. There is not a word about theological matters or about the inner experience of Puritans before or after 1650. That there were individuals in England between 1560 and 1660 – and beyond – who lived a religious life and shared a religious point of view that can most aptly be labelled 'Puritan' and that can be contrasted with a distinctly different kind of religious life and point of view that may be labelled 'non-Puritan,' or even 'Anglican,' is probable. This book, however, is not primarily about such individuals. Here the concern is with national politics before 1641 and after 1660, and it will be argued that there is little reason to think that many of those individuals generally believed by historians to have been influential on the national political stage during these periods can most aptly be called 'Puritan.'

The focus in the second part of the book is on national politics and on the importance to national politics of religious issues. Chapter 4 deals with an aspect of England's political history between 1621 and 1641 – namely, what appear to be the 'religious' preoccupations of those individuals most active in the political arena. Essentially, the chapter asks whether 'Puritanism' is the most apt label for those 'religious' preoccupations. Chapter 5 deals with the same subject matter – 'religion' – as an issue in national politics in the twenty or so years before the Revolution of 1688. The intent of these chapters is largely comparative: Are there significant differences between the way contemporaries seem to have treated 'religious' issues in the political arena before and after the

Interregnum? If so, how do these differences manifest themselves? If not, then what are the implications for the way historians use 'Puritanism' in their accounts of the political history of the early seventeenth century and in their explanations of the English Civil War?

PART I

'PURITANISM' AND 'REVOLUTION' IN ENGLISH

HISTORIOGRAPHY SINCE THE CIVIL WAR

2

Historians and the Idea of 'Revolution'

Between 1660 and 1930 the history of Stuart England was written and rewritten by generations of historians. Yet, despite the changing intellectual preoccupations and conflicting political persuasions of these historians, and the steady increase in the quantity and variety of source material available to them, the essential contours of the story changed very little. If one considers Clarendon's six-volume history of the rebellion to be the start of a tradition, then G.M. Trevelyan's *England under the Stuarts* might reasonably be considered the final statement of a position that, as late as 1925 or 1930, was generally accepted by scholars and by the reading public.[1] There are, of course, historians today who maintain the tradition, but they can no longer be said to present the consensus view of the profession.[2]

In an essay on the historical method of S.R. Gardiner, written in 1915, R.G. Usher wrote that the history of England between 1625 and the end of 1641 had been determined by the authors of the Grand Remonstrance, and that it had not been substantially revised in the following 275 years.[3] Usher's remark was extremely perceptive and draws our attention to the core of the traditional approach to the English civil wars. Historians as diverse as G.M. Trevelyan, C.H. Firth, S.R. Gardiner, T.B. Macaulay, Henry Hallam, John Lingard, David Hume, and even the Earl of Clarendon belong to this tradition. It may seem paradoxical to describe Hume and Clarendon as writing in the same tradition as Macaulay and Gardiner, for while Hume made no secret of his admiration for the 'law and order' Cavaliers, Macaulay proclaimed his conviction that the Roundheads were completely justified in their resort to arms.[4] Yet it can be demonstrated that, transcending their political differences, there is a fundamental consensus in their writing.

Not one of these historians questioned that the early Stuarts, and Charles I in particular, had ruled illegally, or at the very least, on the margins of illegality.

Nor did they doubt that this problem ought to be central to the concerns of any historian of the period. What Hume described as an 'unusual and arbitrary authority' was to Trevelyan, one hundred and fifty years later, 'tyranny' and 'despotism.'[5] Those who formed the overwhelming majority of the Long Parliament in its early months, so has run the tradition, were heroes for their courage in resisting the government of 'thorough,' thereby rendering the constitution invulnerable to future subversion. To Hume, the men responsible for the constitutional reforms of 1641 were entitled 'to very ample praises from all lovers of liberty,'[6] a judgment repeated seventy years later by Hallam, who wrote that members of the Long Parliament in 1641 'acquired a higher claim to our gratitude, and effected more for our liberties, than any that had gone before or that has followed.'[7] Eighty years later still, Trevelyan wrote, 'but in England the revolutionary passions were stirred by no class in its own material interest. Our patriots were prosperous men, enamoured of liberty, or of religion, or of loyalty, each for her own sake, not as the handmaid of class greed.'[8]

An analysis of the historiographical tradition embraced by these historians, even when they were apologists for warring causes, reveals three main areas of agreement. First, they all saw the events of Charles' reign, if not of the Civil War itself, in terms of the struggle between liberty and authority. Second, and related to this, they all shared an assumption that Englishmen have an innate, almost genetic, feeling for liberty quite unlike other peoples' and that as a result there was an inevitability about the ultimate victory of the subjects' rights over the monarch's absolute prerogatives. Third, and this is ironic in view of the use subsequently made by Marxist historians of this belief, they all shared the impression that the two sides in the Civil War attracted two quite distinct social groups.

When Benedetto Croce wrote that 'all history is the history of Liberty,'[9] an opinion repeated by R.G. Collingwood, he was not analysing the English historiographical tradition, but he might have been. From Hume to Trevelyan and beyond, the history of England has been the story of the progressive revelation of liberty, the freeing of the English people from bondage to instrumentalities of church and state. And in this story the seventeenth century has had a major role to play. In Hume's view, in England at the beginning of the century, 'the love of freedom ... acquired new force and was regulated by more enlarged views.' When James I succeeded to Elizabeth's throne, 'symptoms immediately appeared of a more free and independent genius in the nation.' The new prince developed a 'speculative system of absolute government ... [which] might have proved dangerous, if not fatal, to liberty' had he been able to enforce it. The same historian, reflecting on the reign of Charles I, summarized that monarch's problems as deriving from the fact that 'the precedents of many former reigns savoured strongly of arbitrary power, and the genius of the people ran violently towards liberty.'[10]

Henry Hallam, though deliberately writing to refute the biased Toryism of David Hume, shared many of the latter's preoccupations. By abolishing the Court of Star Chamber, Hallam wrote, the Long Parliament abolished 'the whole irregular and arbitrary practice of government, that had for several centuries so thwarted the operation and obscured the light of our free constitution.' Though rule by the first two Stuarts had not materially altered the constitution from its Plantagenet form, yet so precarious had the liberties of the subject become that 1641 'should seem almost a new birth of liberty.'[11] To Hallam, as to almost every historian of the period until 1930, the history of England in the seventeenth century focused on the struggle between the liberty-loving subjects on the one hand and the despotic early Stuarts, the tyrannical army, and the ineptly scheming later Stuarts on the other.

Not only did all the historians in this tradition share a basic theme in the history they wrote, but they all subscribed to a yet more fundamental belief: a fervent patriotism tinged with a conviction of England's 'manifest destiny.' Trevelyan thus described the context for his study of Stuart England: '...the white races of Europe and America, in whom the hope of mankind lay, were developing a political structure and a fashion of public sentiment akin to those of Czarist Russia. But at this moment the English, unaware of their destiny and of their service, tenacious only of their rights, their religion and their interests, evolved a [different] system of government ...'[12] To the Scot, Hume, the connection between English blood and liberty was not so sharp. But even he wrote of how, 'In England, the love of freedom which, unless checked, flourishes extremely in all liberal natures ...'[13] Hallam, of whom Macaulay said that he had never read so impartial an historian of England,[14] had this to say about the English: 'For the English are, as a people, little subject to those bursts of passion which influence the more imaginative multitudes of southern climates, and render them both apt for revolutions, and incapable of conducting them. Nor are they again of that sluggish and stationary temper, which chokes all desire for improvement, and even all zeal for freedom and justice, through which some free governments have degenerated into corrupt oligarchies.'[15]

Even Gardiner, said by some to have 'revolutionized' the study of seventeenth-century England,[16] and who thought of himself as writing the first 'impartial' history of the period, failed to escape the limitations of his assumptions. He believed that a 'national opinion' existed in 1640 which was generally dissatisfied with the ideas and policies of the government. The members of the Long Parliament fully represented the broad national condemnation of Charles' tyrannical government. Gardiner assumed liberty, in its political or religious form, to have been the most cherished value of the English nation and that by threatening this value Charles had displeased the nation. Here his conviction that the quest for liberty provides an unbroken thread through history is reinforced by his assumption that Englishmen, and in particular Puritan Englishmen, had an innate love of liberty. Thus does he write that 'Puritanism not only formed the strength of the opposition to Charles, but the strength of England itself,' and, elsewhere, that 'Milton's voice expressed the deepest feelings of the nation.'[17]

Finally, there is the conviction, shared by all historians from Clarendon to Trevelyan, that when England did divide in late 1642 the cleavage was to a large extent social.[18] Hume elaborates on the observations made by Clarendon: 'The nobility, and the more considerable gentry, dreading a total confusion of rank from the fury of the populace,' supported the king while 'the city of London ... and most of the great corporations took part with the parliament.' Anticipating Tawney, he continued: 'new families, lately enriched by commerce, saw with indignation, that, notwithstanding their opulence, they could not raise themselves to a level with the ancient gentry; they therefore adhered to a power, by whose success they hoped to acquire rank and consideration.'[19] As the politics of the Civil War became more extreme, the social origins of the parliamentary politicians sank steadily lower.

John Lingard, who was moved to include an 'advertisement' before his sixth volume, in which he denied allegations that he was simply trying to refute Hume at every point, and who insisted that he had not read one hundred pages altogether of Hume's *History* in the previous eight years, nonetheless agreed with the latter's social analysis: 'While the higher classes repaired with their dependents to the support of the king, the call of the parliament was cheerfully obeyed by the yeomanry in the country and by the merchants and tradesmen in the towns.'[20] Trevelyan, who so explicitly praised the English for their idealism in contrast to the class-oriented materialism of the French one hundred and fifty years later, nonetheless noted the distinct social composition of the two sides: 'The most devotedly Royalist were the largest owners of land' while 'the towns were the strength of the Roundheads,' though he also saw the division as one of 'North and West against South and East.'[21]

There is enough here to justify the attribution of a 'tradition' to a sequence of historians who differed in many ways. The questions they asked themselves were the same even if the answers they provided were not. This is not really surprising, given the extent to which each was writing in the shadow of his predecessor. Hume, as Trevor Roper has demonstrated, was heavily indebted to Clarendon, while his own history was in turn the standard text for almost a century; and though Hallam, Lingard, and Macaulay were all conscious of what they believed to be Hume's tendency to justify the royal policy, they could not escape his influence. In the same way, Gardiner, though appalled by Macaulay's constant present-mindedness, nonetheless cited him in refutation of Hallam's criticism of Parliament's position in August 1642.[22]

These writers were self-consciously mindful of their predecessors and of correcting their demonstrations of partiality. Indeed, the structure of the argument and sometimes even the phraseology recur from generation to generation. Hume wrote of early seventeenth-century England: 'the minds of men, throughout all Europe, but especially in England, seem to have undergone a general, but insensible revolution' as a result of which large numbers of Englishmen showed signs of a 'more free and independent genius'[23] which the early Stuarts lacked the wit to prevent. Perhaps these phrases of Hume's appeared on one of the hundred pages that Lingard did read, for in his general summary of the origins of the Civil War he wrote: 'Within the last fifty years the minds of men had undergone a wonderful revolution. It had become fashionable to study the principles of government and to oppose the rights of the subject to the pretensions of the sovereign.'[24]

Within a tradition that lasts for more than two centuries it would be rash to suppose the continuance of an identical approach to the study of the past. The worlds inhabited by Clarendon or Hume were different from each other and yet more removed from those of Gardiner or of Trevelyan. Inevitably, these differences are reflected in the histories they wrote. The most fundamental distinction between the earlier as against the later historians in this tradition lies in their attitudes to the events they are describing. Until well on in the nineteenth century, historians wrote of the Civil War primarily to teach their reading public the dangers of civil unrest. As late as 1825, Lingard drew a sharp distinction between the positive reforms of the Long Parliament and its more unfortunate later proceedings, and in doing so he drew a moral: 'To the first we are indebted for many of the rights we now enjoy; by the second we are warned of the evils which result from political changes effected by violence and in opposition to the habits and predilections of the people.'[25]

For Clarendon, Hume, Lingard, and Hallam the heroic resistance to tyranny in 1641 was quickly subverted by ambitious men, or fanatics, or men driven on by 'resentment and distrust.'[26] Until Macaulay's resounding criticism of Hallam in the pages of the *Edinburgh Review*, historians had been extremely reluctant to praise the Parliamentarians more highly than the Royalists. As Hallam put it, the majority party in the House of Commons had little enough reason to trust the king, yet by going to war they were jeopardizing the very liberties they wished to defend. In the last analysis, he believed, the note of anarchy was more to be feared than that of despotism.[27]

In the writings of Macaulay and his successors, attitudes towards the events of the 1640s and 1650s underwent a major change. Whereas previously the habit of historians had been to sympathize with the Roundheads in their dilemma, but to commend the Cavaliers for their wisdom, Macaulay's preference was the reverse. The Parliamentarians in 1642 were simply trying to implement the settlement later made in 1688. The leaders of 1642 and 1689 shared the same object and in the Nineteen Propositions they attempted to 'do directly what at the Revolution was done indirectly' – to give Parliament control over the executive. In defending the Parliamentarians' preparedness to go to war with their king, Macaulay was not just Whiggishly correcting a Tory distortion of the past: rather, he was giving expression to an attitude towards history, change, and revolution that was inconceivable in the eighteenth century. 'The peculiar glory of the Houses of Parliament is that, in the great plague and mortality of constitution, they took their stand between the living and the dead.'[28]

Similarly, in the second third of the nineteenth century, between the time when Macaulay started writing, 1825, and the 1860s when Gardiner began work, historians' basic attitudes to the events between 1640 and 1660 changed, as did their reasons for writing about them. Conscious of at least some of the implications of the American, French, and industrial revolutions, historians began to find change a less frightening concept. Men prepared, as the Roundheads had been, to risk disorder in the cause of liberty, even to break somewhat with the past, were understandable to the nineteenth-century mind as before they had not been. Symptomatic of this changed attitude to the past, this acceptance of the necessity of violence in the cause of liberty, was the increasing use of the term 'revolution' to describe events in England between 1640 and 1660.

The usage of the word 'revolution' in this context goes back to the period itself. Though without the complexities which the term currently connotes, even then it was not unambiguous. Broadly, 'revolution' was used between 1660 and 1700 in one of two ways; either it carried an astronomical implication and meant the 'return or recurrence of a point or a period of time,' when it was used in the singular, or else it carried one of its more common current meanings, 'the forcible substitution of a new ruler or form of government,' in which case it was not uncommon for the Restoration of Charles II to be described as a 'revolution.'[29] Thus Gilbert Burnet, in a sermon delivered towards the end of the Exclusion Crisis, referred to the animosities of the Interregnum having been buried 'by a happy revolution and a gracious oblivion.'[30] Similarly, the anonymous author of a pamphlet reflecting on the political scene in 1689 wrote: 'As the Restoration of King Charles II so the last revolution was the work of the people of England.'[31] It was this latter event, the overthrow of James II, which made the word 'revolution' truly respectable, indeed glorious, and it was not until the work of Gardiner that 'the revolution' was ever associated with anything but the events of 1688-9. By means of this unanimous judgment delivered by the English people, government had finally returned to its origins.

The plural form of 'revolution' was frequently used to denote the troubled Interregnal period. More often referred to as 'our late disorders' or 'our late troubles,' 'revolutions' occurs fairly frequently. One need not look beyond the Declaration of Breda to find a reference to the land transfers resulting from 'the continued distractions of so many years and so many and great revolutions.'[32] Thomas Rugg explained that he wished to record in his diurnal events surrounding the Restoration so 'that after ages may learn constancy from these our inconstant revolutions that have so long had the predominancy in the(se) our nations.'[33] Similarly, the authors of a broadsheet aimed at the electors of the Convention Parliament in 1660 referred to 'the many late various forms and revolutions of our public government.'[34] The restored monarch himself, Charles II, in a speech expressing his gratitude to the City of London, said he had always been comforted by the affections of the citizens 'in these great revolutions which of late have happened in that our kingdom to the wonder and amazement of all the world.'[35]

The ambiguities inherent in the usage of 'revolution' in the seventeenth century are no less apparent in David Hume's treatment of the Civil War period. In addition to the appearance of the phrase 'Revolution of 1688' to describe the terminus of his history, 'revolution' appears many times in his narrative of events between 1640 and 1660. Furthermore, when he refers to the minds of men having undergone a 'general, but insensible revolution,' he meant the 'expansion of letters' and the enlargement of the 'general system of politics' – that is, revolution in the sense of 'change.'[36]

In the course of his *History*, however, he used the word in at least three other senses. Referring to the attacks on the king's principal ministers, Strafford and Laud, he wrote that the House of Commons had, in a matter of weeks, 'produced such a revolution in the government that the two most powerful and most favoured ministers of the King were thrown into the Tower.' He employs a similar use of the term when summarizing the achievements of the first phase of the Long Parliament. As a result of the legislation of 1641, abuses were remedied, grievances redressed, and, more important, 'great provision, for the future, was made by excellent laws against the return of like complaints.' True, he agreed, the means employed were not always praiseworthy, yet 'it is to be considered, that revolutions of government cannot be effected by the mere force of argument and reasoning.'[37]

The second sense in which Hume used 'revolution' was as a description of disorder. The attacks by the populace on the Convocation in May 1640 were, he says, 'presages of some great revolution.' By the end of the year, 'the causes of disgust ... were now come to full maturity and threatened the kingdom with some great revolution or convulsion.' 'Revolution' was the word Hume frequently used to describe the political and civil confusion from 1642 to 1660. Reflecting on the execution of the king, he commented: 'From the memorable revolutions, which passed in England during this period, we may naturally deduce ... that it is very dangerous for princes to assume more authority, than the laws have allowed,' but he also insisted that there is 'another instruction no less natural and no less useful concerning the madness of the people, the furies of fanaticism, and the danger of mercenary armies.' After describing the purge of Parliament by the drayman Pride, Hume wrote, 'These sudden and violent revolutions held the whole nation in terror and astonishment.'[38]

Finally, as had been the case in the Restoration period, 'revolution' meant restoration. Not only did the Revolution of 1689 complete the re-establishment of the old constitution, but the Restoration of Charles II was also this kind of revolution: 'And as the sudden and surprising revolution, which restored him to his regal rights, had also restored the nation to peace, law, order and liberty.'[39]

For all the varied senses in which Hume used 'revolution' to describe events between 1640 and 1660, one thing is clear. Even when it signified the achievement of laudable change, as with the constitutional reforms of 1641, the change was largely restorative. What the legislation of 1641 had really achieved was the better securing, 'by such important concessions ... that moderate freedom transmitted from their ancestors.' There was in no sense a break from the past, but rather a return to it. Charles I had attempted to expand greatly his prerogatives in consequence of which the 'privileges of the nation lay prostrate at his feet.' The nation responded correctly, in Hume's view, and as a result of the 'revolution' of 1641, the government was 'more exactly defined,' but not profoundly changed. The subsequent 'revolutions' between 1642 and 1660 were the work of the fanatical lower orders, and were, in Hume's mind, of no lasting consequences.[40]

Henry Hallam, who wrote his *Constitutional History of England* in the 1820s, was not only writing after the American and French revolutions, but had no hesitation in referring to both those events in the course of his history. Comparing the acts of regicide in 1649 and 1793, he wrote that in the former 'none of that clamorous fanaticism showed itself, which, within recent memory, produced from a far more numerous assembly, an instantaneous decision against monarchy.' He was just as mindful and considerably more appreciative of the American achievement. Speculating on the feasibility of England's having remained a republic in 1660, he wrote, 'the most conspicuously successful experiment of republican institutions (and those far more democratical than, according to the general theory of politics, could be reconciled with perfect tranquillity), has taken place in a people of English origin.' Part of the success of this experiment, he said, derived from 'the good sense and well balanced temperament, which have come in their inheritance with our laws and our language.'[41]

Nonetheless, Hallam followed his foes Hume and Clarendon in their ambiguous and essentially conservative and historically oriented use of 'revolution.' Hallam too used the term in a number of contrary ways. First and foremost was his acceptance of the astronomical overtones of 'revolution.' Indicative of the reverence he shared with his society for the events of 1688-9, these he refers to as the 'Revolution,' whereas the mere restoration of Charles II does not merit capitalization. Hallam went to considerable pains to defend Monk and the other 'conductors of this great revolution' against allegations of irresponsibility in not having sufficiently limited the powers of the later Stuarts. In doing so, he illustrates the other, and more general, use of the expression. The makers of the 'revolution' of 1660 cannot be blamed, for the king was restored 'to nothing but the bounded prerogatives of a king of England,' limited by statutes, including those of 1641, which Hallam too saw as having constituted the only permanent result of events between 1640 and 1660. The early legislation of the Long Parliament, which 'cut away the more flagrant and recent usurpations of the crown,' Hallam described as 'the revolution of 1641,' and here, following Clarendon and Hume, he directed his total admiration, though expressed in slightly ambiguous language. He said 1641 saw no innovations: 'they made scarce any material change in our constitution such as it had been established and recognized under the house of Plantagenet ... the monarchy lost nothing it had anciently possessed, and the balance of our constitution might seem rather to have been restored to its former equipoise, than to have undergone any change.' Yet, at the same time, so firmly did he see this legislation as having 'formed our constitution as it now exists' from which dated 'the preservation of our civil and political privileges' that he also referred to 1641 as having witnessed a 'great innovation,' a 'new birth of liberty.' Here in Hallam we have our first glimpse of the service 'revolution' was to provide as an organizing tool for future historians of mid-seventeenth-century England.[42]

As for the significance of the war, the regicide, and the republic, Hallam did not believe they had any enduring effects. Interesting and remarkable though they were, he felt strongly tempted to jump over this period 'as not strictly belonging to a work which undertakes to relate the progress of the English constitution.'[43]

While Hallam was composing his *History*, another scholar was hard at work in France applying the benefits of French revolutionary consciousness to his analysis of seventeenth-century English history. Francois Guizot, whose *History of the English Revolution* was not published in English until some years later, had none of contemporary Englishmen's reservations about the men of 1642. To him, the English Revolution of 1640 was the 'greatest event which Europe had to narrate' prior to the French Revolution. Guizot believed that the two events were in essential respects similar and that Englishmen could learn about their revolution only by seeing it as the model for the French. He had, furthermore, little sympathy for the view that England's revolution was a 'monstrous apparition in the history of Europe.' On the contrary, he proclaimed that it, together with its French counterpart, 'advanced civilization in the path it has been pursuing for fourteen centuries.'[44] This was not just a selfless venture into scholarship, for the prolific Frenchman hoped that his contemporaries would learn something from the English ability to marry the socially egalitarian benefits of revolution with political stability.

Even when Guizot's work was translated and published in England in the 1840s, his celebration of the civil wars as England's 'revolution' was greeted coldly. As one reviewer wrote, Guizot had fundamentally confused the most unfortunate events in the 1640s and 1650s with the 'glorious Revolution' of 1689. 'I admit,' wrote the Tory politician and critic J.W. Croker, 'that the first helped to produce the other as a dungheap helps to produce asparagus, as filth produces food, but they are not the same thing.'[45]

It was not until the great Victorian historian of early seventeenth-century England, S.R. Gardiner, had completed the majority of his sixteen volumes that it became at least an acceptable proposition that events in England between 1640 and 1660 provided an example of a general phenomenon called a revolution. Given Gardiner's stature and his influence on the study of seventeenth-century England, it is obvious that his attitude to 'revolution' is worth careful attention.

So cautious was Gardiner's methodology that in his multi-volume *History of England* and his *History of the English Civil War* he made few, if any, generalizations about his subject. By his reliance upon narrative, his utter fidelity to chronology, and his determination to write about the past as it appeared to contemporaries, thus eliminating, or so he thought, any sense of the future, Gardiner invariably abstained from making explicit statements about the course of English history. Fortunately, however, there was a market for other kinds of history books in the late Victorian period and Gardiner, like so many of his successors at the University of London, was not totally averse either to trying his hand outside his chosen field or to writing about a comparatively large number of years in a small number of pages.[46] In a variety of works aimed at students, rather than at scholars, of history, he made explicit what was only implicit in his more scholarly tomes.

Commenting on the relationship between the work of an historian and that of a statesman, Gardiner once wrote that even if 'the aims and objects of men at different periods are different, the laws inherent in human society are the same.' These laws were derived from the 'scientific' study of history and were particularly interesting when applied to revolution, for, he wrote, '[a revolution] reveals more clearly than smaller changes do the law of human progress.' As a scientific historian, follower of Ranke, and severe critic of Macaulay and Forster for their 'constant avowed or unavowed comparison of [the past] with the present,' Gardiner nevertheless subscribed fully to the tradition according to which history is the study of political liberty based upon an assumption of irresistible progress.[47]

Gardiner both followed in the tradition and, in an important way, modified it. His conception of seventeenth-century English history differed from his predecessors' in its deliberate and self-conscious celebration of the Puritan Revolution. To Gardiner, the term 'revolution' no longer implied disorder or restoration. He praised the men of 1641 for the modesty of their attempts to compromise with the king, for 'a nation which easily casts itself loose from the traditions of the past loses steadiness of purpose, and ultimately, wearied by excitement, falls into the arms of despotism.' Yet he believed that revolutions were progressive: 'they are to be accounted for as steps in the historical development of nations.'[48] There would always be demands for political change in any society. Sometimes those exercising authority would yield and at other times they would be either unwilling or too incompetent to adapt. Under the latter circumstances, 'some alteration has to be made in the institutions under which government is carried on; and if this alteration is very great, and is effected by force, it is called a Revolution.'[49] England's revolution, like all other revolutions, was the result of two forces, 'dissatisfaction with existing ideas and dissatisfaction with existing practice.' When those in power 'have become obnoxious alike to the men who think and to the men who feel [and do not respond] to constitutional pressure, the fusion of thought and feeling becomes more complete, and the ensuing change takes the form of a revolution.'[50] The violence and duration of revolutions varied, depending upon the extent of resistance from the institutions under attack. In England, in 1641, the monarchy's resistance was considerable.

What was at stake in seventeenth-century England was the question of who should rule. By 1600 the Tudors had assumed unprecedented powers to enable them to deal with the barons and the church. By then, however, Gardiner believed 'it was inevitable that the House of Commons should take a larger part in the direction of affairs than it had done before.' Inevitable or not, the major theme of his history of Stuart England was that government changed from that of a somewhat limited monarchy to 'practically a republic.'[51] The revolution was the process whereby the House of Commons and its supporters ensured that this would happen. It was not just the legislation of 1641 that provided the basis for the future development of England's political and constitutional life. That legislation, on which the Restoration of 1660 was founded, represented a 'great constitutional change,' but did not constitute a revolution because it failed to solve the major problem. When two men ride a horse, Gardiner was fond of saying, they cannot both sit at the front. The Civil War was fought 'to decide, at least for a time, in whose hands was sovereignty in England.' Politically, it was necessary that Charles clearly accept the reformed constitution, that he 'bend or break.' 'It was this part of the Revolution which was not accomplished till the deposition of Charles I, which unhappily took the form of his execution.' Whereas the essence of the French Revolution had been 'that there should cease to be privileged orders,' in England revolution lay in the preparedness of many to fight the king, to defeat him, and ultimately to depose him.[52] This assertion of the supremacy of the House of Commons over the king, temporarily betrayed in 1660, but eventually confirmed in 1688, was the English Revolution. Not that Gardiner, the Nonconformist, was prepared to rejoice in the unlimited sovereignty of Parliament. Answering both Thomas Wentworth's and Oliver Cromwell's quite separate objections to the sovereignty of Parliament, objections which Gardiner himself echoed, were two principal safeguards of the liberties of the subject that flanked parliamentary sovereignty: 'a free press and a free pulpit took their places in the new system' of 1689.[53]

Gardiner's use of 'revolution' to characterize the fundamental development in England's history in the seventeenth century provides us with an essential aid to understanding the way in which he modified the traditional view of the period as a whole, and of its central decades in particular. While he accepted the traditional wisdom concerning what was fit matter for an historian's pen and what were the natural themes about which to write, he took a more recognizably modern attitude to the nature of the change involved. So fundamental was the issue (sovereignty), so decisive was the victory, and so positive a contribution to the English nation's 'natural development' were they that events in England between 1640 and 1649 were comparable to those in France one hundred and fifty years later, and, like them, merited the encomium 'revolution,' a term Gardiner, most unscientifically, never dreamed of defining. What appears to be the crucial ingredient in Gardiner's concept of 'revolution' is the magnitude of the change which, in turn, necessitated the use of violence for its accomplishment. In the area of politics and the constitution, England experienced sudden and violent change which catapulted the country into the modern world.[54]

Gardiner was not the first historian to interpret the history of England in the seventeenth century in revolutionary terms. He was, however, the first academic historian to do so. Writing for an essentially different and more specialized audience than did Macaulay or Gardiner's more popular contemporary, J.R. Green, and with an avowedly more professional purpose, Gardiner not only bore witness to a 'scientific' approach to history for the next generation of English historians, but also created a structure in terms of which the period would be studied for years to come. By declaring the civil wars to have constituted a revolutionary break with the nation's past, Gardiner, without ever writing serious history of the period after 1656, was asserting that in those areas that he considered to be of utmost importance to the historical profession, namely politics and the constitution, England after 1660 had assumed a character that was recognizably modern and, by implication, fundamentally different from that before 1640. The prevailing assumption of continuity had now been replaced by its antithesis – that of revolutionary discontinuity.[55]

Gardiner's sense of the character of the 'Puritan Revolution' and its impact on the course of seventeenth-century English history has been a major influence on all the history of the period written for a hundred years. While few, if any, historians would accept his precise version of events, all, however, write in his shadow, and, whether writing simply to revise or entirely to reject Gardiner's vision, few historians escape his influence.

This latter observation applies especially to the work of the man who for forty years has laboured to attack Gardiner's 'Puritan Revolution' and to replace it with a different kind of event. Since 1940, when Christopher Hill presented his outline of a revisionist approach to seventeenth-century English history,[56] he has produced an extraordinary volume of work designed to develop and embroider his thesis, without departing far from his introductory theme. If Gardiner represents one inescapable influence on contemporary historians, then Hill represents another, and from the tension generated by their structurally similar yet ideologically opposed interpretations is created much of the energy that sustains contemporary debate in the field.

In Hill's view, the 'Puritan Revolution' was the invention of nineteenth-century historians who preferred to listen to what contemporaries had said about politics and religion than to their observations about the social character of the two parties. It is Hill's belief that the seventeenth- and eighteenth-century historians, and especially Lord Clarendon, were much more aware of the social realities of the civil wars than were their Victorian successors. 'Puritan Revolution,' he has written, is a quite misleading expression in that it implies a revolutionary self-consciousness among a segment of those wielding power in 1642 to establish a Puritan society. Instead of a 'Puritan Revolution,' Hill posits a 'bourgeois revolution.'[57]

For all the elaboration and development that has occurred in Hill's work since 1940, his overriding conception of seventeenth-century England has not changed. In the source book he assembled in the late 1940s, he wrote that the documents were chosen to illustrate the story of 'how one social class was driven from power by another and how the form of state power appropriate to the needs of the first was replaced by one appropriate to those of the second.'[58] Over the next quarter century, even though he abandoned expressions such as 'progressive historical function,' 'historic processes,' and 'parasitic feudal land-owners,'[59] and wrote fine studies of the religious and intellectual origins of the Civil War, his basic vision of the period remained unaffected. As he wrote in 1974, he continues to find 'the Marxist conception of a bourgeois revolution the most helpful model for understanding the English Revolution.' More recently, Hill's view has, if anything, firmed. Quoting extensively from Marx, Engels, and Lenin, he has reiterated his conviction that England witnessed a 'bourgeois revolution' between 1640 and 1660, meaning that although it was not 'brought about ... by the wishes of the bourgeoisie ... its outcome was the establishment of conditions far more favourable to the development of capitalism than those which had prevailed before 1640.'[60]

Applying this model to seventeenth-century England, Hill believes that the political conflicts of the period are properly interpreted in social terms and as playing a part in an historical development that extends beyond the boundaries of England and the confines of the seventeenth century. In the hundred years before 1640, the most important development was the rise of capitalism. This involved the emergence of a large number of merchants trading on a vastly increased scale both nationally and internationally, the development, particu-larly in those parts of England close to the rapidly expanding metropolis, of a large number of market-oriented landowners and the appearance of a new industrial class. This new class, described by Hill in 1940 in rather doctrinaire fashion as a 'new class of capitalist merchants and farmers,'[61] has assumed a more heterogeneous character in recent years, but has not changed essentially. Hill believes that seventeenth-century England witnessed a fundamental con-flict between this new and developing capitalist class on the one hand and, on the other, a conservative alliance of court-sanctioned monopoly capitalists, established churchmen, and old-fashioned landowners beyond the economic and social influence of London. The dialectical opposition between these two classes underlay most of the conflicts in sevententh-century England and, in particular, the political conflict of the 1640s.[62] Furthermore, Hill has always seen opposition between these classes in a much broader chronological frame-work. Despite his real sympathy for the 'lunatic fringe' and the long-forgotten minority groups of the past, and his criticism of the 'big battalion' assumptions of Whig historiography, he too sees the past in progressive terms.

In Hill's view, the big mistake that Archbishop Laud made in the 1630s was to 'revive the Middle Ages' both in ceremony and in the economic function of the church. By attempting to abolish impropriations, to restore tithes, and to regain the church's old political ascendancy, Laud was pursuing a retrogressive policy that meant 'dealing violently with history.' To Hill, history consists of a number of stages, each one defined in social terms, with a society's movement from one stage to the next being certain even if the rate of movement, and its precise mode, might vary. In this same study of the church, Hill remarked that 'the old regime might have been slowly modified' had the bishops, especially Laud, not played such a reactionary part. The Archbishop of Canterbury in the 1630s, he wrote, 'by making reform impossible precipitated revolution.'[63]

There is in Hill's approach to history a tension that is never resolved. However muted, it is the Marxist model of a 'bourgeois revolution' that informs all of his work in the period and that leads him to analyse what is idiosyncratic to seventeenth-century England in terms of the general movement in history that entirely transcends any one nation's peculiar experience. At the same time, he is quite aware of the unhistorical implications of economic determinism. In the 1950's, for instance, he frequently criticized the major participants in the gentry controversy, and in particular Professor Trevor Roper, for improper adoption of the Namier approach to history, and for interpreting the political behaviour of Civil War politicians as a mere economic reflex. Referring to Trevor Roper and to Brunton and Pennington's study of the membership of the Long Parliament, he wrote, 'I do not believe that material conflicts are the only ones deserving serious analysis.'[64] In his study of the *Economic Problems of the Church*, also written while the battle over the gentry was raging, he made the same point. The rigid antithesis between 'Puritan Revolution' and 'bourgeois revolution' was 'superficial,' for 'Puritanism, though it embraces nobler ideals than the triumph of capitalism, is unthinkable without a bourgeoisie; and the English Revolution could not have succeeded even to the limited extent it did without the power of Puritanism to awaken and organize and discipline large masses of people who knew what they fought for and loved what they knew.'[65]

Despite Hill's acute sensitivity to the problem and his awareness of the complexity of the relations between religion, science, politics, and economics, in the end he does not succeed in reconciling his Marxist assumptions with his liberal disclaimer. There is a certain disingenuousness in a footnote he added to a discussion of the social origins of the Independents and Presbyterians: 'To discuss the differences between the Presbyterians, Independents and sectaries exclusively in social terms as here, is as historically one-sided as to discuss them in exclusively religious terms, and is very insulting to the genuine religious convictions of most members of congregations,' he wrote, adding, 'but I am abstracting one aspect for analysis.'[66] When an historian devotes forty extraordinarily fruitful years to work that continually 'abstracts one aspect for analysis,' then it is questionable whether disclaimers that rarely, if ever, are translated into the actual history should be interpreted at their face value. In the end, his interpretation of England's political upheavals in the mid-seventeenth century as a 'bourgeois revolution' will have to be taken, as it was originally intended, as a fundamental attack on the idea of a political and religious revolution first coherently articulated by S.R. Gardiner.

This is not to say, however, that Hill's approach to history, and to seventeenth-century England in particular, has not changed since that initial bold statement of a revisionist interpretation in 1940. First, he has become more sensitive to the gap between what contemporaries believed themselves to be doing in the 1640s and the long-term historical significance of their actions. Second, he has become aware of the asymmetrical relationships between social classes on the one hand and political alliances on the other. In 1940 these all seemed fairly clear. Just as there were two distinctly opposed social classes, so were there two political sides fighting the Civil War. The political division reflected the geographical division, which in turn expressed the basic social reality, as the new class strove to overturn the old social order. By the 1970s, Hill had accepted two propositions that confused the stark simplicity of the earlier picture. He agreed that 'revolution' in the modern sense was not a seventeenth-century concept and thus that contemporaries were not self-conscious revolutionaries. In defence of this stand he argued that the modern sense of 'revolution' was probably not clarified until Marx wrote the *Communist Manifesto*, but that assuredly there were revolutionaries before 1848. Moreover, he conceded that there were doubtless bourgeoisie on opposing political sides in the 1640s, but that fact did not really deprive the revolution of its bourgeois character. Denying the existence of a 'pure social revolution,' one in which the social character of the struggle is reflected unambiguously in the composition of the political parties, he quoted Isaac Deutscher with approval: 'A bourgeois revolution creates the conditions in which bourgeois property can flourish.' Although his expectations about the relationship between social classes and political groups have modified, he wrote in the 1970s about the broad question as he might have in 1940. 'The Revolution was caused, ultimately, by economic developments which could not be absorbed within the old regime.'[67]

We have thus far suggested that for the most part Hill has for forty years projected an interpretation of seventeenth-century English history that is fundamentally opposed to Gardiner's. There is, however, one aspect of Gardiner's approach that Hill accepts. As he once wrote, while Tory historians such as Clarendon perceived the social nature of the revolution but refused to accept its 'progressive nature,'[68] Whig historians like Gardiner quite properly grasped its contribution to the forward movement of history.[69] It scarcely needs to be said that Hill has fully accepted Gardiner's sense of the structure of seventeenth-century English history. For both of them, the early seventeenth century saw a conflict between two forces – albeit differently conceived – that reached a climax in the early 1640s. One group, identified by both historians as representing the future, be it that of parliamentary liberty or of a new social class, successfully seized political power from the king and his supporters, viewed by both historians as backward looking and reactionary. Both historians have seen the events of the 1640s – Hill extends this to the 1650s – as revolutionary in that they involved a profound break with the past on a scale quite different from any other disturbance in England's history before or since. A corollary of this belief in the revolutionary nature of the period is their interpretation of the Restoration as a misnomer. To Gardiner, as we have seen, the willingness to fight the king and eventually to dethrone him was the principal event in England's history, an event that paved the way for the country's future political development. Hence the Restoration of 1660 was incomplete and signified only a temporary and confused pause in the progress of English history which was not resumed until the constitutional settlement of 1689 finally confirmed the political ascendancy of the House of Commons. So too with Christopher Hill. For all the continuity that he sees in seventeenth-century England, 'sharp and sudden change did in fact occur.'[70] Nothing was really restored in 1660 – only the names were the same, for, he writes, 'the Restoration of 1660 was a restoration of the united class whom Parliament represented, even more than of the king.' To Hill, 1660 marked the triumph of a new social class and as it came to power England entered into the modern world. As late as 1980 he was making essentially the same point when he noted that 'there was continuity between the power structure and the financial structure of England in 1649-53 and the 1660's; there was much less continuity between prerevolutionary and postrevolutionary England.'[71]

The belief, shared by Gardiner and Hill, in the peculiar aptness of 'revolution' as a label to describe events in England between 1640 and 1660 has been affirmed by the majority of historians who have studied the period in recent times. It is not possible to subject to close analysis all of these historians, nor is it easy to escape accusation of bias by choosing several illustrations. Let us, however, risk blame and consider the views of Professors Stone, Aylmer, and Zagorin, three widely acclaimed historians whose work is within the mainstream of prevailing attitudes and assumptions.

All three, like most though not all historians of seventeenth-century England currently working, believe in the English Revolution of 1640-60. Furthermore, they have all been sufficiently interested in the broad implications of the term 'revolution' to justify its usage in some detail. Indeed, Lawrence Stone and Perez Zagorin have produced studies in revolutionary theory.[72]

As with Gardiner a hundred years ago, Gerald Aylmer's broadest interpretative statements about seventeenth-century England are to be found in a general work, *The Struggle for the Constitution*, in which he states clearly his view of the significance of this period in England's entire history. England's experience in the past two hundred years has been relatively peaceful, Aylmer believes, because its great revolution occurred in the mid-seventeenth-century, a revolution in which absolute monarchy was conquered by parliamentary government which, in turn, eventually led to 'political democracy' of the twentiety century.[73] To Aylmer, the revolution was political and constitutional in character and occurred in 1649. 'The King's death and the abolition of the monarchy form the most important single political event of the century ... the balance of political power was more decisively affected by this than by any other event in our history ... to some extent it set the pattern for [the French and Russian Revolutions] and it had a great influence on the American Revolution.' While Aylmer's fundamental perception of seventeenth-century English history is not very different from Gardiner's, he is well aware of the Marxist insight which he attempts to graft on to the other view. He writes that, in 'limited ways,' events during the two decades can 'be thought of as a shift of power and still more of opportunity, towards the business and commercial interests.' The smoothness of this graft is not aided by his knowledge of the re-emergence of the landed aristocracy after 1660. As he also writes, 'to a limited extent, the Restoration does seem to signify a shift in power back from the middle to the upper class' when viewed beside the relative positions of these two groups in the 1640s and 1650s. Given the irreconcilable nature of the assumptions of Gardiner and Hill, it is not surprising that an attempt to marry these interpretations should not be entirely successful. Although Aylmer is not certain about the degree of social change, he is in no doubt that decisive change did occur. And here he sees more clearly than some that intrinsic to 'revolution' is decisive and permanent change. Thus he begins his narrative of events after 1660 with an analysis of the differences between 'the period before the Civil War' and 'that after the Restoration.' One of the greatest of these differences, he writes, is that 'Puritanism came increasingly to be the religion of a single social class. It became the creed of a substantial section of the middle class, and virtually ceased to be a movement cutting across social divisions, generating energy and piety throughout the nation.' The problem of Puritanism will be considered in some detail later in this study, but one implication of Aylmer's statement is of the utmost importance. As he sees clearly, the relationship between the 'revolution' of the 1640s and the 'restoration' of 1660 is inverse. Insofar as 'revolution' implies radical and permanent change, there are similar limitations on the extent to which institutions, property, and values are restored.[74]

Of all the historians who have written on seventeenth-century English history, Lawrence Stone, possibly more than any other, has had a more genuine respect for and has made greatest use of the concepts and methodology of the social sciences. Certainly he has been most preoccupied with the relationship between revolutions in general and the English Revolution in particular. To Stone there is no doubt that events between 1640 and 1660 constituted a 'revolution,' although in his most systematic discussion of the subject he concedes that according to the one definition of 'revolution' he chooses to cite, that of Sigmund Newmann, England's revolution does not fully qualify. According to Newmann, a revolution is 'a sweeping fundamental change in political organisation, social structure, economic property controls and the predominant myth of a social order, thus indicating a major break in the continuity of development.' But, as Stone points out, many of the political changes of the 1640s were temporary and 'in terms of distribution of wealth, England in 1660 was scarcely different from England in 1640.' Yet, despite the definition, he continues to assert that among the 'many rebellions in early modern Europe,' England's revolution was distinctive for its 'political and religious radicalism.'[75]

In probing the various achievements of the 1640-60 period to locate the precise 'revolution,' Stone creates more problems for himself than he can solve. First, he sees the 'revolution' occurring both before the outbreak of the first Civil War, in 1640-1, as well as after the second Civil War in 1648-9. Second, hard pressed to identify permanent achievements of the 'revolution,' he distinguishes between its deeds and its words. His analysis of the accomplishments of the revolutionaries, for instance, differs little from Aylmer's. In the abolition of the institutions of monarchy, the House of Lords, and the Established Church, he writes, lies the heart of England's 'revolution.' Yet, aware that these institutions were, to a greater or lesser extent, not only restored in 1660, but that they still exist three hundred years later, he went on to add that 'the revolutionary nature of the English Revolution is perhaps even more convincingly demonstrated by its words than by its deeds.' To illustrate this point, Stone then addresses himself to the problem of the extent to which contemporaries between 1640 and 1660 were self-consciously radical or revolutionary as distinct from restorative. He refers to the sermons before the Long Parliament of Jeremiah Burroughs and Thomas Case, and to the zealous rhetoric of the Rump politicians who proclaimed their desire to export political revolution throughout Europe, and concludes that here were examples enough of 'the language of revolution in the modern sense, and the language of the "cultural revolution" at that.'[76] This idea of a political as well as an intellectual and rhetorical revolution has to be considered in the context of other remarks Stone has made about the changes in English society between 1560 and 1640 and between 1621 and 1721. Describing the context of the 'crisis of the aristocracy,' he wrote, 'granted that change is a continuous process, that every shift has both earlier antecedents and later developments, it is nevertheless between 1560 and 1640, and more precisely, between 1580 and 1620 that the real watershed between medieval and modern England must be placed.' Finally, there is the 'seismic rift' that Professor Stone has identified opening up 'within the English political nation from 1621 to 1721,' when the 'political and religious structures of the nation' were repeatedly shaken and, once, destroyed.[77]

All in all, it is not absolutely clear what to make of this imagery. 'Revolution' is frequently associated by theorists with the process of modernization, the purpose served by the metaphor 'revolution' closely resembling that served by 'watershed' between mediaeval and modern periods. Yet if Stone locates the 'watershed' between 1580 and 1620 and the 'revolution' in the rhetoric and actions of the 1640-60 period, all of this within the context of a 'seismic shift' between 1621 and 1721, then it is not certain just what function the term 'revolution' serves. How does a historian of politics between, let us say, 1560 and 1760 reconcile these competing metaphors? Obviously, Stone believes that there was a 'revolution' in England in the seventeenth century, but it is not clear just where he locates it nor what makes the 'revolution.'

Finally, there is Perez Zagorin's idea of 'revolution.' He, like Aylmer and Stone, appears to be in no doubt that between 1640 and 1660 a 'revolution' occurred in England. In his study of the beginnings of the English Revolution, he cites Ranke, Trotsky, and Deutscher in support of his suggestion that 'the great revolutions are those in which the pace of change is suddenly accelerated and in which, as Macaulay wrote, the "experience of years is crowded into hours." ' England's revolution, like the American and French ones that followed, 'was a decisive event in the emergence of a liberal political order in the world.' Zagorin, like Aylmer, accepts Gardiner's plan of seventeenth-century English history, central to which was the concept of 'revolution' straddling the century like a giant colossus. The events of 1640-60 were revolutionary in the range of their 'constitutional and religious experimentations, the fertility of [their] public discussion and the extremity to which [they were] carried by the abolition of kingship and the establishment of a republic.' In both their 'practical attainments and ideal aims,' the revolutionaries deserve the title for expressing 'the aspirations of the epoch at whose threshhold [they] stood.'[78]

Like Stone, Zagorin has been attracted to the more theoretical study of 'revolution' as a phenomenon and, in the process, has developed his own definition that is broad enough to include under its umbrella not only what he refers to as the 'English Revolution of 1640' but also other events, such as the Pilgrimage of Grace of 1536. Intrinsic to Zagorin's concept of 'revolution' as a 'generic class,' of which there are many instances of specific 'revolutionary occurrences,' is the notion that there is a distinction to be drawn between 'revolutions' such as the Pilgrimage of Grace and 'great revolutions' such as England's in the mid-seventeenth century, which are of 'substantial magnitude and consequence.' Thus, while Zagorin clearly conceives of there being failed revolutions – revolutions that result in no significant social, economic, political, or religious change – he does not appear to view England's 'revolution' as having failed or as having left no mark on the country's institutions.[79]

In this complex issue of England's revolution, any attempt to identify representative historians would be a distortion. Each scholar makes a distinctive contribution, and no two agree on very much. On one fundamental point, however, it does seem valid to suggest that Aylmer, Stone, and Zagorin share with most of their colleagues an acceptance of 'revolution' as the most apt label for events between 1640 and 1660. It follows from this that, in common with Gardiner and Hill – though Stone is more ambiguous than the others – they all assume as an implication of 'revolution' that political institutions or ideas, social structure, or whatever the historians' own assumptions make paramount are fundamentally different after 1660.

There is one other group of historians of the seventeenth century to whom the concept 'revolution' is vital – the 'general crisis' historians. Best exemplified by Professors Hobsbawm and Trevor Roper, this view asserts that England's revolution needs to be understood in its broader European context. What occurs in England between 1640 and 1660 is just the most spectacular and decisive example of a broader 'crisis' confronting states across Europe. That which Hobsbawm sees as essentially socio-political is to Trevor Roper political, yet they share the belief that so profound is the 'crisis' that the result is a fundamental discontinuity in the society's experience. Perhaps no historian who takes as his governing assumption the fact of 'revolution' between 1640 and 1660 articulates the discontinuity more crisply than Trevor Roper when he writes that the seventeenth century 'is broken in the middle, irreparably broken, and at the end of it, after the revolutions, men can hardly recognize the beginning.'[80]

While most historians who have written about seventeenth-century England in the past hundred years have taken for granted that events between 1640 and 1660 constituted a revolution and that, as a consequence, England after 1660 was more or less unrecognizable when compared with England before 1640, nevertheless this assumption is not universal. Let us now turn our attention to the much smaller group of scholars to whom these decades witnessed no more and no less than a 'civil war' or a 'great rebellion,' terminology which, significantly, would have been entirely familiar to contemporaries.

The attack seems to be informed by one of three distinct points of view. The first was enunciated by Professor J.H. Elliott in an article in which he addressed the 'general crisis' historians and questioned the applicability of 'revolution' to any events in seventeenth-century Europe.[81] He suggested that the application of this late eighteenth-century word – in its modern sense – to the mid-seventeenth century tempted historians into anachronism by attributing to an earlier period the characteristics of a paradigm abstracted from a later period. Professor Elliott did not quote Guizot in his article, but he might well have. In the preface written in 1826 to his *History of the English Revolution*, Guizot explained why only a nineteenth-century Frenchman could properly understand events in England in the mid-seventeenth-century. Only one who had lived through and experienced the 'passions and vicissitudes of [France's] revolution' could sympathetically portray it for, he believed, 'the first [revolution] would never have been thoroughly understood, had not the second taken place.'[82] What concerned Elliott was the historians' tendency to ascribe to seventeenth-century movements a progressive, ideological commitment to revolutionary change that is the hallmark of the French and later revolutions, yet which, he suggested, is not readily apparent in the earlier period. To Elliott, continuity might be a more helpful guide to seventeenth-century England, as to the rest of Europe, than revolution.

The second critique of 'revolution' is a little more oblique. G.R. Elton, in an essay dealing with the origins of the Civil War, and J.R. Jones, in a study of the events of 1688, have expressed their concern with those historians who assume that because events took a particular course it follows that such a course was inevitable.[83] In particular, Elton has said, historians' analyses of the 1603-40 period have not benefited from their preoccupation with the divisions of the Civil War and their insistence on seeing the forerunners of these divisions four or more decades before they appeared. It is a mistake, Elton says, to forget that in 1624 the government worked in harmony with the House of Commons, and that in 1640 it was the king who was isolated from the great bulk of his subjects within whose ranks no division may be discerned. Thus, the Apology of the Commons, far from being the first step in the 'high road to civil war,' was, in fact, a minority report that had been decisively rejected by the House.[84]

The same resistance to the Marxist-Whig view of the revolution of 1640-60 as 'one of the stages in the process of historical changes which produced the world we live in' is expressed by Jones, although he is concerned not with the causes of the great event but with its consequences. As befits the first revisionist historian of the 'Glorious Revolution' since Trevelyan, he does not share the almost universal tendency of historians to view 1688 as just 'a post-script' to the English Revolution of 1640-60. The defeat of James II, the collapse of his policies, the success of the revolution and its settlement were not, he insists, 'historically inevitable.' On the contrary, he argues, developments betwen 1640 and 1660 had been neither 'decisive nor conclusive' and, furthermore, 'the establishment of absolutism was a much more practicable proposition in the decades after 1660 than in the years before 1640.'[85]

Although neither Elton nor Jones is explicitly addressing himself to the usefulness of 'revolution' as a label for events between 1640 and 1660, both, by implication, are rejecting it. What occurred in the 1640s did not have the long-term, fundamental roots that one normally associates with revolutions, says Elton, nor did it, in Jones' view, achieve anything permanent or decisive. To both historians, there is no reason to believe that 1640-60 saw England take particularly significant steps into the modern world.

The idea that informs both Elton's and Jones' scepticism concerning the extent to which there was a revolution in seventeenth-century England also lies behind some of the recent revisionist work on pre-Civil War politics and is one of the points at issue in the controversy that has recently enlivened the pages of the *Journal of Modern History.* In playing down the role of the House of Commons as the locus of power in the decades before 1641, in stressing the importance of the peerage during the same period, and in rejecting the notion of 'adversarial politics' before 1646, the revisionist historians are, implicitly or explicitly, diminishing the extent of 'revolution' between 1640 and 1660. Thus, for example, Paul Christianson challenges the notion that 'some sort of revolution ... preceded the outbreak of civil war in England,' and argues that the Civil War began 'as a rebellion led by what contemporaries called the greater and lesser nobility.' J.H. Hexter, in his brilliant rebuttal of the revisionists, while agreeing with many of their critiques of the various forms of the Whig version of the Civil War, affirms sharply the revolutionary nature of events in the 1640s: the Civil War, he asserts, was revolutionary with the central issue, going back at least a generation, involving 'liberty and the rule of law.'[86]

The third assault on the idea of 'revolution' is frontal and is launched from the rapidly filling ranks of the professional local historians. This point of view, most commonly associated with the work of Alan Everitt, takes the position that the politics of Westminster in seventeenth-century England does not provide a paradigm, and often has little connection with political conflicts within local communities. Everitt is one of the few historians to insist that any explanation of England's 'crisis' of 1640-60 must make sense of the ' "conservative reaction" of 1659-60 as well as the revolutionary developments of 1640-

49.'[87] To understand the politial developments in Kent, Cheshire, or Sussex between 1640 and 1660 it is necessary, argue their historians,[88] to remember the essential localism of these societies, the remoteness of London and its issues, and the extreme variations from community to community. National issues are important and may certainly not be ignored, but they were always perceived at the provincial level through local filters no two of which were identical.

While this emphasis on the local rather than the national does not lead inevitably to a rejection of 'revolution,' nevertheless historians such as Everitt and Morrill tend to be struck more forcibly by the evidence of continuity in the local communities than by revolutionary discontinuity. What Everitt sees as the central conflict in Kent between 1640 and 1660, that between loyalty to the state and loyalty to the county, neither begins nor ends in this period. No major new families are established in Kent and the old gentry emerge more powerful than ever, while 'the variety, the cohesion and the obstinacy of that local life which formed the basis of their power, and which had defeated first the king, then parliament and finally Cromwell was not fundamentally altered until the nineteenth century,'[89] when, one assumes, England may finally have experienced its revolution.

J.S. Morrill, the historian of Cheshire in the Civil War years, is a little less certain about his county's experience during the period. On the one hand, he asserts that between 1640 and 1660 'the whole of society experienced a much more profound crisis than Professor Everitt has allowed' and that by the 1650s there had been sufficient 'administrative, ecclesiastical and social innovations' to make 'the rebellion worthy to be called a Revolution.' Yet, on the other hand, in his fantasy about the imaginary historian who conscientiously studies the pre-1640 period and then takes up his studies again in 1660, he agrees that such an historian could deduce little about the intervening years from Restoration sources. 'The Revolution,' he writes, 'left few permanent traces on the institutions of church and state ... across the country the old ways predominated.' Here, too, it would seem, although radicalism and innovation prevailed for a brief period, continuity rather than discontinuity were the dominant motif.[90]

It has not been the purpose of this historiographical analysis to determine whether or not 'revolution' is an appropriate label for events in England in the mid-seventeenth century. For well over a century it has been the favourite organizing device for historians in their approach to the whole period, although relatively few have attempted a systematic definition of the term and those who have tend to agree neither with each other nor with the social scientists. We have seen that there are some scholars, such as Christopher Hill, to whom permanent change, the crossing of the threshhold of the modern world, is intrinsic to their concept of 'revolution.' To others, such as Lawrence Stone or J.S. Morrill, it is not so much change permanently achieved, as change, foreshadowed or attempted, that forms the revolutionary core. Furthermore, if we try to lean too heavily upon the insights of the social scientists we risk a serious fall. According to the social scientist most admired by Professor Stone, Chalmers Johnson, events in England between 1640 and 1660 constitute not a revolution but a complex rebellion, since the prevailing ideology was not characterized by a 'conscious espousal of a new social order.'[91] As we have seen, according to the definition that Professor Stone actually cited, that of Sigmund Newmann, there was no 'revolution' in England in the seventeenth century.[92] However, despite all of the problems associated with the use of the term, it seems clear that historians will continue to apply it to England's mid-seventeenth-century civil wars, and, if the term is carefully defined, it will doubtless continue to serve a useful analytical purpose.

Nor has it been the intention of this study to consider the more general question of whether continuity or discontinuity characterizes Stuart England. It would not be fruitful to suggest that one model rather than the other provides the only guide to an understanding of the period. Just as Everitt is well aware that 'the hidden forces of social and economic change ... were neither reversed nor halted ... in 1660,'[93] so Christopher Hill reminds us that Isaac Newton was an alchemist and John Locke believed that a patient suffering from kidney pains could cure himself by burying a stone jug filled with his urine.[94]

Yet there does seem to be some point in urging historians to be more conscious of the connections between their assumptions and their discipline. To describe events in England between 1640 and 1660 as comprising a 'revolution' is to resort to a metaphor. It is not unusual, of course, for historians to employ metaphors: indeed, it is inconceivable that historians should not write metaphorically since the use of such imagery does not just enhance language but is intrinsic to it. However, the metaphor 'revolution' is unusually complex. The word itself enters the English language in its modern sense one hundred and fifty years after the death of Charles I in reference to a complicated series of events in late eighteenth-century France. When historians describe equally complex developments in England between 1640 and 1660 as 'revolution,' it is incumbent upon them to be clear about the implications of their language.

Furthermore, 'revolution,' in the sense in which Gardiner and Hill use the term, enters the language still later and carries an even heavier burden of significance. To the Marxists and to the Whigs, a 'revolution' not only involves permanent change, but also a specific function in the longer-term historic process. When these historians base their whole approach to seventeenth-century England upon such a heavily laden concept, the simple lines of metaphor override the complexities of the past.

Thomas Kuhn's exploration of the development of scientific method and knowledge is of some relevance here. In his *Structure of Scientific Revolutions*, Kuhn argues that normal scientific research is predicated upon the general acceptance, by the community of scientists concerned, of paradigms or models 'from which spring particular coherent traditions of scientific research' and which provide generally agreed 'rules and standards' for the discipline.[95] Before a paradigm is developed, as for instance occurred with electricity in the mid-eighteenth century, there can not really be scientific research as we understand it or even a science of that field. Data-gathering is without orientation and each researcher has to start afresh since there is no common body of knowledge to be assumed. However, after a paradigm has become established, Kuhn points out, members of the particular community of scientists periodically become aware of the existence of anomalies, natural phenomena that cannot be explained by reference to the paradigm. When the incidence of anomalies reaches a certain proportion, the scientific community experiences a kind of crisis that is resolved only by the acceptance of a new paradigm which both contradicts the old one and explains the anomalies. Scientists, he suggests, then embrace the faith of the new paradigm as fervently or dogmatically as they had the old one, and the advance of knowledge proceeds. The crucial point here is that paradigms cannot be supported by logic or by another paradigm. The final arbiter, he writes, is 'the assent of the relevant community.' Once the paradigm is accepted, then 'normal science' proceeds with its task of 'forcing nature into the preformed and relatively inflexible box that the paradigm supplies.'[96]

It would seem that historians of seventeenth-century England also have their paradigms and that the most generally accepted one for the past hundred years or so has been that of 'revolution,' which is normally associated with 'discontinuity.' Furthermore, it appears that historians of seventeenth-century England have taken to their research the basic assumption that there was a 'revolution' between 1640 and 1660 and that, as a corollary, they do not expect to analyse and explain post-1660 England in the same terms they use for pre-1640. The degree of change is far greater than can normally be expected during a couple of decades. The paradigm of revolution has defined the boxes in terms of which historians of Stuart England see their evidence.

Notwithstanding Elton's persuasive remarks on the historical discipline's enviable independence from *a priori* systems or models, paradigms would still appear to be indispensable.[97] Historians could no more do without the models in terms of which they make sense of the past than could Kuhn's physical scientists. However, it is important to recognize that they are simply models, or metaphors, and that they not be confused with the reality they purport to characterize. As Colin Turbayne has pointed out, there is a crucial difference between 'using a model and mistaking it for the thing modeled. The one is to make believe something is the case; the other is to believe that it is.'[98] David Fischer has made the same point in regard to historians' abuse of analogies. He agrees that it makes no sense to talk of abolishing metaphors. A more realistic policy, he writes, would be for 'historians themselves to search out the metaphors in their language and raise them to the level of consciousness, where they can be controlled.'[99]

Finally, Kuhn's notion of 'anomalies' can provide us with some insight into the current historiography of seventeenth-century England. As a direct consequence of the assumption by historians that discontinuity prevails, there are some questions softly asked and yet less audibly answered. As Everitt observed, the Restoration of 1659-60 needs to be considered by any theory which purports to explain the events of 1640-2.[100] More important for this study is the question of religion and its significance in any attempt to explain England's political history in the seventeenth century. Which historian has 'explained' the 'revolution' and not placed 'Puritanism' in the forefront of his analysis? Yet, how much attention is ever paid by political historians to late seventeenth-century Puritanism? We are told that society becomes more secular, but it has never been clearly explained just why Puritanism, so potent amongst the political elites in the 1640s, is so weak there in the 1660s. In terms of the metaphor of revolution, it is not surprising that the character and distribution of religious piety, like so many other elements in society, should change profoundly. But if we employ another paradigm, that of continuity, in place of revolution and look at the evidence through its filter, then it can be argued that the question 'What happens to Puritanism?' assumes a rather different character and, indeed, the whole history of Puritanism in the seventeenth century assumes a quite different form.

3

Historians and the Idea of 'Puritanism'

For almost a hundred years, as we have seen, most historians of Stuart England have accepted that spanning the central decades of the seventeenth century was a complex sequence of events that constituted a 'revolution.' As a result of this belief, much of the history of seventeenth-century England written since the late nineteenth century has been predicated upon its corollary – that there is an overriding and fundamental discontinuity between the early and later decades of the period. Christopher Hill, for example, has written of the revolution of ideas that took place in England between 1640 and 1660 that 'it was so great an intellectual revolution that it is difficult for us to conceive how men thought before it was made.' Nor was it solely a 'revolution in thought,' for the years 1640 to 1660 were 'comparable in many respects with the French Revolution' and witnessed also a 'revolution in science' and 'revolution in prose.' More recently, Hill has written: 'the apparent similarity between the England of 1640 and the England of 1660 is illusory. The institutions are the same – monarchy, House of Lords, House of Commons, episcopal state church, common law; but the social context has changed.'[1] A similar and fundamental discontinuity between the early and later decades of seventeenth-century England is also implied in T.S. Eliot's 'dissociation of sensibility' which he saw occurring in this period as the unity of thought and feeling evident in the Metaphysical poets was fatally and permanently severed by Dryden's time.[2] One of Eliot's followers, S.L. Bethel, referred to the 'almost violent contrast between the first and second halves' of the seventeenth century and stated the fact of discontinuity in its most blunt form: 'In 1660 King Charles II returned from exile and the new age really began.[3]

The paradigm of 'revolution' has had an equally dramatic effect on the way in which historians have viewed the history of English religion in the seventeenth century. This effect can be demonstrated in two ways. First, much more attention has been paid to problems ultimately religious in nature and origin in the hundred years before 1660 than in the hundred years following the Restoration. Second, and not unrelated, there is scarcely any area of interest to the historian of the earlier period in which he does not turn to religion for at least part of his explanation. The growth of capitalism and of the market society, the spread of education, changing attitudes to marriage and the rise of 'affective individualism,' the rise of Parliament, the growth of science – these and many other generally accepted phenomena in early seventeenth-century English history have all been at least partly explained by reference to causes that were ultimately religious in character.[4] After 1660, in contrast, there is no such dependence upon religion. While historians of the period after the Restoration do not ignore the question of the way men perceived their relationship with God, nevertheless it becomes a matter of secondary importance. As Lawrence Stone has expressed it, one result of the English Revolution, 1640 to 1660, was that 'religion now came to be regarded as a useful buttress of law and order and the status quo and an aid to economic prosperity, rather than as a means to communicate with God and to achieve salvation in the next world.'[5] The growth of political stability or of the origins of the Industrial Revolution in the eighteenth century, unlike comparable problems a hundred years before, do not usually cause their historians to give a great deal of attention to religion.[6]

Of all the many different varieties of religious experience that flourished in England between 1560 and 1660, Puritanism has most fascinated modern historians. Who, in recent times, has ever attempted a history of the early seventeenth century in England, or of the origins of the civil wars, or of a whole gamut of more social and economic problems, without paying fulsome attention to Puritanism? Undeterred by the real problems of definition,[7] historians of England during the century before 1660 almost invariably see Puritanism as providing either the essential context for political and social change or as being itself the cause of the change. Yet it is an easily demonstrable feature of seventeenth-century English historiography that few, if any, historians of the post-1660 period – and, significantly, they are usually different scholars – ever feel much obligation to Puritanism. To historians of the post-1660 period – and particularly to political historians – neither religious belief, in general, nor Puritanism in its new guise of Nonconformity, in particular, demand the kind of attention that scholars of the pre-1660 period without question assign the phenomenon. Whereas for the earlier period all historians of politics and society feel obliged to come to grips with the problems raised by the varieties of religious belief, after 1660 the history of religion tends to be left to the denominational scholars.

This point can be most readily illustrated by a brief comparison of the work of two political historians, David Underdown and J.R. Jones. In *Pride's Purge*,

Underdown has presented a fine analysis of English upper-class politics in 1648/9. Jones, in *The First Whigs*, an equally valuable study of the Exclusion Crisis, has analysed political divisions within the same upper classes thirty years later. While both books are political studies of a relatively small social class separated by just one generation, there is a major difference in the importance assigned to religious belief in the narrative and analysis of the two scholars.[8]

Underdown's study of Pride's Purge is a model of its kind. His analysis of the parliamentary politics of the late 1640s is particularly clear-minded and has resolved much of the confusion that long surrounded discussion of Civil War politics at the national level. Furthermore, his quantitative social analysis of the various political groups is revealing, although, as he has concluded, far from definitive in establishing connections between socio-economic interests and political behaviour. Underdown does not believe that religious divisions were the decisive ones in the Long Parliament in 1648/9, and he is well aware of the difficulties in generalizing about the religious convictions of most members of Parliament. The religious beliefs of almost one half of the entire membership of the Long Parliament in late 1648 are, he admits, 'unknown.' Nevertheless, he is firmly convinced that 'Puritanism' is central to an understanding of the political history of the period. 'Most of the active Parliamentarians *were* Puritans – religious idealists who strained towards the Godly Reformation.' Nor were just the leaders Puritans, for, he believes, 'the overwhelming majority of the members who remained at Westminster after 1642 were Puritans in the broad undifferentiated sense used by Baxter.' Discussing the religious aims of the middle group in 1644, he writes 'that they had none that were more specific than those dictated by the undifferentiated moral Puritanism of the majority of members.' 'Most members were Puritans in a general sort of way,' he estimates of 1649, 'but not so completely absorbed by the finer shades of controversy as the clergy.' Eleven years later, however, the nature of the religious beliefs of at least the upper levels of English society had changed dramatically. In his brief remarks about the response of the gentry to the reconvening of the Long Parliament in 1660, Underdown writes that they, reuniting 'in defence of liberty and property,' are still 'religious men,' but men for whom 'religion no longer determined their political outlook (if it ever had) except insofar as it had confirmed the fears they felt for Quakers and other sectaries on political and social grounds.'[9]

Here we are confronted with a clear exposition of the fundamental discontinuity historians have consistently found in the religious persuasion of the political elites of seventeenth-century England. Underdown's political analysis of the 1640s takes for granted that 'Puritanism' is the *sine qua non* of revolution. 'Every major event in the Interregnum,' he writes, is the product of 'the two conflicting forces of Puritan idealism and gentry constitutionalism.'[10] Yet, a decade later, this burning piety has been almost extinguished. By 1660, Puritanism is no longer integral to any explanation of events.

Just as Underdown may be seen as typifying historians of pre-1660 England in his evaluation of and dependence upon 'Puritanism,' J.R. Jones may be said to represent historians of the Restoration period in his downgrading of the religious influence. In his study of the politics of the Exclusion Crisis, Jones rarely employs the word 'Puritanism' and refers to the influence of Dissent as being important, but no longer a dominant factor, in English political life. He identifies five component sections of the 'Whig party' in the late 1670s and, of these, only the minority 'old Presbyterians' exhibited a 'genuine and positive zeal for religious reform and Protestant unity' comparable to that of the Puritans. It is clear, furthermore, that this group has become, by 1678, an anachronism, for the predominant forces behind Shaftesbury's alliance were secular and political.[11] The aspirations of Shaftesbury and of the Whig party, although reminiscent of the parliamentary alliance of 1641/2, are not dependent upon the forces of religious experience for their explanation. To Jones, as to most other historians of the period, the political nation is essentially secular. Puritanism, a fundamental in every analysis of the 'revolution' of the 1640s, has become, one generation later, essentially peripheral.[12]

The contrast between the two historians' views of Puritanism is clearest in the way they treat the one individual who was a prominent member of the Long Parliament from its first sitting in November 1640 and also a member of the three Exclusion Parliaments forty years later. Denzil Holles had a rather chequered political career, having been one of the members of the House of Commons imprisoned by Charles I after the dissolution of Parliament in 1629, one of the five members of the House of Commons accused of treason by Charles I in January 1642, one of the eleven members impeached by the army in June 1647, and, ultimately, a member of the Cavalier and Exclusion Parliaments as Baron Holles. While neither Underdown nor Jones focuses directly on Holles, there is nevertheless a clear distinction between the ways in which they interpret him. To Underdown, Holles was a Puritan, a 'fiery spirit' who was among the most militant opponents of the king in 1642 and who, as he became frightened by the likelihood of social revolution, became a leading Presbyterian. Notwithstanding the steady tempering of his zeal as the decade progressed, Underdown clearly sees Holles as he sees hundreds of other members of his social class – as a religious zealot. Jones, in contrast, views Holles as an anachronism, one whose views on life and on political society had been rendered obsolete by the secularism implicit in the political activism of Shaftesbury and his Whig party. To Underdown, the importance of religious factors in the politics of the 1640s is fundamentally different from its importance to Jones in the political history of the same society one generation later. Nowhere does Jones make this more apparent than when he makes the explicit comparison, writing that 'the causes of the Exclusion Crisis were not identical with those of the civil war ... for instance, few of the younger Whigs were absorbed by religious questions.'[13]

It is possible that historians have presented seventeenth-century English religion in terms of this discontinuity because that is a precise description of how it was. It is conceivable that the thousands of gentry and merchant families who comprised English political society saw their lives in the period culminating in the 1640s primarily and increasingly in terms of a 'Puritan' zeal to create the New Jerusalem, and that, after a decade of rule by the 'saints in arms,' they regained their senses and once again put property and order ahead of the zeal for reform. If this is what happened in England between 1650 and 1670, then it has certainly never been carefully described, let alone explained. If it is true that most parliamentarians in the 1640s were Puritans, then there is a major problem. If Puritanism was powerful enough to bring about the upheavals of the 1640s, then why did it decline so quickly? If the political alliance that was powerful enough to wage war with the king in 1642 derived its strength from Puritanism, and if Puritanism is a label for a coherent theological point of view that caused believers to manifest extraordinary and distinctive piety and a self-conscious zeal to reform the church and to erect the godly commuity, then what becomes of it in and after 1660?[14] Is it reasonable to assume that such a broad segment of the gentry, that was represented, for example, in the Long Parliament and was so thoroughly and militantly Puritan, should, within half a generation, be equally thoroughly reconverted to secular constitutionalism?

One purpose of this study is to suggest an approach to the problem 'What happens to Puritanism?' not by describing the process of reconversion of this large social group, but by questioning the premises upon which the question is based. In short, it can be argued that nothing decisive happens to the religion of English political society in the aftermath of the civil wars and that the post-1660 religious persuasion of the members of the country's elite classes had not fundamentally changed since 1640. If we look at the evidence relating to the impact of men's religious experience on their political behaviour before and after the Civil War in terms of continuity rather than of discontinuity, it can be suggested that the question 'What happens to Puritanism?' is not so much answered as made irrelevant.

Before considering an alternative approach to this problem, however, let us examine how we have reached our present dilemma. In particular, let us look at the way in which the individual experiences of seventeenth-century 'Puritans' were transmogrified by historians into the abstraction 'Puritanism' and, in the process, came to assume a central role in any explanation of the origins and character of what its foremost exponent, S.R. Gardiner, referred to as the 'Puritan Revolution.'

Between the 1560s and the 1640s, the frequency with which contemporaries used the word 'Puritan' to describe others' – usually their enemies' – positions was matched by the variety of ways in which they employed the term. Any attempt to derive a definition of the term 'Puritan' from contemporary usage is doomed to failure in the same way and for the same reasons as would be an attempt to define 'communist' or 'socialist' from a review of letters to the editors of a variety of newspapers from the late 1940s to the present day. 'Puritan' was a term of opprobrium, with theological, ecclesiological, political, and social connotations, and was used to describe individuals at almost every point on the political, religious, and social spectrum, from James I and Archbishop Whitgift on the one hand to Thomas Cartwright and John Milton on the other.[15] On this, historians agree. Even when the word was used most dispassionately between the 1560s, when it was coined, and the mid-seventeenth century when it fell out of common circulation as a label for contemporary positions, there was considerable variation in its meaning. In the 1560s a Puritan was one who abhorred the 'popish apparel' prescribed for the clergy, whereas a decade later it usually meant a 'Presbyterian.'[16] In the course of the next half-century the word was used variously and by the early 1640s, as Henry Parker's classic analysis testifies, it was applied indifferently to politicians and clergymen, the respectably pious and the uncouth fanatics. 'By a new enlargement of the name, the world is full of nothing else but Puritans, for besides the Puritans in Church policy, there are now added Puritans in Religion, Puritans in state, and Puritans in morality. By this means whole kingdoms are familiarly upbraided with this sin of Puritanism.'[17]

After the Restoration of Charles II, 'Puritan' ceased to be used much to describe contemporary religious or political positions largely because of the self-conscious emergence of Presbyterian, Independent, and other sectarian groupings that rendered the term obsolete. Amongst historians and other propagandists who between the Restoration and the mid-nineteenth century wrote about England during the century before 1660, the use of 'Puritan' to describe groups or persuasions was occasional, while references to 'Puritanism' were almost non-existent. This abstraction, 'Puritanism,' which in the past hundred years has been crucial to nearly every historian's account of the origins of the English Civil War, was, before the mid-nineteenth century, rarely used. When it was employed, 'Puritanism' served an incidental and summarizing function, which contrasts sharply with its more recent *deus ex machina* role.

Whether or not historians have chosen to use the word 'Puritan' to describe a religious position in the pre-1640 period is interesting, but is ultimately less important than is the fact that they all have agreed that the civil wars could not be fully understood without some attention to religious disagreements. Broadly speaking, it is possible to discern three distinct points of view on this subject among historians between 1660 and 1860. First, there are those historians who accepted the Royalist propaganda about the civil wars and to whom the achievements of 1641 were the necessary safeguards of the constitution, but who bemoaned the willingness of the parliamentary party to jeopardize law and order after that date. To these historians, including Clarendon, Hobbes, and Hume, it was the factious work of the preachers which stirred up the lower orders and hence brought about the disasters of the next eighteen years.[18] Then there were those historians who identified with the religious position of the Puritans, accepted the parliamentary propaganda linking Charles' court with popery, and identified the godly party with the Parliamentarians.[19] By the nineteenth century a third point of view had developed which did not neglect the role of Puritans in bringing about the violence of the 1640s, but saw them as one group amongst a number. To historians writing in the first half of the nineteenth century, such as Hallam, Lingard, and Macaulay, there was a Puritan party in England before 1640, a group neither factious nor incompatible with the Church of England, but one that was less than co-extensive with that much larger parliamentary party that waged war with the king in the years after 1642.[20]

When Thomas Hobbes enumerated the various causes which led the people of England to be seduced from their allegiance to their sovereign, his first three categories were religious. Hobbes made no use of 'Puritan' in his explanation of the civil wars, but he did see the Presbyterian ministers, and the Independents and other sectaries, along with the papists, as having been extremely important. While the papists were always looking for opportunities to foster disorder, the better to facilitate 'the restoring of the Pope's authority,' the Presbyterians were playing a more dynamic role. Working with 'a great many gentlemen,' the Presbyterian clergy, strongest in London and in the other cities and market towns of England, brought the people 'to a dislike of the Church-government, Canons and Common-prayer book' as effectively as the gentry made them 'in love with democracy by their harangues in the Parliament.' Hobbes did not believe that the teachings of the Presbyterians constituted a religion at all, as he understood the term. Since all virtue resided in obedience to the laws, and since even religion derived its authority from the nation's laws, it followed that the Presbyterians were not truly religious. On the contrary, they were 'the most impious hypocrites ... covered with the cloak of godliness.' Their opinions, and those of the sects later in the 1640s, were not a form of religion, but rather a 'divinity, or church philosophy.'[21]

To Hobbes, the civil wars were about sovereignty. His history was a practical demonstration of the truth of Hobbism. The alternative to the Leviathan was anarchy. Forces that we would describe as broadly 'religious' played a fermenting role in society, as did the universities, the prosperous merchants, the declining gentry, and the failure of both sides to read Thomas of Malmsbury, but in no sense did the civil wars occur because of an attempt to implement the godly community. In adopting the program of the 'number of poor parish priests that were Presbyterians,' the Parliamentarians simply intended 'to make use of their tenets, and with pretended sanctity to make the King and his party odious to the people, by whose help they were to set up democracy and depose the King.'[22]

Clarendon is not usually regarded as having much in common with Hobbes. Although they were both believers in strong authority, Clarendon shared the abhorrence of Restoration society for the writings of Hobbes who, in turn, implicitly criticized Clarendon for his wrong-headed support for the idea of mixarchy, or mixed monarchy, 'though it were indeed nothing else but pure anarchy.'[23] In his conception of the nature of the Puritans' religion before 1640 and its connection with the civil wars, however, Clarendon shared some of Hobbes' scepticism. In particular, he echoed Hobbes' profound anti-clericalism and his conviction that the civil wars would not have occurred without the preaching of the 'factious and schismatical' clergymen.[24]

In Clarendon's well-known celebration of the state of affairs in England during the 1630s, his optimism embraced the spiritual sphere as fully as the secular. Charles, he suggested, was even more fortunate than Elizabeth, whose prosperity was clouded by 'the doubts, hazards and perplexities upon a total change and alteration of religion, and some confident attempts upon a further alteration by those who thought not the reformation enough.' The outlook was more favourable by the 1630s as the nation was 'little inclined to the Papists and less to the Puritans.' Clarendon, of course, was not likely to include the lower orders in any analysis of a well-ordered community, and thus his remarks about the happy acceptance of the 'government and discipline' of the church applied only to those 'persons of any valuable condition.'[25]

His explanation of how so felicitous a kingdom so quickly degenerated into the anarchy of civil war is not very different from Hobbes'. There was an unholy alliance between a number of politicians seeking place and a group of clergymen seeking religious reform, whom he occasionally refers to as Puritans. This alliance, taking advantage of the alarm caused by the Laudian reforms and the elevation of some clergymen into positions of political authority, while professing merely the 'reformation of disapproved and odious enormities,' was in actual fact 'removing foundations.' Few members of either House were, in Clarendon's view, religious reformers, but were moved to adopt dangerous constitutional positions because the liberty of subjects was jeopardized by the 'countenancing [of] Popery to the subversion of the Protestant religion.'[26]

Clarendon focused on William Prynne as an example of the way clergymen influenced the politicians. Prynne's 'divinity' had been 'marred by the conversations of factious and hotheaded divines.' Under their influence, he had developed a 'proud and venemous dislike against the discipline of the Church of England.' In due course, 'as the progress is very natural,' Prynne had come to challenge the 'government of the state' as well.[27]

The preachers, however, had not had their most dramatic effect upon the likes of Prynne. Men of quality, after all, were immune to their kind of irrational influence almost by definition. The real import of the preaching was to be seen in its effect upon the people. With the weakening of Laudian controls in 1640, 'pulpits were freely delivered to the schismatical and silenced preachers, who till then had lurked in corners or lived in New England.' These preachers then drove out all 'learned and orthodox men' and, pretending 'reformation and extirpating of Popery, inspired seditious inclination into the hearts of men against the present government of the Church and with many libellous invectives against the State too.'[29]

In Clarendon's view, religion – though he would not so dignify the teachings of the Puritan divines with the term – was influential in stirring up the urban classes and lower orders generally, whereas ambition motivated their betters. His narrative of events in the eighteen months before August 1642 is in terms of a dialogue between two groups. On the one hand were the members of Parliament, most of whom, like the Earl of Bedford, 'had no desire that there should be any alteration in the government of the Church.' On the other hand were their clerical supporters outside Parliament, the 'seditious and schismatical preachers,' frustrated with their allies for their 'want of zeal in the matter of religion.' Such was the tension between the two wings of the alliance by April 1642, says Clarendon, that the Parliamentarians published a declaration promising the calling of the Assembly of Divines. This had become essential 'to confirm and encourage the factitious and schismatical party of the kingdom, which thought the pace towards the reformation was not brisk and furious enough and was with great difficulty contained in so slow a march.'[29]

The similarities between Hobbes and Clarendon are never more apparent than in their comments upon the irony of the preachers' position in 1641. To Hobbes, the differences between 'Bishop and Presbytery' were slight and were certainly not likely to affect the individual's chance of salvation. Together, he wrote, they preach every 'duty necessary to Salvation except only the duty we owe to the King on which point each condemns itself' by their mutual preparedness 'either to rule or destroy the King.'[30] The Protestant attack on Rome and the Presbyterian rejection of the Laudian church were equally seditious in that they denied the absolute sovereignty of the monarch. Clarendon too was struck by the same contradiction between rhetoric and the reality of the preachers' position. While they urged the Bishops' Exclusion Bill on the grounds that secular authority was inconsistent with ecclesiastical function, the reformation in England in 1641 was being 'driven on by no men so much as those clergy,' men such as Burgess and Marshall, who had far more influence on Parliament than ever Laud had had 'upon the counsels at Court.' Clarendon indeed speculated that perhaps he had discovered the sin against the Holy Ghost. In a judgment closely resembling that of Hobbes, he condemned those ministers of the church who 'by their function being messengers of peace' nevertheless, in the greatest apostacy conceivable, became the 'trumpets of war, incendiaries towards rebellion ... [by] preaching rebellion to the people as the doctrine of Christ.' To both these writers, of course, the truly religious party was the king's. As Clarendon wrote, 'men were drawn by the impulsion of conscience' to support the king who were 'zealous for the preservation of the law, the religion, and true interest of the nation.' To Hobbes, what religion there was in England in 1642 was on the king's side as no one could be religious who did not obey his sovereign.[31]

If Thomas Hobbes wrote *Behemoth* as a cautionary tale for a society that had not had the benefit of what he himself had written on the nature of political obligation, then David Hume was equally insistent that readers of his *History of England* learn the lesson of the dangers of 'religious enthusiasm.' For it was precisely that – Puritan zeal – which transformed a legitimate determination in 1641 to protect the rights of Englishmen into the hypocritical willingness in 1642 to encourage 'such violent convulsions ... [that are] the disgrace of that age and of this island.' Whereas to Hobbes, virtue consisted largely in obedience to authority, to Hume it resided in reasonableness. His history of seventeenth-century England was intended to prove the point.[32]

Hume praised the manner of England's Reformation for being more rational than that in any other country, by which he meant that in retaining certain of the old ways the new church acquired an instantaneous veneration in 'the eyes of the people.' This very reasonableness, however, provoked a group of reformers, the Puritans, who in the early Elizabethan period adopted extremely anti-Catholic views and were essentially 'enthusiasts, indulging themselves in rapturous flights, ecstacies, visions and inspirations,' with a natural aversion to institutions or forms 'which seem to restrain the liberal effusions of their zeal and devotion.'

While Hume, like Clarendon, makes some use of the labels 'Puritan' and 'Puritanical' when referring to critics of the church prior to the 1630s, he almost never uses 'Puritanism,' nor is he consistent when he describes individuals as 'Puritans.' In the course of his narrative of England's history in the late 1620s, Hume wrote 'that the appellation puritan stood for three parties which, though commonly united together, were yet actuated by very different views and motives. There were the political puritans, who maintained the highest principle of civil liberty; the puritans in discipline, who were averse to the ceremonies and episcopal government of the church: and the doctrinal puritans, who rigidly defended the speculative system of the first reformers.' Yet, notwithstanding his awareness of the complexity of the label, Hume frequently used it in its simple and undifferentiated form, leaving his reader to guess to which group he is referring. At other times he simply described the connection between kinds of 'Puritan' groups that only compounds the confusion. Thus, for example, he wrote of alliances on the eve of the meeting of the Long Parliament, 'though the political and religious puritans mutually lent assistance to each other, there were many who joined the former and yet declined all connexion with the latter.'[33]

Hume was most fascinated – and appalled – by the religious Puritans, and upon them he laid the blame for the disasters of the Interregum. He, like Clarendon and Hobbes, attributed class differences to the opposing parties in the civil wars. These differences, furthermore, were mirrored in similar, and not unrelated, differences in religious preference. Just as it was essentially the lower orders who provided the main strength of the parliamentary alliance, so these were the kinds of people among whose 'distempered imaginations ... the fanatical spirit let loose, confounded all regard to ease, safety, interest; and therefore dissolved every moral and civil obligation.' To him it was clear that without religious differences, the political and constitutional adjustments of 1641 would have been completed and the king's prerogatives thereafter permanently checked. But it was religion or, more accurately, a particular form of religious experience by which men were affected, for 'all orders of men had drunk deep of the intoxicating poison' which caused them to believe that 'in the acts of the most extreme disloyalty towards their prince, consisted their greatest merit in the eye of Heaven.' It was easy, thought Hume, to demonstrate that as far as 'the people' were concerned, the controversy in and after 1642 was 'almost wholly theological.' Without religious fervour, 'the generality of the nation could never have flown into such fury in order to obtain new privileges and acquire greater liberty than they and their ancestors had ever been acquainted with.' According to Hume, the political division of 1642 corresponded to the religious division in the nation. Whereas 'the Presbyterian religion was new, republican, and suited to the genius of the populace; the other had an air of greater show and ornament, was established on ancient authority, and bore an affinity to the kingly and aristocratic parts of the constitution.'[34]

Hume's explanation of the civil wars was clearly consistent with those of Clarendon and Hobbes in that all three saw a form of religious fanaticism appropriate to the less respectable elements of society as motivating these groups to fight for the parliamentary side. Hume, however, differed from his predecessors in his more developed repudiation of the kind of religion experienced by the Parliamentarians and by his inclination to characterize even their leaders as 'enthusiasts.'

While Hume's explanation was couched in terms of the familiar alliance between 'zeal and ambition,' he did not share his predecessors' view of ambitious politicians cynically manipulating the gullible masses. As early as 1625, he wrote, 'the puritanical party, though disguised, had a very great authority over the kingdom; and many of the leaders among the commons had secretly embraced the rigid tenets of that sect.' And even though the 'religious schemes of many of the puritans, when explained, appear pretty frivolous' he had in mind the surplice, altar rails, and the like – yet were they pursued by 'some men of the greatest parts and most extensive knowledge.' There cannot have been many of this rank who were susceptible to the Puritan cause, because elsewhere he seems quite clear that the 'nobility and more considerable gentry' supported the king, 'dreading a total confusion of rank from the fury of the populace.' The fury, which activated the few gentry and their more numerous allies from 'the vicious and enervated populace of the cities,' was a form of religion characterized by Hume as stimulating 'unsurmountable passion [which] disguised to themselves, as well as to others, under the appearance of holy fervours, was well qualified to make proselytes and to seize the minds of the ignorant multitude ... Equally full of fraud and of ardour these pious patriots talked perpetually of seeking the Lord, yet still pursued their own purposes; and have left a destructive lesson to posterity how delusive, how destructive, that principle is by which they were animated.'[35]

Clarendon, Hobbes, and Hume did not doubt that the civil wars were the fundamentally malevolent result of a dangerous and anti-social form of religion that had had a limited effect upon the 'better sort' but had spread like wild-fire in the more congenial – and less civilized – atmosphere of London and the other corporations, and among the lower orders generally. What is important to note in the approach of these three historians is not their emphasis upon religion as a cause of the wars, but their characterization of the 'Puritan' religion as essentially an emotional, irrational, and incoherent form of madness. The contrast between this conception and that of scholars writing in the Puritan-Nonconformist tradition is striking. One of the best accounts of the origins and character of the civil wars and of one man's involvement in them to come from this tradition is Lucy Hutchinson's *Memoirs of Colonel Hutchinson*. Writing more or less contemporaneously with Hobbes and Clarendon, Hutchinson shared with those writers their conviction of the religious origins of the wars, yet could not have been more different in the way in which she characterized the Puritans.

To Hutchinson, the English civil wars could be understood only in the broader context of English history, which she presented in terms of two distinct, but complementary, lines of development, one sacred, the other secular. To illustrate England's recent religious history, she employed the common astronomical metaphor, the movement of the sun around the earth. 'The dawn of the gospel began to break upon this isle after the dark midnight of papacy' during the reign of Henry VIII, whom she condemned for merely managing to change 'their foreign yoke for home-bred fetters, dividing the pope's spoils between himself and his bishops.' For this reason, the morning of true religion, 'when light and shades were blended and almost undistinguished,' was 'more cloudy than in other places.' As late as 1620, when Lucy Hutchinson was born, it was still 'early in the morning,' but 'the Sun of truth was exalted in his progress and [was] hastening towards a meridian glory.' In her own lifetime, she wrote, she considered herself privileged to have witnessed 'the admirable growth of gospel-light,' a characterization that would have astounded most of her contemporaries.[36]

Her view of England's secular history was more conventional. From the union of Normans and Saxons emerged a people whose valour was such that they 'have showed abroad how easily they could subdue the world, if they did not prefer the quiet enjoyment of their own part above the conquest of the whole.'[37] More important than their courage, however, was their political organization. With a constitution comprising the better parts of monarchy, aristocracy, and democracy, 'popular liberty' could never be so seriously threatened that 'it trod on those that trampled it before. For the generous people of England, as they were the most free and obsequious subjects in the world to those princes that managed them with a kind and tender hand, commanding them as freemen, not as slaves, so were they the most untameable, invincible people, in defence of their freedoms against all those usurping lords that scorned to allow them liberty.'[38]

During the reigns of the first two Stuarts, these streams combined so that when John Hutchinson and the other Parliamentarians finally took up arms in 1642 it was to protect 'the great cause of God's and England's rights.' Although the tone of the courts of James and Charles differed greatly, Hutchinson did not believe their fundamental objectives varied. James, she said, was always mindful of the fate of his mother and 'harboured a secret desire of revenge upon the godly in both nations.' Thus he steadily proceeded to 'undermine ... the true religion ... and the liberty of the people.' The two were connected, she believed, since 'it was impossible to make them slaves, till they were brought to be idolators of royalty and glorious lust; and as impossible to make them adore those gods while they continued loyal to the government of Jesus Christ.' Under Charles, the threat was even more serious, since 'this king was a worse encroacher upon the civil and spiritual liberties of his people by far than his father.' Specifically, the direction from which the threat to both civil and religious liberties came was popery. In Hutchinson's view, there was between 1603 and 1640 a deliberate and almost successful conspiracy to subvert Protestantism and to reconcile England with the Church of Rome. Her illustrations of this conspiracy included the Hampton Court Conference, as a result of which 'the nonconformists were cast out of doors ... and the penalties against papists were relaxed'; the fact that 'Arminianism crept into the corruption of sound doctrine'; 'secret treaties were entertained with the court of Rome'; 'the mixed marriage of papist and protestant families, which, no question, was a design of the papist party to compass and procure'; the Spanish match and, worst of all, the marriage between Henrietta Maria and Charles I. It was bad enough that Charles was the king, he being a 'prince that had nothing of faith or truth, justice or generosity in him.' The influence of his wife, however, was disastrous. She managed to 'enslave' her husband in his affections while her passion was solely 'to promote her designs' which were the implementation of her priests' plans 'of advancing her own religion, whose principle it is to subvert all others.'[39]

The heroes in this sorry tale were the Puritans whose banners she proudly unfurls. 'Puritans,' she says, was a label applied by the 'children of darkness' – the 'needy courtiers, the proud encroaching priests, the thievish projectors, the lewd nobility and gentry' – to the 'children of light,' who included all who either 'grieved at ... the unjust oppressing of the subject' or were 'zealous for God's glory or worship.' Hutchinson's own use of the term was rather less catholic, although not entirely consistent. On occasion she appears to have accepted contemporary usage of 'Puritan' as referring to the broad political alliance of the saints and the patriots who opposed the court. At other times, however, she gave 'Puritan' a much more specifically religious connotation, as when describing her father-in-law she boasted of his 'Puritanism' as 'the reproach of the world, though the glory of good men.' In general, however, she preferred to describe those who, like her husband, exhibited a 'passionate zeal for the interest of God' as the 'godly.' This was a specifically religious label that signified an individual in whom there was apparent 'that universal habit of grace which is wrought in a soul by the regenerating Spirit of God, whereby the whole creature is resigned up unto the divine will and love, and all its actions directed to the obedience and glory of its Maker.'[40]

Such people were clearly a minority within the broader parliamentary or

Puritan alliance, although they appeared to be more numerous than they were because, she confessed, there were many who 'put on a form of godliness' when they were unable to secure preferments. Such hypocrites showed their true colours later in the 1640s when the Presbyterians attempted 'a violent persecution upon the account of conscience' of the saints in the New Model Army. It was this apostasy by the Presbyterian faction that caused them 'to break their covenant with God and men, and to renew a league with the papish interest' and so 'destroy that godly interest which they had at first so gloriously asserted.'[41]

It is clear that to Lucy Hutchinson, as we have already seen to her contemporaries, Hobbes and Clarendon, it was the zeal of the godly that disposed the Parliamentarians to fight against the court and its supporters among the 'malignant nobility and gentry.' Furthermore, the purity of the 'good old cause' became increasingly clear through the 1640s when only the saints could stay the course. Even the Rump Parliament she praised as manifesting 'the hand of God' until 'Cromwell's ambition' interrupted its deliberations.[42] Where she differed from Clarendon and Hobbes was in her judgment of the sectaries. She accepted the sectarian position and absorbed their propaganda into her history, whereas Hobbes and Clarendon accepted the Royalist propaganda and saw John Hutchinson and his ilk as seditious disturbers of the public order.

Lucy Hutchinson did not write a formal historical account of the civil wars, nor did she write for publication. The significance of her *Memoirs* lies in the way she represented the rarely expressed – and yet more rarely licensed – sectarian view of the civil wars and of the connection she perceived between the 'Puritan' interest and the wars. Written within the same broad tradition, albeit more critical of the actions of many of the Puritans, Daniel Neal's four-volume *History of the Puritans or the Protestant Nonconformists* presented the first elaborate defence of the Puritan position. Hoping by his account to defend the cause of full political and social freedom for Nonconformists, Neal's *History* is notable both for the assumption of continuity that informs his sense of the Nonconformist tradition and for the limits he attributes to the involvement of the godly in the civil wars.

As each volume of Neal's *History* was published through the 1730s, he devoted a considerable part of its preface to a plea for the relaxation of the Test Act and other parts of the penal code towards the Nonconformists. This body of legislation, he wrote, had quite properly been passed to protect England against the unceasing conspiracy of popery, but was both unnecessary and unjust when directed at the Nonconformists whose loyalty was unquestioned.[43] With this in mind, Neal wrote to defend the Puritans against the aspersions of Tory historical accounts which blamed them for all that was anarchic and dangerous in the civil wars.

There is an ambiguity in Neal's use of 'Puritan' that we have already seen in Hutchinson, an ambiguity which throws some light on the way he connected the civil wars with various forms of religious experience. The Puritans whose history he wrote he sometimes distinguished as 'doctrinal puritans.' Following Fuller, he defined such Puritans as those 'who endeavoured in their devotions to accompany the minister with a pure heart and who were remarkably holy in their conversations.'[44] A Puritan, therefore, was 'a man of severe morals, a Calvinist in doctrine and a nonconformist to the ceremonies and discipline of the church, though he did not totally separate from it.' Not that Neal regarded non-separation as intrinsic to his concept of a Puritan, since he criticized Queen Elizabeth sharply for her persecution of the early Dissenters; compelling things indifferent by law 'made them separate.' Because there were many who could not worship in the 'popish churches' of Elizabethan England, there developed that separation from the Church of England 'which continues to this day.' Just as 'puritans' were not to be defined by their disavowal of separation, neither, ironically, were the 'doctrinal puritans' to be distinguished from conformists by doctrine. In the Elizabethan period, according to Neal, the differences between Puritans and conformists concerned church government, apparel, and 'the natural right every man has to judge for himself and make profession of that religion he apprehends most agreeable to truth'[45]

During Elizabeth's reign, and indeed until the eighteenth century, the number of such 'doctrinal puritans' was, Neal implies, small. Between 1603 and 1640, however, the 'number of puritans increased prodigiously,' for several reasons which tend to confuse his concept of 'Puritan.' In the first place, there emerged a new kind of Puritan, a 'state puritan,' whom he defined in exclusively secular language. Such Puritans, he said, were all those 'who found it necessary, for the preservation of their properties, to oppose the court and to insist upon being governed according to the law.' In addition, said Neal, the ranks of the 'doctrinal puritans' were filled by 'most of the country clergy' who, although 'well enough affected by the discipline and ceremonies of the church,' nevertheless 'adhered to Calvin in disputes with the Court Arminians.' Finally, there were recruits to the Puritan ranks from moral men who were called Puritans even if they only 'kept the sabbath, frequented sermons, maintained family religion.' Not surprisingly, therefore, when Laud 'drove so near the precipices of popery and tyranny, the hearts of the most resolved Protestants turned against him and almost all England became puritan.'[46]

As a result of adopting these separate categories of 'Puritan,' Neal both affirmed that by 1640 most Englishmen were Puritans, and also that the vast majority of members of the Long Parliament were conforming members of the church who aimed 'to set bounds to royal prerogatives, to lessen the power of the bishops, but certainly not to overturn civil or ecclesiastical government.' Neal's account of the religious principles of the politicians in the Long Parliament was quite deliberately based upon Clarendon's *History* so that 'it might be without exception.' As late as 1641, wrote Neal, the members of Parliament wanted only a 'reformation of the hierarchy,' for this was all 'the body of puritans, as yet, wished for or desired.'[47]

But while Neal claimed to be basing his version of the nature of the religious piety of the parliamentarians upon Clarendon, he refuted him on many crucial points. In this way, he was able to demonstrate that contemporary Nonconformists did not deserve the suspicion engendered by versions of the civil wars such as Clarendon's. He agreed with Clarendon that there were few religious reformers in the Long Parliament, but denied that either that tiny handful or those Puritans outside the House wanted a Presbyterian settlement. Elizabethan Puritans, he conceded, had espoused Presbyterian principles, but their seventeenth-century followers had not. Presbyterianism became an issue in the civil wars solely because of the Scottish alliance. Evidence of this, he suggested, was the fact that when the Scots withdrew in the late 1640s, 'it dwindled by degrees, till it was almost totally eclipsed by the rising greatness of the Independents.' Clarendon's charge that the Puritan clergy had a 'formed design' to subvert church and state was, he wrote, quite wrong. Clarendon was also incorrect when he misjudged the reality of the popish threat. The court had been involved in the Irish rebellion in October 1641 and the king did not scruple to employ papist soldiers in his army. In the end, Neal, like Hutchinson, simply incorporated the parliamentary propaganda of 1642 into his *History*. Such was Charles' 'attachment to the papists,' he wrote, that he was prepared to sacrifice all.[48]

In a history that was essentially a plea for toleration for Dissenters, many of the guises that Puritans assumed in the 1640s and 1650s were an embarrassment to Neal. Presbyterianism, we have seen, he wrote off as being Scottish and essentially un-English. After the Solemn League and Covenant was signed, he said, many of the Puritans 'did not fight for a reformation of the hierarchy nor for the generous principles of religious liberty to all peaceable subjects, but for the spiritual power the bishop had exercised.' While approving some aspects of the Independents' position, he did not praise 'the enthusiastic follies that were afterwards a reproach to the army.' These blemishes should not, he asserted, be held against the 'present body of Protestant dissenters ... [who] are content that their actions be set in a fair light as a warning to posterity.'[49]

Among these historians, there was fundamental agreement on the importance of religion to any explanation of the civil wars, although at the same time there was an equally profound disagreement on the way the religion of the

Puritans was to be conceived. There are, in addition, two other generalizations that might be made. First, it is clear that early historians of the Civil War period, like contemporaries, did not often make use of the abstract concept 'Puritanism,' and that even on those rare occasions when that word entered their language it was incidental to their essential analysis. Thus Hume, having dealt in some detail with the anti-Catholicism of the parliamentarians in the 1620s, wrote, 'the extreme rage against popery was a sure characteristic of puritanism.'[50] Second, there was general recognition by these writers that 'Puritan' was a label applied to a great variety of individuals by their opponents, and that it came to refer to an increasingly broad spectrum of causes, ranging from the support of separatism to the dogged protection of the rights of property. Despite their differences, it is doubtful if any of the historians who have been considered here, or indeed any of the many others who could equally well have been considered, would have disagreed with Richard Baxter's description of the way the secular and the sacred streams of English history separately fed the parliamentary flood of 1640-2:

The Parliament consisted of two sorts of men, who by the conjunction of these causes were united in their votes and endeavours for a reformation: one party made no great matter of these [Laudian] alterations in the Church; but they said, that if parliaments were once down, and our propriety gone, and arbitrary government set up, and laws subjected to the prince's will, we were then all slaves, and this they made a thing intolerable ... these the people called Good Commonwealth Men. The other sort were the more religious men, who were also sensible of all these things, but were much more sensible of the interest of religion; and these most inveighed against Innovations in the Church, bowing to Altars, the Book for Sports on Sundays, the casting out of ministers etc.[51]

Even in the early decades of the nineteenth century, as 'isms' multiplied, historians of Stuart England continued to shy away from the use of 'Puritanism.' In the pages of Lingard, Hallam, and Macaulay are to be found both the disinclination that we have seen in earlier writers to resort to the broad abstractions, along with a similar ambiguity and variety of judgments.

Lingard, like virtually all historians since the Restoration, perceived the civil wars as disastrous, and saw the emergence of opposition to the court as the result of the merger of two parties. The 'saints or zealots formed a powerful phalanx' in the House of Commons in the 1620s, and generally 'fought under the same banner ... with the members of the country party who, whatever might be their religious feelings, professed to seek the reformation of abuse in the prerogative and the preservation of the liberties of the people.' These Puritans were, however, only a minority of the population since, while they regarded the bishops' war as 'an impious crusade against the servants of God,' the majority of English subjects were indifferent to it. Within the Long Parliament, Lingard was inclined to believe, 'only a few' such as Fiennes and the younger Vane were 'both enthusiasts in religion as well as politics,' although, consistent with Hume's view, he believed religion was a more powerful motive among the lower orders. Most, if not all, of the troops in Cromwell's regiment in 1642, for instance, were 'enthusiasts both in religion and politics.'[52]

Hallam paid rather less attention to the Puritans than many of his predecessors and was as critical of them as any. In a rare reference to Puritanism, he wrote that 'the morose gloomy spirit of puritanism was naturally odious to the young and to men of joyous tempers.' It was the austerity of Puritanism, so 'intolerable to the youthful or gay,' that contributed so greatly 'to bring about the Restoration.' Worse even than this, however, was Puritan intolerance. 'The remorseless and indiscriminate bigotry of presbyterianism might boast ... that it trampled on the old age of Hales and embittered with insult the dying moments of Chillingworth' whom elsewhere he had described as 'two remarkable ornaments of the English church.' If Hallam was critical of the Presbyterians, he was scathing in his remarks about the Independents. These, he wrote, 'comprehended, besides the members of that religious denomination, a countless brood of fanatical sectaries, nursed in the lap of presbyterianism, and fed with stimulating aliment she furnished, till their intoxicated fancies could neither be restrained within the limits of her creed nor those of her discipline.'[53]

While Hallam was absolutely clear that he disliked the Puritans, he was less certain whom they were. Archbishop Abbott's connivance in some 'irregularities of discipline in the puritanical clergy,' he said, gained him 'the favour of the party denominated puritan.' By the time the Long Parliament met, there was a 'puritan party' in the House of Commons among whose ranks were Presbyterians who were 'by far the less numerous, though an active and increasing party.' Outside Parliament, 'heated puritans' used the more modest program of their betters to perpetrate 'tumults,' whereby 'indecent devastation [was] committed in churches by the populace.' This 'ecclesiastical democracy' was the occasion of the first split within the alliance that had revived the constitution. When members of the House of Commons came to subscribe to the Solemn League and Covenant in 1643, he wrote, many did so with the greatest reluctance owing to their 'dislike of the innovation' and to the fact that most laity in England disliked the Presbyterian system. As in so much of Hallam's *History*, there is a resonance here between his judgments and those of Hume. His condemnation of the Independents typifies his view of Puritan involvement in the English civil wars. The Independents, he wrote, prospered 'through ambition in a few, through fanaticism in many.'[54]

Macaulay, in his famous review of England's history up to 1685, did not once employ the term 'Puritanism' and presented a somewhat confusing sense of 'Puritan.' First emerging in the Elizabethan period, Macaulay's 'Puritans' were 'bold and inquisitive spirits' who 'from interest, from principle, and from passion' were hostile to the royal prerogatives. So powerful was their influence that, by the 1560s, they 'began to return a majority of the House of Commons.' Within two generations, however, the Puritans had come to embrace an extremism that Macaulay found objectionable. Driven almost into a frenzy by persecution, the extreme Puritan in Laud's time 'was at once known from other men by his gait, his garb, his lank hair, the sour solemnity of his face, the upturned white of his eyes, the nasal twang with which he spoke, and above all, by his peculiar dialect.' When the parliamentary alliance took shape in 1642, Macaulay did not see religious factors as having been crucial, although he did see a religious dimension to the political conflict. Supporting Parliament, he wrote, were found the 'whole body of Protestant Nonconformists, and most of those members of the Established Church who still adhered to the Calvinistic opinion which, forty years before, had been generally held by the prelates and clergy.'[55]

Where religion surfaced in the political consciousness of the parliamentary alliance was within the New Model Army and among its allies. Following Lucy Hutchinson more closely than any other of his predecessors, Macaulay saw the religious minority of 1642 become the Independents of 1646 and the 'most powerful faction in the country.' Displaying a 'stubborn courage characteristic of the English people,' Cromwell's 'Puritan warriors,' inspired by 'rigid discipline ... in company with the fiercest enthusiasm,' obliged their leader to take a 'fearful vengeance on the captive King' en route to the creation of the commonwealth.[56]

For two hundred years after the Restoration, virtually no historian attempted an explanation or a characterization of England's civil wars without paying considerable attention to religious conflict, but none went so far as to describe the entire parliamentary alliance of 1642 as 'Puritan.' Sometimes referring to 'Puritans' sympathetically as the godly and sometimes with unconcealed hostility as fanatics, scholars nonetheless agreed that they had to be included in any history of England in the first half of the seventeenth century. But it was not until almost the middle of the nineteenth century, first with the influential, eccentric historicism of Thomas Carlyle and then with the much more 'scientific' and academic approach of S.R. Gardiner, that historians began to rely upon the abstraction 'Puritanism' rather than upon the beliefs and actions of individual 'Puritans' or groups of 'Puritans' to explain events of the period.[57]

In rehabilitating the reputation of Oliver Cromwell, Carlyle scornfully rejected what he referred to as the 'Dryasdust' school of history, doubtless including in that category such important opinion-shapers as Hume and Hallam, by making 'Puritanism' intrinsic not only to his interpretations of Cromwell, but also to his version of the English Civil War. As far as Carlyle was concerned, all earlier English historians had failed lamentably in their task and had succeeded in reducing their subject merely to a 'dull dismal labyrinth' in which the 'English mind' must, if honest, confess it has found 'of knowable, of lovable, or memorable – next to nothing.' He regarded Puritanism as the 'last of all our Heroisms' and viewed the history of England in the early seventeenth century as consisting of the struggle of 'devout Puritanism against dignified Ceremonialism.' The following extract from the great Victorian hero-worshipper best illustrates the way Carlyle's passionate historicism provides an essential link in the historiogaphy of 'Puritanism' between Macaulay and his predecessors on the one hand and, on the other, Gardiner and his successors up to the present time. Describing the events in Cromwell's life prior to the first extant letter of 1636, Carlyle dates Cromwell's conversion to 'Calvinistic Christianity' in the 1620s. It was then, Carlyle says, that Cromwell placed his own 'deliverance from the jaws of Eternal Death' and in doing so transformed the scale of his existence:

> That the 'Sense of difference between Right and Wrong' had filled all Times and all Space for man, and bodied itself forth into a Heaven and Hell for him: this constitutes the grand feature of those Puritan, Old-Christian Ages; this is the element which stamps them as Heroic, and has rendered their works great, manlike, fruitful to all generations. It is by far the memorablest achievement of our Species; without that element, in some form or other, nothing of Heroic had ever been among us.

Though it would be foolhardy to attempt to chart Carlyle's influence, it can safely be said that after his edition of Cromwell's letters and speeches appeared in 1845 neither the Lord Protector nor what Carlyle regarded as his hero's principal driving force, 'Puritanism,' was quite the same. Extravagantly but vividly conceptualized by the irascible Scot, Puritanism was then channeled by the historiographical rigour of the great Nonconformist scholar, S.R. Gardiner.[58]

Notwithstanding the fact that Gardiner wrote more than twenty volumes on or around the subject, he did not once attempt to define 'Puritanism.' Nevertheless, he clearly believed it to have been a force which alone made intelligible the movement of seventeenth-century English history, especially the civil wars. Early in the first of the four volumes on the Civil War itself occurs a passage expressive of Gardiner's unique perception of the connections between 'Puritanism' and the development of English history. 'Puritanism,' he wrote, 'not only formed the strength of the opposition to Charles, but the strength of England itself.' In words reminiscent of Hume, Gardiner went on to suggest that, without

Puritanism, Englishmen would not have resorted to violence over the issue of 'parliamentary liberties and even parliamentary control.' While those were important, a compromise could surely have been agreed upon. Englishmen fought for something more valuable than political rights or property – their 'Puritanism.' And, Gardiner wrote, 'it is the glory of Puritanism that it found its highest work in the strengthening of the will ... to struggle onwards and upwards towards an ideal higher still.'[59]

Throughout his long narrative of political events from the accession of James to the 1640s, Gardiner constantly returned to 'Puritanism' as an essential driving force for change. By the end of 1604, James had 'decided against the Puritans' at the Hampton Court Conference and rebuked a House of Commons that was sympathetic to them. In so doing, he was initiating a policy that embittered 'the moral earnestness of Puritanism,' which not only made a schism 'sooner or later unavoidable' but, more importantly, set in motion a struggle that would result ultimately in the Revolution of 1688. In the end, Gardiner suggests, it was the members' encouragement of Puritanism that played a large part in causing the initial alienation of the king from his subjects.[60]

Similarly, twenty-five years later, 'the real line of separation between the King and the House of Commons had lain in the religious question.' Thus, after Parliament had been dissolved in 1629, Charles placed his trust in Bishop Laud, and supported his ecclesiastical policy of strict uniformity. For the young king, 'the fervent individual zeal of Puritanism was an unfathomable mystery, and its fierce dogmatism a hateful annoyance. When it had been driven out of the land, England would be herself again, as loyal and obedient as she had been to her Tudor sovereigns.' Thirteen years later it was still religion which separated the two parties, although by this time, of course, the king had attracted a considerable following. Pym, the leading member of the parliamentary alliance in 1641/2, was not seen by Gardiner as atypical of his following. 'Pym's difficulties arose from his recognition that more than the form of government was at stake, and from his belief that religion – or, in other words, Puritanism – must be upheld if the nation were to live, even against the will of the nation itself.'[61]

It is apparent that Gardiner's 'Puritanism' represented a force considerably more potent, more persuasive, and more historically purposeful than the ideas and beliefs of Puritans as analysed by scholars over the preceding two centuries. It is also clear that at least part of the reason why 'Puritanism' was so influential, and explained so much, is owing to the ambiguity with which Gardiner used the word. He did not ever define 'Puritanism' and he early lost sight of the distinction between the label 'Puritan' as used opprobriously by contemporaries and the abstraction 'Puritanism' which came to be his ultimate explanation of the civil wars. The problem is further compounded by his use of other terms –

Protestantanism, Calvinism, Presbyterianism, and Independency – to describe the religious views current in England between 1560 and 1640.

Gardiner's first use of 'Puritan' is conventional enough, In dealing with Elizabethan religious problems, he writes that the majority of the clergy in the 1560s were unimpressive Marian conformists and that the hope of the church in the future lay with 'the young men of ability and zeal who were growing up to manhood in the Universities. But such men were generally found among the Puritans, as the Nonconformists and the Presbyterians began to be alike called in derision.' Within the same discussion, however, Gardiner refers to both 'Protestantism' and 'Puritanism.' Thus when the prophesyings were put down by the government and Archbishop Grindal disgraced, 'all hope of bringing the waters of that free Protestantism which was rapidly becoming the belief of so many thoughtful Englishmen to flow within the channels of Episcopacy was, for the present, at an end.' Nowhere does Gardiner state clearly the connection between 'Protestantism' and 'Puritanism,' although there is reason to believe that in the Elizabethan period, at least, they were quite distinct. For while he analyses in some detail the 'undoubted reaction against Puritanism which marked the end of the sixteenth century,' an antagonism that was conspicuous especially among the country gentlemen in the House of Commons, he wrote elsewhere of the 'tide of Protestantism which swept over the nation in the years of triumph which followed upon the ruin of the Armada' and which clearly shaped many men, such as the young John Winthrop.[62]

In his discussion of politics in the two decades before the outbreak of the civil wars, however, it is not clear just what the distinction could have been. We have already seen that Gardiner believed the principal issue in the 1629 political crisis to have been religious. Yet the precise nature of this religious division is not clear. After describing the Arminianism of men such as Montagu and Cosin, Gardiner wrote that 'the gulf between [their] religion and the religion of the ordinary English Protestant was wide and deep.' This distinction, between the belief of Arminians and that of 'ordinary' Protestants, is easy to grasp. Unfortunately, Gardiner continued, 'as the central point of the Puritan system lay in preaching and conversion, the central point of the system of their opponents lay in the Sacrament of the Lord's Supper.' Elaborating upon the ritualism urged so lovingly by Cosin, Gardiner added, 'such a doctrine would offer a refuge to many who but for it would have fled from the uncongenial teaching of Puritanism into the arms of the Church of Rome.' At this point, Gardiner appears to be equating 'Puritanism' with 'Protestantism.'[63]

Then, as his narrative approached 1642, Gardiner further compounds his difficulties by secularizing his Puritans. The closest he ever comes to defining the term occurs in a passage in which he referred to Sir John Coke: 'many counted him a Puritan, or, in other words, an opponent of the existing ecclesiastical system.' If, in Gardiner's opinion, all opponents of the Laudian church were Puritans, then it is not difficult to see why he could write that 'Puritanism formed the strength of England itself.' Yet he was well aware that opposition to the ecclesiastical elements of 'thorough' was much more complex than the opposition to its political side. In one insightful passage, Gardiner analysed the 'ecclesiastical opposition' in 1640 as comprising four separate components. First, he wrote, 'many persons wished to see the Prayer Book replaced by the unceremonial worship of New England or Geneva.' Second, there was a larger number who 'wished to retain the Prayer Book with certain alterations.' A third category included all those who would not alter the Prayer Book 'but would interpret the rubrics as they had been interpreted in the days of their boyhood, when the communion-table stood in the centre of the church.' Finally, 'behind all these there was a body of resistance not called forth by any ecclesiastical or religious feeling whatever, but simply rising from the dissatisfaction of the gentry with the interference of the clergy.' If all who subscribed to one or other of these opinions was rightly to be labelled a 'Puritan' and if the body of beliefs held in common by them all may be described as 'Puritanism,' then it is difficult to see what useful purpose is served by the term or how it is to be distinguished from 'Protestantism.'[64]

Elsewhere, however, Gardiner appeared to be aware of the problem, as, for instance, when he wrote, 'those who were united in political opposition to the Crown were divided by their religious sympathies. The feeling of irritation against Laud's meddlesome interference with habitual usage was indeed almost universal; but Puritanism was after all the creed only of a minority.' And elsewhere he referred to the 'thousands in England who were not Puritans [but] were violent enemies of Laud.'[65]

What was a religious minority in 1640, however, within two years became increasingly identified with the entire parliamentary alliance. Gardiner's narrative of 1640-2 is studded with references to the 'aggressive Puritanism of the Commons,' a 'Puritan House of Commons,' 'the strong Puritan feeling of the Commons,' and at one point he concedes that because the elections to the Long Parliament had taken place 'when the Court was at the highest of its unpopularity ... it was consequently more Puritan in its composition than the country itself.' At this point, opposition to the court has become equivalent to 'Puritanism.' This identification is apparent in his analysis of the degree of support for the Scottish war in the summer of 1640. He agrees that the court belief that opposition to its policy was largely 'confined to the upper classes' had some validity because 'Puritanism had no deep root in the minds of the agricultural poor.' Compounding this confusion of political and religious dissatisfactions,

Gardiner went on, 'country gentlemen and small freeholders might be averse to Laudian innovation in the Church and to unparliamentary exactions in the State, but the labourers and the small handicraftsmen of the country-side cared very little about the matter.'[66]

Finally, let us examine Gardiner's treatment of the religious position of two members of the alliance. The diarist, Simonds D'Ewes, was one of the more moderate members of the parliamentary alliance of 1642. Essentially a cautious man, he had responded to the king's attempt to arrest the five members in January 1642 by rushing to his lodgings to make a will. Although almost all of Gardiner's many references to D'Ewes involved his making either constitutional points – sometimes in opposition to Pym – or occasional remarks about the excesses of Laudian episcopacy, nevertheless Gardiner claimed that in the end it was D'Ewes' 'Puritanism' that led him to remain with Parliament. In summarising D'Ewes' dilemma in August 1642, Gardiner wrote: 'if his reverance for law and precedent drew him to the side of Charles, his Puritanism fixed him reluctantly by the side of Pym, and with him, as with so many of his contemporaries, the religious motive was the strongest.'[67]

Gardiner's treatment of Pym's religious position raises precisely the same problem. Scholars have for three hundred years found Pym's public and political life more accessible than his private life, and Gardiner was no exception. Gardiner wrote that 'he combined a firm persuasion of the truth and importance of the Calvinistic creed with a knowledge of the world.' Apart from this, Gardiner has little to say about the parliamentary statesman's piety or view of the world. Nonetheless, after equating his religion with 'Puritanism,' and suggesting that it was this which caused Pym to act as he did in 1641/2, he concluded, 'the one thing which he asked for the Church was that it should be sincerely Protestant. All else was but a matter of expediency.[68]

Gardiner's analysis of Pym's religion illustrates the fundamental problem with his treatment of 'Puritanism.' While the concept was absolutely central to his vision of the history of England from 1560 to 1660, and although he used the term in an innovative way, so varied was his employment of the term that it became drained of significance and unable to carry the explanatory weight that he assigned it. The problem is that Gardiner described as Puritans those individuals, like Cromwell, about whose religious convictions there was a good deal of evidence, as well as those individuals far more numerous whose personal and religious lives remained shrouded in mystery. It is true that, as Gardiner pointed out, Pym was deeply committed to maintaining the Protestant religion in England and to protecting it from what he believed to be the continual threats from popery. To describe this view, as Gardiner did, as 'Puritanism,' which he elsewhere referred to as the religious convictions of a dedicated minority, was to introduce a confusing ambiguity that has muddied the waters of Civil War historiography for a hundred years.

Since Gardiner completed his *History*, there has been a steady erosion of belief in his essentially religious conception of the civil wars, but a widespread acceptance of what he regarded as a principal driving force for change in seventeenth-century England – 'Puritanism.' As we have seen in the previous chapter, the development of new disciplines and the extension of old ones have caused scholars to look with caution upon the largely two-dimensional assumptions of Gardiner's narrative. Not all historians today would accept his assertion that for both sides 'the religious difference was complicated by a political difference' or that 'the religious question was at the bottom of the quarrel.'[69] Yet despite this widespread reluctance to interpret the wars as essentially the expression of religious divisions, since Gardiner first brought 'Puritanism' to the forefront of historians' consciousnesses, few have challenged the validity of the concept. Differences between quasi-Marxists like Hill, liberals like Stone, psycho-historians like Walzer, and literary scholars like Haller fade in the face of their undeviating acceptance, as a phenomenon to be explained as well as an heuristic device, of the metaphor 'Puritanism.'

And just as we have seen in the previous chapter that 'revolution' served a purpose as an organizing device, so too has 'Puritanism.' It can scarcely be denied that when the events of 1640 to 1660 are placed in the broad context of the political and religious history of England in the modern period they seem extraordinary and thus in need of extraordinary explanations. The socially and politically radical movements of the 1640s, the trial and execution of the monarch, the preparedness to write and rewrite constitutions – these and other developments have been judged by historians as being without precedent in England's past and hence as revolutionary and sorely in need of a kind of explanation that lies beyond the normal categories. Hence, while land redistribution and social change, mercantile and other economic developments, intellectual ferment, political and constitutional change all have their place in the litany of causes, they are never quite enough. The crucial factor to which most twentieth-century historians have had recourse to transform these rational causes into the irrational and unpredictable effects of 1640-60 is 'Puritanism,' that curious mixture of ratiocination and simple piety.

While it is intellectually satisfying to use a concept like 'Puritanism' to throw light on both the emotional intensity of the civil wars, as well as on the radicalism of post-war movements, nevertheless the term is not without its difficulties. 'Puritanism' would be a more plausible phenomenon if either Gardiner or his successors had ever succeeded in devising a generally acceptable definition that had both precision and specificity rather than simply the generality of a broad behavioural tendency or of a certain theological or political preference. Gardiner himself used the term in such a variety of ways as to render the derivation of a definition by implication impossible. Nor have twentieth-century scholars been very much more successful. Christopher Hill, in whose vision of the history of Stuart England Puritanism plays a vital function as the ideological spearhead of the progressive movement for political and socio-economic change, provides us with an apt illustration of the difficulties inherent in defining the term.

In the first chapter of his *Society and Puritanism in Pre-Revolutionary England*, Hill attempts to define a Puritan on the basis of a large number of contemporary references either to that term, or to its derivative, 'Puritanism,' at various times from the 1560s to the Civil War period and beyond. As is usually the case with Hill's work, there is a remarkable richness of documentation with sources containing 'Puritan' allusions ranging from the Grand Remonstrance to a letter from a gamekeeper to the Earl of Suffolk. There is, however, a problem. The conclusion, which is crucial for the remainder of Hill's argument, does not seem to follow from the sources quoted. Having dismissed the arguments of Charles and Katherine George[70] that 'Puritan' has been too loosely employed and too widely ascribed to contemporaries by scholars, Hill goes on to illustrate the great variety of uses for the term. So compelling does he appear to find his sources, some of which describe 'Puritan' as a purely papist term of opprobrium, others as a political or social label, that he writes that 'one is inclined to agree with Giles Widdowes who, in 1631, wrote "the name [Puritan] ... is ambiguous, and so it is fallacious." Elsewhere, too, Hill has shown a similar awareness of the breadth of meaning in contemporaries' uses of 'Puritan.' 'Newcastle coal exporters referred to London merchants who opposed their monopoly as "Puritan." ' Notwithstanding his diverse evidence, Hill's recognition that 'for contemporaries the word [Puritanism] had no narrowly religious connotation,' and his frequent reference to 'the shrewd Henry Parker and his four-part categorisation of Puritanism,' still he concludes, surprisingly, 'so I agree with contemporaries in thinking that there was in England in the two or three generations before the civil war a body of opinion which can usefully be labelled Puritan. There was a core of doctrine about religion and Church government, aiming at purifying the Church from inside.' He identifies a 'mainstream of puritan thought' with a number of theologians whose ideas he agrees were 'not monolithic,' but who 'adopted comparable attitudes' to a number of key problems. These attitudes appealed to a large lay 'body of opinion without which the civil war could never have been fought.'[71]

There are at least two problems with Hill's definition. First, while it is undoubtedly true that there were some contemporaries who would have shared it, there were just as many to whom it would have made no sense. In this category, for instance, would be included those to whom 'Puritan' was a term employed by Catholics in the 1620s to deride those Protestants most suspicious of the Arminian innovations in the church. This was Francis Bacon's sense of the word when he wrote to the Duke of Buckingham in early 1623, 'let me advise you that the name of Puritans, in a Papist's mouth, do not make you to withdraw your favour from such as are honest and religious men (so as they be not of turbulent and factious spirits, nor adverse to the government or the Church) though they be sometimes traduced by that name.'[72] As Hill has demonstrated, 'Puritan' was used so broadly that it does not seem possible to derive a precise and substantive definition from the inconsistent contemporary usages. It is true that contemporaries used 'Puritan' frequently and it is doubtless possible for an historian to infer from each individual usage a specific content. Problems arise, however, when one tries to infer from widely differing usages what Hill refers to as a 'core of doctrine.'

More recently, Patrick Collinson has also addressed himself to this problem. In answer to Paul Christianson's plea to narrow usage of 'Puritan' to include only those reformers 'who worked within the Established Church for ministerial parity and a severely attenuated liturgy,' Collinson has argued that the widespread and pejorative use of the term between 1560 and 1642 should lead us to expand rather than to contract its meaning. Accepting the contemporary sense of 'Puritanism' as 'at once polemical and nominalistic,' he has written, 'we should regard the incidence of the term in contemporary discourse as indicative of theological, moral and social tension which should be the prime object of our investigation,' adding the worrisome rider, 'especially if we wish to understand what followed, in the 1640s and beyond.' From the context of this observation, it would appear that Collinson is rejecting Christianson's modest efforts to confine the usage by present-day historians of 'Puritan' to a relatively small number of people, preferring instead the more widespread attribution of 'Puritan' and of 'Puritanism' preferred by contemporaries. Thus the phenomenon, still undefined, continues to serve for Collinson a crucial analytical and explanatory function. He has, however, drawn an unwarranted conclusion from his argument. No one could reasonably disagree with his first observation that the frequent and pejorative usage of 'Puritan' and of 'Puritanism' is evidence of the fact contemporaries felt strongly about issues, some of which were moral and theological. Yet to argue further, on the basis of these diverse contemporary usages of 'Puritan,' that there was in England between 1560 and 1640 a definable theological point of view that we might label 'Puritanism,' and which might be called upon to explain in part or in full 'what followed, in the 1640s and beyond,' seems unjustifiable unless the precise theological content of the label, as valid for 1563 as for 1640, can be identified.[73]

The second and more significant problem with Hill's definition of Puritanism is the question of the content of this 'core of doctrine about religion and church government.' If there was such a 'core of doctrine' subscribed to by all individuals between 1560 and 1660 who are described by historians as 'Puritans' – and the list must surely include Sir Francis Knollys and his namesake Hanserd, Thomas Cartwright, Henry Vane, John Milton, Denzil Holles, and Hugh Peter – then it is incumbent upon the users of 'Puritanism' to articulate this 'core' and to distinguish it from its implied antithesis 'Anglicanism,' on the one hand, and from the more or less related terms 'Protestantism' or 'Calvinism' on the other. This scholars have failed to do, at least to the satisfaction of any but themselves.

Hill, having asserted the existence of such a doctrinal core, tends to avoid describing it in any detail. Instead, being more interested in 'non-theological reasons for supporting the Puritans, or for being a Puritan,' he prefers to accept its existence and then to explore the social aspects of what he assumes follows from the doctrinal core, such as the Puritan reliance upon preaching rather than the Anglican preference for sacramentalism. Although he does not dwell upon the theology of Puritanism, he makes it abundantly clear that he believes there is one. Referring to the Georges' stress on the common Protestantism of Puritans and Anglicans alike, Hill denies that 'there was nothing in Puritanism significantly different from the position of the hierarchy before the Laudian innovations.'[74]

Other historians, too, have agreed with Hill that Puritanism referred ultimately to a theological position held by a self-conscious group of Englishmen between 1560 and 1660 in contradistinction to another theological position maintained by the hierarchy of the church, together with those who were satisfied by that church. Such an historian is J.F.H. New, who in his *Anglican and Puritan* examines attitudes to man, the church, sacramental faith, and human destiny and finds Puritanism and Anglicanism to constitute 'two antagonistic bodies of opinion.' The problem with New's analysis is twofold. First, he tends to treat the period from 1560 to 1640 as though there was no significant theological development. Hill recognized this problem by the somewhat cumbrous device of referring to the post-Presbyterian 'Puritans' as the 'new Puritans,' though, as he did not carry the distinction between 'new,' and 'old' Puritanism into his analysis it did not serve a major purpose.[75] Second, while demonstrating the theological differences between the two extremes of England's Protestant church between 1560 and 1640 – and note that he does not regard Separatists as Puritans – he has done little to establish the existence of two fundamentally opposed parties, the tension between which can be linked to the origins of the civil wars. Significantly, when New considers the argument of the Georges, he rejects it, noting that their thesis 'leads to the conclusion that Puritanism had little or nothing to do with the gestation of the Civil War.' This, he suggests, cannot be correct since 'all the great authorities from Gardiner to Hill have recognised the connection between Puritanism and the coming of the Civil War.' J. Sears McGee expresses a very similar objection to the Georges' repudiation of the idea of a specifically 'Puritan' theology when he writes that to accept it would require us 'to take matters of religion off our list of causes for the Civil War despite the certainty of contemporaries that religion was an issue of overriding importance.'[76] This remark brings us to the heart of the matter. The creation by modern historians of 'Puritanism' as a dominant force in opposition to another force which has anachronistically been labelled 'Anglicanism,' together with their inclination to see mirrored in this tension the origins of the civil wars, has had two effects on the writing of seventeenth-century English history. It has reinforced the model of this history as based upon a fundamental discontinuity, and it has confused rather than clarified the important question of the religious character of the civil wars by a blanket application of 'Puritanism' to the entire parliamentary alliance of 1642.

The basic problems surrounding the term 'Puritanism' are somewhat magnified by the fact that not all scholars agree that there was a clear-cut theological or ecclesiastical distinction between the 'Puritans' and their opponents. William Haller, for instance, whose two studies of 'Puritanism' are justly famous, believed that Puritan preachers were distinguished from others more by 'the manner of their preaching than by their doctrinal position.' Haller was here referring to the Puritan preference for 'spiritual' sermons which he contrasted with the 'witty' sermons of the more orthodox preachers. Nowhere did he define precisely the 'Puritanism' whose rise he described, but he did provide a fairly close description. The fact that Puritans tended to break up into factions ranging from extreme Separatist to Presbyterian should not, he believed, 'confuse our understanding of Puritanism.' 'The disagreements that rendered Puritan into presbyterian, independent, separatist and baptist, were in the long run not so significant as the qualities of character, of mind, and of imagination which kept them all alike Puritan,' Haller did not see theological differences separating Puritans from their less critical brethren. Instead, he was inclined to see 'Puritanism' as a 'way of life' which eventually was 'to subdue English civilisation to an attitude of mind, a code of conduct, a psychology, a manner of expression, the vitality of which far outran the particular form of religious life which sprang up from time to time in the course of its irresistible advance.' In Haller's view, 'Puritanism' lost none of its potency for want of a theological core. It was, he wrote, 'a great dynamic force ... in the corporate life of the English people,' 'a cyclonic shattering storm of the spirit' which, he claimed, alone could explain the otherwise inexplicable surge towards liberty in the 1640s.[77]

Paul Seaver is another historian who has been somewhat perplexed by the problem of a distinctively Puritan 'core of doctrine.' For, while he has cited New's study with approval and has asserted that 'doctrinal differences between Anglican and Puritan were by no means negligible,' yet he seems at a loss to know just where they lay. Summarizing the issues over which 'the Puritans and their orthodox brethren' quarreled, from the vestiarian controversy of the 1560s to the Laudian innovations, he wrote that 'the impression that they are scarcely fundamental remains.' Puritan clergy were, of course, characterized by a respect for preaching, but he notes that Puritanism 'encompassed laity as well as clergy' and thus was a 'movement that was unlikely to adhere rigorously and uniformly to a set of doctrinal propositions.' Further complicating the question was the fact that throughout the century 'Puritanism was a dynamic element in English life ... there were Calvinist Anglicans who were not Puritans' and, late in the period, 'Puritans ... who were no longer orthodox Calvinists.'[78]

Another problem arises when historians attempt to establish a fundamental conflict in pre-Civil War English society between 'Puritanism' and 'Anglicanism,' for the implied 'Anglicanism' of the 'Anglicans' is not, strictly speaking, comparable with the implied 'Puritanism' of the 'Puritans.' Contemporary official 'Anglicanism' – and, recalling the great difference between the 'Bullingerism' of Whitgift and the 'Arminianism' of Laud, it is important to recognize that it changed greatly between 1560 and 1640 – is the set of theological, doctrinal, and ecclesiological positions broadly shared at any one time by the bishops and a handful of approved spokesmen such as Richard Hooker, essential to whose position is not so much a theological point of view as an institutional connection. 'Puritanism,' in contrast, is the theological or ecclesiastical viewpoint at any one time of a group that is potentially very much larger and may include any who opposed officially sanctioned positions of the church on a wide range of subjects, selected by historians over the years, that includes sabbatarianism, millenarianism, usury, divine right monarchy, grace, attitudes to work and to poverty. This is not to say that there were at any time between 1560 and 1640 more 'Puritans' than 'Anglicans' but that from the historian's vantage point there are potentially more. Only a handful, probably only a hundred or so, at any one time could represent official 'Anglicanism,' whereas every other member of the church who disagreed with the established view on any one of dozens of subjects can be reckoned by the historian as a 'Puritan.'[79]

It would be possible to consider the work of a much larger number of scholars of the period 1560-1660, or of 'Puritanism,' but it is unnecessary. Ever since Gardiner first used 'Puritanism' to label a dynamic force which moved inexorably through English society, when he lost sight of its esentially metaphorical character and equated the dancer with the dance, most scholars have found the term extremely useful if utterly indefinable. Even at a fairly simple level, such as the question whether Separatists from 1560 to 1640 may legitimately be regarded as Puritan, there is no agreement. Seaver, Hill, and New exclude them from their analyses of pre-1640 Puritanism, without considering the implications of so doing. If Separatists are not Puritans in 1630, are they still not in 1650? If they are not, then what does one call all those who came to the forefront of political life in the late 1640s, those, who, to Cromwell, had 'the root of the matter' in them? If Henry Vane is a Puritan in 1649, why are not Separatists so labelled in 1590? Other scholars, such as Haller and Woodhouse, include Separatists as Puritans, thus solving the problem just raised, but at the same time making it even more difficult to devise a definition that is both inclusive and meaningful. The problem is most apparent in Woodhouse's attempt at a definition. Having insisted that Puritanism was an 'entity,' he then went on to say, 'it is unnecessary to posit a unity in all Puritan thought; it is sufficient to recognise a continuity.' If this is true, then how does one distinguish between Puritanism and Protestantism?[80]

The scholars whose use of 'Puritanism' has so far been considered represent only a small fraction of those who, in the past hundred years, have seen in this phenomenon a major force for change in England between 1560 and 1660. Yet greatly to increase the survey would not substantially alter the conclusions. Despite the freedom with which the term is used, few, if any, scholars have been successful in defining or explaining it. But, as we have seen, despite historians' inability to define the term, it is nevertheless a crucial component in almost every explanation of the English civil wars, in every characterization of them, and in almost every political, social, and religious history of England between 1560 and 1660 written in the past hundred years.

There are, of course, exceptions to this generalization, perhaps the most notable one involving the work of Nicholas Tyacke. Although his major work has yet to appear, he has already made a convincing case for his central proposition 'that religion became an issue in the Civil War crisis is due primarily to the rise to power of Arminianism in the 1620s.' To Tyacke, the central religious force for change emanated from Arminianism. He stands orthodox opinion on its head by arguing that, until the mid-1620s, Calvinism 'linked nonconformists to the leaders of the established church' and that this nexus was not broken until the Laudian establishment espoused Arminian views and proceeded to castigate hitherto conventional theology as 'Puritan.'[81]

Examples of this widespread scholarly habit of reifying 'Puritanism,' of objectifying it, of tracing its life-cycle, and of using it to explain other phenomena abound. Thus Hill writes, 'thanks to Protestantism and especially Puritanism, the well-to-do were becoming more sensitive to the age-old problem of poverty.' Michael Walzer illustrates the same use of the concept when he writes that between 1530 and 1660, 'the crucial years of struggle and change in England ... Puritanism provided what may best be called an ideology of transition. It was functional to the process of modernisation not because it served the purposes of some universal progress, but because it met the human needs that arise whenever traditional controls give way and hierarchical status and corporate privilege are called into question.'[82] Haller and Woodhouse, despite their different assumptions and preoccupations, are equally convinced that Puritanism was an objective reality, and in Woodhouse's case, susceptible to minute spectographic analysis. Most importantly, both scholars were convinced that in Puritanism lay the essential explanation for the liberal aspirations of a Milton or of a Lilburne.[83]

Given the fact that 'Puritan' is a term as old as Civil War history itself, it is not surprising that historians should have attempted to derive a broad generalization from the large number of specific examples. That is, after all, how knowledge accumulates. In the case of 'Puritan,' however, it does not seem a legitimate procedure because it ignores the fundamentally political and opprobrious dimension to the original word. It is, it would seem, no more possible to derive a positive content for 'Puritanism' from a hundred individual 'Puritan' case-studies than it is to assign to 'radicalism' a specific content by considering the beliefs of a hundred individuals labelled 'radical' between 1880 and 1980. 'Puritanism,' like 'radicalism,' is not an entity, but a reference to one end of a political or religious spectrum. To label an individual a 'Puritan' or a 'radical' is to compare him with his fellows, but to say little or nothing of the content of his actual beliefs.[84]

More important than the reasons why historians have inclined to 'Puritanism' as a description of what is extraordinary in English society between 1560 and 1660 is the effect their so doing has had upon our perceptions of that society. Acceptance of 'Puritanism' as an entity is normally predicated upon the existence of another entity, antithetical to 'Puritanism,' rarely labelled but epitomised by the 'judicious Hooker.' Once this basic conflict has been established, it is hardly surprising that historians should then see it embodied in that other major conflict, Court versus Country, or Royalists versus parliamentarians. As a result, the opposition to the Established Church becomes identified with opposition to the government of Charles I, and 'Puritanism' comes to refer not just to Hill's 'core of doctrine concerning religion and church government,' but as well to purely secular and political matters. Simultaneously, opponents of the social and political policies of the government, including many, if not most, members of the Long Parliament, come to be explained in terms of their presumed connection with 'Puritanism.' The careful distinction that scholars for two hundred years drew between the secular and the religious streams that fed the flood-water of 1642 has been blurred. Thus, everyone who took sides against Charles I in the Civil War is taken to be a 'Puritan,' unless, in the case of those like Henry Marten, there is clear evidence of the inappropriateness of the label.

Anthony Fletcher, in his study of Sussex from 1600 to 1660, illustrates this tendency. He writes of the elite group in his county: 'religion in the last resort was dearer to the Puritan gentry and townsmen of the county than politics or economic interests. Their faith called for constant striving in their daily lives. While they were convinced that the cause was good, it also sustained them in the hazardous decision to challenge their sovereign in the civil war.' In his more recent account of the immediate political origins of the English Civil War, Fletcher exhibits a similar faith in the ultimate importance of 'Puritanism' as a cause of the war even though his meticulous narrative does not warrant the belief. Having argued that John Pym was able, almost single-handedly, to persuade his parliamentary colleagues of the imminence and of the reality of the popish conspiracy, and having established that what sustained the parliamentary leadership throughout 1641 was its 'obsessive anti-Catholicism,' Fletcher nevertheless asserts that it was a 'Puritan assembly' that Pym was leading and that what ultimately made war inescapable was the fact that 'the Puritan core of the parliamentary party could not abandon their belief in the supremacy of truth.'[85]

J.S. Morrill, too, has suggested that the religious division presupposed by 'Puritanism' coincides with the political division of 1642 and thus has made his contribution to the dilution of the significance of the religious label. Morrill has written that for most activists in the counties in 1642 'religion was the crucial issue.' He continues: 'Quite simply, in most counties the active royalists are the defenders of episcopacy who saw in puritanism a fundamental challenge to all society and order, and the parliamentarians are those determined to introduce a godly reformation which might, for a few, leave room for bishops, but in most cases did not.' Morrill went on to add that what these 'puritan activists did agree on' was the need to create a 'new, militant evangelical church.'[86]

The problem, however, is that Morrill's evidence in support of this position is less than overwhelming. He does not sufficiently distinguish between country opposition to Laud's 'neopopish' clericalism, on the one hand, and 'Puritanism' on the other. Moreover, he confuses the propaganda of some 1642 Royalists concerning their parliamentary opponents with what can actually be documented about their beliefs. In the end, he says, referring to William Brereton, John Pyne, and John Hutchinson as models, it was the minority of 'men who felt most strongly about religion who began the war.'[87]

Morrill would have done well – as would most other historians – to have

heeded the warning that accompanied his own analysis of the religious affilia-
tions of the Cheshire gentry. In his study of that county, he wrote, 'in religion
most of the known Puritans were Parliamentarians and the handful of known
Laudians were Royalists.' But, he went on, 'the evidence of religious conviction
is scarce and some of the sources sometimes used by historians are not altogether convincing.'[88]

And here we arrive at the crux of the problem. The habit that historians have
acquired, since Gardiner, of elaborating upon his concept of 'Puritanism,' and
of attributing this form of religious persuasion to all opposition to Charles I in
the pre-Civil War period, has in fact explained less rather than more of what
happened in seventeenth-century England by making Puritans more common,
and hence less unique, than they indeed were. If, instead of attributing 'Puritanism' to the bulk of Charles' opponents in 1642 on the basis not of solid evidence
concerning their personal zeal, but on the strength of their political position, we
assume the Puritans really were only a minority group before 1640, as so many
historians have said they were after 1660, then several things will follow. First,
we may be able to develop language with which to analyse the religious concerns
of the great bulk of political society in the period before 1640 that makes sense of
their political behaviour, but does not require them all to have been 'Puritan.'
Second, we may provide a framework within which the political crisis of
1620-42 is intelligible and not so radically different from the crisis of 1678-88. In
other words, we may develop an approach to seventeenth-century English
political history that is less fundamentally dichotomous than has been the case
since the late nineteenth century.

Both of these goals may more readily be accomplished by ceasing to lay stress
on the concept of 'Puritanism' which was, as we have seen, developed in the
nineteenth century, and, instead, by listening more closely to contemporaries
and to their early historians. For, common to all classes in English society in the
generation before 1642, and taken just as seriously by their historians for the
next two hundred years, was not the fervent desire to build the new Jerusalem
but the resolute determination to hold onto the Protestant church they had
inherited from Elizabeth and to protect it from the imminent threat of popery.

PART II

THE RELIGIOUS FACTOR IN ENGLISH POLITICS

BEFORE AND AFTER THE INTERREGNUM

4

Puritanism, Anti-Catholicism, and English Politics, 1621-41

We have seen that historians' attitudes to the importance of religious forces in the developing political crisis in England between 1621 and 1641 have changed in two ways since S.R. Gardiner first elaborated the concept of 'Puritanism.' First, they have become increasingly sceptical of Gardiner's single-minded conviction of the primacy of religion as the key to the principal political divisions during the generation before 1642. Yet simultaneously, with few, if any, exceptions, they have seized upon the 'Puritans,' and upon 'Puritanism,' when groping for the extraordinary cause of the 'revolutionary' events of the 1640s. Thus, most modern historians who have addressed themselves to England's political history in the years 1621-41 place the 'Puritans' in the forefront of their narrative and assume that the growing belligerency of the parliamentarians derived to a large extent from their 'Puritanism.'

Lawrence Stone, for example, has spent a large part of his professional life pursuing interests that Gardiner would have regarded as either inaccessible or irrelevant to the historian. Nevertheless, in Stone's tripartite study of the causes of the English Revolution, 'Puritanism' comes as close to being indispensable as any of his explanatory factors. In Stone's view, what made events in the 1640s revolutionary was the energy provided by ideas in general, and by Puritanism in particular. Though not the sole 'ideological underpinning of the opposition to the government,' Puritanism appears to be, in Stone's view, the crucial one, for he writes, 'it is as safe as any broad generalisation of history can be to say that without the ideas, the organisation, and the leadership supplied by Puritanism there would have been no revolution at all.' In their portrayal of English society during the hundred years before 1640, Stone and Gardiner see this vaguely-defined but all-powerful force in strikingly similar terms.[1] Between 1529 and 1629, Stone writes, 'there was the spread throughout large sectors of the propertied and lower middle classes of a diffuse Puritanism whose most important political consequence was to create a burning sense of the need for change in the Church and eventually in the State.' Even when he descends from the metaphorical overview to the level of short-term political explanation, Stone is no less dependent upon the 'Puritans.' Just as it was the 'Puritans' who provided the 'clerical and secular leaders of the opposition, in and out of Parliament, to Queen Elizabeth's religious and foreign policies,' so too, forty years later, 'Puritans' 'led the attack on Buckingham's character and policies' in the 1620s.[2]

Consistent with Stone's interpretation is Mary Keeler's analysis of the members of the Long Parliament during the crucial months leading up to the outbreak of war. She is similarly reliant upon the 'Puritans,' although she has given even less attention than had Stone to the problems raised by the term. Basically, she does not seem to believe that religion was the most important force motivating members' political behaviour between 1640 and 1642. Not more than a small number of members, she writes, were first elected for religious reasons and the large number known for their 'anti-Laudian views' who were chosen as burgesses received the call, she believes, 'more because they stood for the townsmen's developing sense of independence, apparently, than because they were stiff-necked puritans.' Religious influences operating upon members of the Long Parliament were at their most potent, she writes enigmatically, 'when they combined with forces that were essentially political or economic.'[3]

Keeler seems to feel an intellectual commitment to 'Puritanism' as a vital force. However, this commitment is undermined by her apparent disbelief in its content, a view which is reinforced by an examination of the hundreds of biographies that provide the substance of her study of the membership of the early Long Parliament. Let us look, for example, at her analysis of the county of Bedfordshire and its four representatives at Westminster. In her broad characterization of the county and its members, she writes that, with one exception, 'all were puritans.' When one looks at the biographies of the individuals concerned, however, including old Sir Oliver Luke, Roger Burgoyne, and Sir Beauchamp St John, one finds no reference at all to their religious opinions, presumably because there is no information available. Why then does Keeler describe them as 'Puritans'?[4]

The answer to this question may be found in her analysis of the religious attitudes of the membership at large, an analysis which gives the impression of remarkable precision. Keeler is well aware of the problems inherent in any attempt to gereralize about the religious convictions of the 547 members since only a 'comparatively small portion of the membership' have left behind much evidence of their religion, while the 'thoughts of many ... on matters of religion were far from fixed.' Nevertheless, she believes that the division in late 1642 between Royalists and Parliamentarians coincided almost precisely with the religious division. As early as the autumn of 1641, 'the split between those willing to accept the established Church of England and the nonconformists was already apparent.' Though somewhat ambiguous as to the degree of causality involved, Keeler is in no doubt that the two sides that emerged in 1642 could be characterized by religion. It 'may be conceded,' she writes, that those who 'stayed loyal to King Charles were loyal also to episcopacy.' The picture was not completely simple, she points out, because within the Royalist ranks were some who 'inclined towards puritanism,' and some who 'leaned towards Rome.' Summarizing the religious position of the king's party in the early Long Parliament, Keeler concludes that 'possibly 200 of the total membership may be classified as Anglican, of whom at least 30 favored modification of the Laudian system.' When the 3 who were 'definitely inclined towards Roman Catholicism' and the 35 who were unclassifiable are omitted, there are left some 289 members – all ultimately Parliamentarians – of whom she says, they 'were nonconformists of some type' [who] were 'willing to abolish episcopacy, whether or not they had decided upon the form of church government which should replace it.' Refining her classification with a quite breathtaking example of historical hindsight, she goes on, 'included in this group were about 123 who survived Pride's Purge of 1648 and are generally considered Independents' and perhaps 166 who 'if only because Colonel Pride secluded them from the House have come to be known as the Presbyterians.'[5]

The weakness in Keeler's analysis of the religious position of the Parliamentarians on the eve of the civil wars is common to many other historians of English politics during this period. Though scrupulous in explaining the difficulties preventing her from providing information about the personal religion of more than a handful of members of the Long Parliament, and though apparently half-convinced that secular motives were, in the last analysis, more potent than religious ones, nevertheless she assumes that the leaders of the Parliamentarians were 'Puritan' and that the civil wars were fought between largely Anglican Royalists and mostly Puritan or Nonconformist Parliamentarians. In the end, she describes the MPs from Bedfordshire as 'Puritans' not because of their religious beliefs, about which she appears to know very little, but because of their political behaviour between 1642 and 1648.

J.H. Hexter's analysis of the religion of John Pym is similarly informed by the same questionable assumption – that it is not necessary to know what a man's religious beliefs were to label him a 'Puritan.' Hexter does not pretend to be better informed about King Pym's personal piety than other scholars have been. While confident in his assertion that Pym detested 'anabaptism, Brownism and the like,' and also that the bishops were responsible for introducing popery into the church, Hexter can add little about his personal beliefs. Knowing more than had ever been known about Pym's political skills, but not significantly more about his religious beliefs, nevertheless Hexter could summarize these beliefs: 'In a word, Pym was not a fanatic and not a sectarian. Probably he was not even a Presbyterian. He was a militant Puritan.'[6]

The most recent work on the politics of the early Long Parliament, that of Anthony Fletcher, recognizes that there are problems in labelling Pym a 'Puritan,' but manifests the common tendency to attribute 'Puritanism' widely to others within the parliamentary alliance. Thus Fletcher suggests that Pym was almost an 'outsider' amongst his parliamentary colleagues, never understanding the 'county viewpoint'; for while Pym was driven throughout his career by his belief in conspiracy, a belief that Fletcher never describes as 'Puritan,' his supporters both in Parliament and in the local communities are persistently referred to as 'Puritan.' In this respect, Fletcher's dependance on 'Puritanism' for his ultimate explanation for the political origins of the Civil War shares a great deal with Gardiner a hundred years before.[7]

In addition to the historians of the Long Parliament, those scholars who have chosen to work on successive Parliaments in the 1620s have also seen within the rapidly expanding ranks of the 'Puritan' members of Parliament a principal reason for the increasing pretensions of the House of Commons. Robert Ruigh, for instance, in his excellent study of the Parliament of 1624, makes steady reference to the dynamic role played by the 'Puritans.' Throughout James' reign, Ruigh suggests, the House of Commons had become increasingly assertive because it 'reflected the economic and religious views of merchants and Puritans whose numbers increased with every session.' Unfortunately, Ruigh, unlike Keeler, does not attempt to quantify them, but he does suggest that in 1624 their numbers were high. In his discussion of the petition to the monarch against the recusants, Ruigh points out that within each successive Jacobean Parliament the 'Puritan faction had grown stronger' and hence the 'vocal Protestant (if not Puritan) majority' were covering such old ground that they did not discuss their demands in much detail. Here Ruigh seems unclear as to how best to characterize the anti-recusant fervour of the parliamentarians. Elsewhere, however, he seems more certain. Discussing the king's irritation at the way Prince Charles appeared to be in complete alliance with the members of the House of Commons, Ruigh writes that the heir to the throne appeared to have 'cast aside all restraints and joined the Puritan hue and cry against papists.' Nor was James I the only one to be alarmed by the 'odd couple' of 1624. Many others were convinced, writes Ruigh, 'that the Prince and the Duke [of Buckingham] had formed an alliance with the Puritan faction which would alienate them from the king.'[8]

There is the lack of clarity in Ruigh's use of 'Puritan' to describe the religious

views of parliamentarians in 1624 which points to the central problem bedevil-
ling all modern scholarship that attempts to deal with the question of the role of
religion in the coming of the civil wars. First, Ruigh, like most contemporary
historians, sees the increase in the number of 'Puritans' between 1603 and 1624
as an essential ingredient in any explanation of political developments during
that period. Second, he seems fairly certain that there is a real and significant
distinction to be drawn between 'Puritans' and 'Protestants.' This point is clear
from the way he deals with proceedings in the House of Commons in the first
days of the session. On the very first day, he says, the 'Puritan element ... seized
the initiative and, capitalising on the religious fervour of the majority, had
engaged the Commons to advocate measures distasteful to the King.' Their
triumph, however, was short-lived. The 'Puritans' had to give way to the 'old
parliament men' and lawyers, whose ascendancy over the House of Commons
was quickly confirmed. Men such as Coke, Sandys, and Phelips, chairmen of
the key committees, were, says Ruigh, 'neither courtiers nor precisions.' Ruigh
does not actually label these men, but he would probably accept the label he
bestows upon Sir Benjamin Rudyard – 'dedicated Protestant.' Yet while he is
absolutely certain that, although all 'Puritans' are 'Protestants,' not all 'Protestants' are 'Puritans,' and that it is in the activities of the 'Puritans' that the
historian can find the explanation for much of the political development of the
1620s, he neither provides a close description of the 'Puritans' nor does he
describe the difference between them and the 'Protestants.'[9]

It is worthwhile at this point to take note of a remark made by Robert Zaller
in his careful study of the Parliament of 1621. Zaller makes less use of the
'Puritans' for his explanation of parliamentary assertiveness than does Ruigh
and, while he acknowledges their presence in the 1621 House of Commons, he
sees the form taken by the parliamentarians' religious preoccupations as transcending 'Puritanism.' In an insightful remark Zaller writes: 'there was of course,
a strong Puritan element in the Commons: but doctrinaire Protestantism was as
little the cause of the anti-Catholic hysteria as a passionate commitment to the
ideals of democracy was in the rabid anti-Communism of the American Con-
gress in the 1950s.' Zaller makes no effort to develop this distinction between
'doctrinaire Protestantism' or 'Puritanism' and 'anti-Catholicism,' but the scar-
city of his references to the 'Puritans' and his emphasis on the all-pervasive fear
of popery suggest that this distinction is fundamental to his entire analysis.[10]

To these generalizations, Conrad Russell's recent meticulous study of parliamentary politics in the 1620s is a notable exception. His explanation of
political tensions in England in the five Parliaments he has examined makes
virtually no reference whatsoever to the influence of 'Puritans' and even less to
that of 'Puritanism.' 'If the word "puritan" is defined to mean those who took

their Protestantism seriously,' he observes, 'then the bench of bishops is the most logical place to find "puritans," ' not the House of Commons. Sensitive to the difficulties inherent in the term 'Puritan,' Russell is persuaded that, however the expression is defined, there is no 'puritan' opposition' in late Jacobean Parliaments. By a 'narrow definition,' he asserts, there was probably not a Puritan member in Parliament – that is, 'avowed opponents of episcopacy or the Prayer Book.' If a broader definition is employed, for example a general preference for church reform, 'puritanism was an official creed' and George Abbott was a 'puritan archbishop.'[11]

Russell is one of a small group of historians whose recent work in the area of early seventeenth-century English politics has had the effect of reducing the extent to which self-conscious opposition between court and country provides the most appropriate model. What these revisionist historians are saying is that it is not entirely helpful to interpret political events before 1642 as though the Civil War divisions were already apparent or inevitable. While historians in this category such as Russell, Sharpe, Christianson, and Kishlansky are not primarily interested in 'Puritanism,' a consequence of their approach is that they tend to reject the notion that the 'Puritanism' of the Parliamentarians in the 1640s was adumbrated by the 'Puritanism' of their oppositionist predecessors between 1603 and 1629. Thus Kevin Sharpe remarks that 'if revolutionary puritanism was a cause rather than a consequence of the Civil War, it was the child of a decade beyond the 1620s.'[12]

The suggestion being made here that, with the exception of this group of recent historians, most historians who have dealt with England's political history in the period prior to the civil wars have felt a certain obligation to the 'Puritans' for their explanations, without being able either to define them or even describe them intelligibly, has also been made by George Yule. He has accused Whig historians, for instance, of paying 'lip service to Puritanism' when they see it as one of the main ingredients of the Civil War but fail to provide any serious analysis of the phenomenon. Such historians, he says, citing Keeler in particular, see 'Puritanism' as playing a general political role, leading to toleration, and not as a form of religious conviction at all. It is Yule's belief that while the 'religious attitudes of the puritan gentry are not easy to come by,' nevertheless 'the intensity of the religious feelings of members of the Long Parliament have been greatly underestimated.' As evidence of this assertion, Yule cites a speech by Benjamin Rudyard – Ruigh's 'dedicated Protestant' – to the Long Parliament: 'we are assembled here to do God's business and the King's in which our own is included as we are Christians, as we are subjects. Let us first fear God, then we shall know the King the more ... let Religion be our *primum quaerite* for all things else are but *etceteras* to it, yet we may have them too, sooner and surer, if we give God his Precedence.'[13]

Yule rightly criticizes modern historians for relying upon 'Puritans' for much of their explanation of early seventeenth-century history without paying any attention to the quality of the religious belief inherent in the term. By implicitly secularizing the 'Puritans' and by attributing their beliefs to all or a large section of the 'country' alliance of the 1620s or of the 'parliamentary' alliance of 1642, historians have both lost sight of what might legitimately be said about the experience of being a 'Puritan' and also have confused rather than clarified the religious origins of the English civil wars. However, in accepting the conventional belief that most members of the Long Parliament who supported the war against the king were Puritans, in his strictly religious sense of the word, Yule is straining the evidence. To Yule, the Parliamentarians who opposed the king shared a 'distinctive style of puritan spirituality' which, emanating from a 'Puritan theology,' caused them to speak in Parliament 'as if they were a compound of David and Nehemiah.' Yule, it is clear, is right to insist that the label 'Puritan' refers ultimately to an individual's sense of his relationship with God. It is, in the last analysis, a religious label deriving from a distinctive theology or theological emphasis which may or may not have political or social repercussions. However, while one can readily accept Yule's stipulations concerning the connection between the label 'Puritan' and an individual's personal piety, it is more difficult to accept his conclusion that 'Puritan' can be applied fruitfully to the bulk of the members of the House of Commons prior to 1642.[14]

This is the question to which we now address ourselves. Accepting as our definition of a Puritan that, following Collinson and many others, he is a 'hotter sort of Protestant,' with a self-conscious commitment to the further reformation of the English church along the lines of the best-reformed churches,[15] let us consider the extent to which the political history of England at the national level between 1621 and 1641 can best be interpreted as the result of such a group extending its influence over the body politic. In the definition of a 'Puritan' here adopted, two points are worth observing. First, there is the self-conscious godliness that is a marked characteristic of John Hutchinson, as interpreted by his widow, and of Richard Baxter. When these authors used the term 'Puritan,' which is not very frequently, or 'godly,' which they greatly preferred,[16] they applied it to ididviduals characterized by their personal 'godliness' or 'election' that stemmed usually from a belief in having experienced conversion. Second, there is the 'Puritan' zeal to reform society. For an historian to label an individual a 'Puritan,' either in the 1570s and 1580s or in the 1620s and 1630s, it is necessary for the scholar to demonstrate that such an individual wanted not merely to prevent the erosion of existing church practices and structures, but to carry on the work of reform aborted in the first years of the reign of Queen Elizabeth. Given this fundamental concept of 'Puritanism,' we approach the central question that occupies this chapter: To what extent may the religious aspirations of the parliamentarians in the generation preceding the outbreak of the English civil wars be properly labelled 'Puritan'?

In surveying the broad sweep of England's political history as it manifested itself in the House of Commons during the twenty or so years that preceded the outbreak of hostilities in the late summer of 1642, three occasions stand out when polarization seems to have become firmer and more militant. James I's third Parliament, after sitting for more than four months between January and June 1621, and after voting the king two subsidies – roughly £160,000 – immediately upon its resumption in the following November found his request for emergency funds for the defence of the Lower Palatinate, while he continued to advance the alliance with Spain by means of the marriage of Charles to the Infanta, to be unsatisfactory. This led to a sharp exchange between the king and the House of Commons in December 1621, in the course of which the Commons transformed the relatively tentative assertions of a committee of 1604 into a more definitive declaration that 'the liberties, franchises, privileges, and jurisdictions of Parliament, are the ancient and undoubted birthright and inheritance of the subjects of England,' and that the 'arduous and urgent affairs concerning the King, State and defence of the Realm, and of the Church of England, and the maintenance and making of laws ... are proper subjects and matters of counsel and debate in Parliament.' James, perceiving the Commons' Protestation as a potential invasion of 'most of our inseparable rights and prerogatives annexed to our Imperial Crown,' promptly dissolved the Parliament.[17]

Four Parliaments but only eight years later it was Charles I's turn to find himself in what he regarded as an intolerable relationship with his representative institutions. This time, however, when the Speaker informed the House of the king's command that they be adjourned, he was actually resisted. Making the unjustifiable assertion that 'it was not the office of the Speaker to deliver any such command unto them, but for the adjournment of the House it did properly belong unto themselves,' they forcibly held the Speaker in his chair while they passed their Three Resolutions.[18] Clearly, the representatives of the parliamentary classes had, in eight years, experienced a quantum leap in either their understanding of their political and constitutional rights or their appreciation of the crisis confronting them, and of the strong measures required to protect themselves.

Then, twelve years later, after Charles I had attempted to govern in the French manner without troubling himself with a Parliament, there occurred a third parliamentary occasion when it finally became clear that the old homogeneity of the governing classes was irremediably split. The passage by the House of Commons of the Grand Remonstrance in November 1641 has long been seized upon by historians for two reasons. Its narrow victory provides a convenient means of dating the first appearance in the House of Commons of a sizeable Royalist party, and it provides an invaluable source for probing the way that at least 159 members of the House of Commons perceived their country's immediate past and its all too probable future.[19]

The enthusiastic approval of the king's government that characterized the early days of the Parliament of 1621 had, by late May, given way to resentment and frustration. In January, members seemed prepared to believe that their fears about the European situation were shared by the king, and that his decision to call Parliament was a sign that he had abandoned his formerly passive acceptance of the plight of his son-in-law Frederick and of the European Protestants generally. When James assured the members that the restoration of the Palatinate was his highest concern and that if he could not achieve this by peaceful means then he would not spare 'my crown, and my blood and the blood of my son,' the fears of both Houses were assuaged and two subsidies quickly resulted. Sir Thomas Roe's sentiments when the House of Commons sat as a Committee of the Whole to consider supply were typical. He urged 'let us give liberally and freely that the papists may see that the King and his subjects are in unity and that the King hath the hearts, the hands and purses of his subjects to help him.' Parliament did just as Roe urged, in the expectation that their grievances would be settled and that the considerable body of legislation that had been accumulating since 1610, and earlier, would be passed.[20]

On neither count were the parliamentarians satisfied. In late April, when addressing his fellow landowners at Rotherham, Thomas Wentworth felt hard-pressed to justify the subsidy: 'But it may be objected that we have given away your money and made no laws,' he said, and it is unlikely that he himself was much reassured by the short list of achievements he could cite after almost twelve weeks in session. A month later, Sir Richard Grosvenor made no secret of his dissatisfaction. With an adjournment only a few days off and the concerns of his neighbours very much in the forefront of his mind, he told the House, 'we have given subsidies and have brought home nothing for them.'[21]

Thus the response of the House of Commons to the request of the king for more money when Parliament reconvened on 21 November is scarcely surprising. When the king asked Parliament for emergency funds to support a mercenary army in the Lower Palatinate, he unwittingly provoked a fierce outburst from members of the House of Commons who gave expression in no uncertain manner to their deepest fears and apprehensions. And much more important than the absence of statutes correcting immediate grievances was the view, widely shared by many members, that the world they had known for sixty years was under attack from all sides and that only immediate and resolute action by the government could now save it. Despite the king's rhetoric, it seemed clear by late 1621 that he had no serious intention of intervening to support what many saw as the cause of true religion. This provides the religious and emotional context which renders explicable the determination of members of the House of Commons to affirm what they believed to be their inalienable constitutional rights in the face of the king's unmistakeable displeasure.

From the first days of the Parliament it was clear that many members firmly believed that the threat to the Protestant cause on the Continent, represented by the emperor's deposition of the Elector Frederick, was matched by a rapidly growing fifth column of 'popish priests and Jesuits.' The problem of how best to implement the anti-recusant legislation was seen by many as at least as important as any other issue before Parliament. In the first week of February, the House of Commons had appointed a subcommittee for recusants whose function was to decide how to frame a petition to the king informing him of the 'insolencies of the papists' and of the need to take greater steps to ensure his safety. One of the first speakers to address this subcommittee was the member for Bath, Sir Robert Phelips. This year, he said, made him especially nervous, because 'we are now about the climacterical year, for religion had continued here about sixty-three years,' adding gloomily, 'I fear it is near a period.' Sir James Perrot followed Phelips and explained to the committee just why the 'insolencies' of the papists were growing at this time. The first reason, he asserted, and this was to be a constant refrain throughout the Parliament of 1621, was that the anti-recusant legislation was not enforced. In addition, he said, 'their books are suffered to be printed even in the High Commission prisons where there is continual resort to Mass' and the papists' children are permitted to attend seminaries from which they return 'Jesuits or Jesuited.' It is worth noting that the sixth reason presented by Perrot was that 'we suffer abuses in our own religion as non-residency and plurality of benefices which is a cause that people are not taught.' Even the concern for a godly preaching ministry was for Perrot primarily a defence against the unceasing proselytizing of the papists.[22]

The result of the hearings of the subcommittee on recusants was a petition to the king which, after some debate by the House of Lords, was presented, unamended, to the king on 17 February. Broadly, the principal heads of the petition, rather like those of the petition of 1610, were as follows: the king was to command all recusants to depart from London and from the court and to return to their own houses; they were to be deprived of their arms; the King was to forbid the hearing of Mass by English subjects at their own houses, or at the houses of foreign ambassadors; the anti-recusant laws as a whole, and the laws against Jesuits in particular, were to be rigorously enforced, and informers upon the laws to be encouraged.[23]

The petition to the king was only a small part of this Parliament's efforts to cope with what members saw as their most serious domestic problem. In addition to the petition, the House of Commons also approved a bill seeking an explanation of a statute passed in the third year of James I's reign, entitled an Act for the Better Discovery and Repressing of Popish Recusants, and a Sabbatarian Bill. As well as these legislative achievements, there was also the remarkably vindictive treatment of the hapless Edward Floyd who, for a few chance remarks accidentally reported to a committee of the House, was subjected to the most vicious and unconstitutional punishment.[24]

Floyd's case is interesting not only for the light it throws on attitudes within the House of Commons in May 1621, but also for what it tells us about the House of Lords. Edward Floyd, a Catholic barrister and a prisoner in the Fleet prison, was reported to a House of Commons committee as having in 1620 uttered some uncomplimentary remarks about the unhappy fate of the king's daughter and son-in-law. He was accused, for instance, of having narrated to an acquaintance with utmost relish the plot of a stage-play in which Princess Elizabeth was 'depicted with a child under each arm and one in her belly with the Palsgrave following with the cradle.[25] For this, and for having referred to the couple as 'Goodman and Goodwife Palsgrave,' he was summoned before the House, accused, tried utterly unconstitutionally, and sentenced to be pilloried, 'set on horse-back, with his face to the horse tail,' and fined £1000. Floyd's self-defence was not greatly helped by the revelation that investigation of his study had revealed 'rosary beads, a crucifix, relics of my Lady's gown, petticoat, smocks, hair and a piece of the cross.' When the Lords heard of this, they were furious because the lower House had pre-empted their judicial function. When the more temperate and balanced House of Lords finally heard the case late in May, they also found Floyd guilty of having uttered 'ignominious and despiteful words and malicious and scornful behaviour towards the Prince and Princess Palatine, the King's only daughter and their children.' Instead of merely pillorying him and fining him, the Lords elected to disbar him from bearing arms as a gentleman, increased the fine to £5000, and sentenced him to life imprisonment in Newgate. Dislike of the papists was not a gentry monopoly.[26]

But none of this flurry of activity was successful in calming the anxieties of many of the members. The king's answer to the petition was not seen as positive, nor did it seem to lead to any increase in the execution of the anti-recusant legislation. Furthermore, Floyd's fine was remitted by the king and he was released from prison within two months. The bills, once passed by the House of Commons, either stopped with the Lords or were not accepted by the king. It is clear that as the first session came to a close in early June, the anxiety level in the lower House was extremely high, as members saw their culture in utter jeopardy. 'For fear, I was never a coward,' said Sir Edward Sandys, 'but yet never more afraid. All things in the country are out of frame, religion is a rooting out in Bohemia, the Palatinate, France. It was a misery to see so many of all sorts of French in Westminster Hall as we came through yesterday, fled from their country for religion. We are next door to them. But our gates, the port towns are forsaken ... there is not one man in them worth £300.' To Dr Gooch, the outlook was just as grim: 'What find we, our friends decreased, our enemies increased, ourselves are weakened ... If we think not that Man of Rome and his son of Spain to be our enemies we're deceived. For it's this country that drew the one from his spiritual monarchy and hindered the other from being that which he hath ever aspired unto, viz to be monarch of the west.' But on the last day of the session, as the members somewhat reluctantly accepted the adjournment, it was Sir James Perrot who placed the foreign and domestic peril in sharpest focus. He urged that 'special care might be taken for true religion [which] stands at this present so endangered abroad and so doubtful at home.' In particular, he urged his colleagues to pledge their 'estates and lives' to subdue those 'who seek the overthrow of religion.' Perrot's impassioned plea was so enthusiastically received by the House that a subcommittee was instantly appointed to compose a Declaration which, after the House of Lords had actually been adjourned, was applauded by the members though it could never be given an official status. The thrust of this Declaration aptly summarized the religious concerns of the majority of members, at least of those who were reported as having addressed the House. They were deeply concerned about 'the present estate of the King's children abroad and the general afflicted estate of the true professors of the same Christian religion professed by the church of England in foreign parts.' So strongly did they feel this concern, they went on, that if the king's attempts to solve these problems by treaty were not soon successful, they would help their brothers abroad 'both with their lives and fortunes.'[27]

It was this offer by the House of Commons that underlay the crossed purposes of the king and the lower chamber when Parliament resumed sitting on 20 November. The Lord Keeper's speech on that day made it clear that James remembered vividly the pledge. 'His Majesty is assured you will be ready with your lives and fortunes to get that which by treaty he cannot.' The 'breach is now grown so desperate as that it cannot otherwise be repaired ... with a sword in the one hand and a treaty in the other.' Not surprisingly, the king had moved the session forward by three months to enable his subjects to provide supply 'to pay Count Mansfield's soldiers.' Despite their declarations, however, the request for more money to be followed by another recess before Christmas struck the members as unappealing.[28]

To most members of the House of Commons there were three problems with James' suggestion. First, there was the response of those like Sir Thomas

Wentworth who, we saw above, had been irritated in late April by the failure of the Parliament to be compensated for its two subsidies by the passage of legislation. Seven months later he 'moved for a session because we have sat long and done nothing and yet been at great charges.' Second, there were the reactions of those like Sir James Perrot to whom it was just as important to preserve God's religion at home as in Europe: 'I like it well to help abroad, but let us have an eye at home also ... Let us be free of the Jesuits, the Pope's Janissaries and their adherents ... And that first our religion be secured at home and then to provide for others abroad.' Finally, there was widespread reaction that although it was gratifying that the king had finally recognized that war was a more realistic policy than treaty, yet he was preparing to wage the wrong kind of war with the wrong monarch. The real enemy was the king of Spain, not of Bavaria. What good was it, so the argument ran, to commit untold future resources to a land war in the midst of German states while still carrying on peaceful relations with Spain, even to the extent of continuing with the marriage treaty. To Thomas Crew, the three objections were one: 'Everyone would give with a swift and open hand ... [if] all the Jesuits might be banished and the papists depressed, [if] the bills ingrossed might be signed by the King ... [if we were] not to fight with a concealed enemy but with the King of Spain and not with the Duke of Bavaria,' and if the king would give assurances 'that we might see the Prince matched to one of the same religion.'[29]

Crew's predictions proved to be accurate, for when the House of Commons sat as a Committee of the Whole on 28 November, members were vying with each other in generosity. Would one subsidy be sufficient or would one or more fifteenths be also necessary? Little opposition was expressed to Sir Thomas Jermyn's view that 'to give bountifully now is the way to accomplish our desires.' John Pym's contribution to the debate was that the sum should be increased because it would be some time before it would be collected. He moved 'that it be a subsidy to be paid in February.' This, of course, was not the end of the story. Attached to the subsidy were two orders. First, recusants were to be assessed for this subsidy as though they were aliens – they should pay double the amount 'because they are aliens in heart [and] because they never bear office in the commonwealth, therefore they are free of many charges.' More important than this, however, was the second decision to appoint a subcommittee to draw up petitions to the king that would give expression to their vote 'to have a session before Christmas and to petition to the King about religion.' Under these circumstances, and by this committee, was the statement composed that became the petition of the House of Commons of 3 December 1621 which provoked what some historians have regarded as the first major political crisis of the seventeenth century.[30]

The constitutional implications of the petition and of the Protestation of December 1621 have long been familiar to historians and, notwithstanding the work of recent revisionist historians, the point does not require extensive elaboration here.[31] By approving the petition, followed by the protestation two weeks later, the House of Commons, while not exactly making the subsidy conditional upon the king's acceptance of their advice, nevertheless saw fit to make strong recommendations to him on matters that were clearly part of his prerogative. Specifically, the House of Commons urged the king 'that the bent of this war and point of our sword may be against that prince ... whose armies and treasures have first diverted and since maintained the war in the Palatinate' and also that 'to frustrate [Popish] hopes for a future age, our most noble Prince may be timely and happily married to one of our own religion.' Then, when the king refused to permit the House of Commons to continue the discussion about Spain or about the match, members came to adopt a clear position on their right to consider such matters. The king was fully aware that both the petition and the protestation tended to 'breach of prerogative royal' and, although the paper skirmishes continued for several weeks as the two sides tactfully restated their positions, the petition effectively brought the Parliament of 1621 to a premature conclusion with no bills passed save the earlier double subsidy.[32]

What is important to our discussion here is the religious context of the constitutional dispute. To the extent that religious forces might be said to have motivated members of the House of Commons in adopting their position in early December 1621, how may these religious forces best be characterized? Are the stated positions of the parliamentarians best described as 'Puritan,' following upon the definition cited above? If not, what alternatives do we have?

There can be little doubt that members of the House of Commons knew both that they were adopting a constitutionally controversial stance and that they were doing so in defence of their religion. When the petition was first read to the whole House on 3 December, Sir Edward Sackville, a courtier, was quick to point out that 'we have been careful all this parliament not to touch the King's prerogatives but what greater prerogative is there than to make war, matches and alliances?' His warning, and that of others, was to some extent heeded, for the petition finally adopted had a paragraph added which expressed their hope not 'to press upon your Majesty's undoubted and regal prerogative.' This window-dressing surely deceived few and it is certain that they were all aware of the essentially innovative and thus dangerous implications of both the petition and the Protestation.[33]

It is equally clear that what sustained these gentry in their explorations on the frontiers of the constitution was not revolutionary fervour or a love of innovation of any sort, but a self-conscious 'zeal of our true religion, in which we have been born and wherein (by God's grace) we are resolved to die.' They believed in December 1621, as they had at moments of tension earlier in the year, that they and apparently only they – not the court – were prepared to come to the defence of the 'beleaguered isle.'[34]

Central to the awareness of the House of Commons of their immediate political situation was a sense of 'imminent peril,' as Perrot expressed it. The most fundamental reality about England in 1621 was the growing 'insolencies of popish recusants' who, if not restrained, 'will increase and grow in number and arrogancy.' Every member, it seemed, had his favourite horror story or, failing that, could always fall back on the Gunpowder Treason. Sir Edward Giles told the House on 26 November of the confession by a west country Jesuit who had revealed that 'there is amongst us 500 [Jesuits] ... and that there would be shortly a King, that would profess the Catholic religion.' In the debate on the petition on 3 December, Thomas, Peter Wentworth's son, supported its presentation to the king, reminding his auditors of the events of the exploits of Guy Fawkes. 'These walls (methinks) do yet shake at it. And I would know whether those 30 barrels of gunpowder under these walls do not require this?'[35]

Debate on the petition in the House of Commons on 3 December focused on the papists because the document itself was about nothing else. Members' concern with papists abroad was simply a variant of their concern with papists at home. The February petition concerning recusants had not produced the effect that 'the danger of these times doth seem to us to require,' stated the preamble to the December petition, which again placed the domestic perils in the context of the declining fortunes of continental Protestants. The fourteen causes of the 'growing mischiefs,' the four effects, and the ten remedies were all pleas to the king to abandon his naïve *de facto* toleration of popery at home and his weak-kneed treaty with papists abroad. There is no sign here of any attempt to change England's religion. 'Subversion of the true religion' was, after all, the ambition of the 'pope of Rome and his dearest son.'[36] Quite unlike the 'Puritan' members of the Elizabethan Parliaments whose intention is said to have been to perfect the church established in 1558, Pym, Phelips, Grosvenor, and Wentworth were attempting to preserve the church in which true religion had flourished for over sixty years. They can be described as 'religious' men in the sense that they believed themselves to be motivated by, amongst other things, a desire to protect religion, but not, by any reasonable definition of 'Puritan,' as 'Puritans.' Perhaps there were some within their ranks who were genuine 'Puritans' to whom preservation of the church was only the immediate goal, to be followed by its further reformation. That does not, however, seem to be the case with the majority of members whose anti-Catholicism stemmed from a widely-shared identification of the interests of the elite classes with the maintenance of a monarchical, English, national, erastian, and, above all else, Protestant church and state. To the great majority of parliamentarians in 1621, unlike some of their Elizabethan predecessors and certain of their successors in the later 1640s, the idea of religious reform was inconceivable. The idea of the past that they shared, their perception of the present, and their fears for the future were all couched in terms of their continuing struggle with, and their all too likely annihilation by, the political and religious forces wielded by the Rome-Madrid axis.[37] Sir Edward Coke had read the House a lecture on the history of England since the accession of Queen Elizabeth in the debate on 27 November in which he took as his theme the constant provocations initiated by the Catholics, beginning with the Papal Bull of 1570, and what he regarded as the series of completely legitimate responses by the English Parliament in the form of anti-recusant legislation. The climax of Coke's history was 1605 when the papists' attempted coup was designed 'to take revenge against us in these places when we made laws against them.'[38]

Our consideration of the preoccupations of the members of the House of Commons in 1621 has confined itself entirely to matters that might broadly be defined as religious. Obviously, this approach excludes a whole range of other matters, not remotely connected to religion, that were of major concern to the members. The campaigns against Mompesson and Bacon, the alarm at the 'decay of trade,' the abuse of patents, and innumerable other fears, whose importance is testified by the eighty-one bills that were passed by the House of Commons and sent to the upper house, were part of the broader political picture that has been deliberately excluded here. This, of course, permits us to focus more sharply on our central problem – the part played by religion in the political history of England during the twenty years prior to the outbreak of the civil wars.

Confining ourselves thus to religion, what can be said of it regarding the parliamentarians in 1621? First, it seems that at least those members whose views we have considered believed themselves to be deeply concerned about religion. Second, it seems that the occasions of greatest tension between the House of Commons and the king arose when the question of religion was being discussed. It was the passage of the Bill for the Better Discovery and Repressing of Popish Recusants by both Houses, and the consideration by a committee of the House of Commons of an even broader bill to summarize the entire body of anti-recusant legislation passed since 1558, that caused James to adjourn Parliament lest the legislation interfere with the Spanish treaty. Similarly, it was the petition of 3 December, which was largely concerned with the popish peril, that led finally to the dissolution of James' third Parliament. Third, it is also clear that when parliamentarians talked about religion, for instance, when they appointed a committee on religion, their intention was not to reform the church but to preserve it.

In 1621 the enemies of true religion were not masquerading as Protestant members of the Church of England, and were certainly not the bishops. The cause of God's religion, established by Elizabeth, appeared to be threatened by recusants, papists, and, yet more sinister, the rapidly filling ranks of Jesuits and other priests, who were eroding from inside England the church that was openly assaulted from outside. Given the reforming zeal that is the hallmark of 'Puritanism' as defined or presumed by most historians, that label scarcely seems the most appropriate way to designate the essentially defensive religious zeal of the parliamentarians in 1621.

The second political and constitutional crisis of the 1620s occurred in the third Parliament of Charles I, noted principally by historians for its Petition of Right. Much has been written about this Parliament and no good purpose would be served by rehearsing its familiar story except where it throws light on our particular theme.[39] The first session of this Parliament had begun in March 1628 and in the course of three months had spent its energies on rectifying the constitutional iniquities of the government's policy since 1626. As Sir Robert Phelips had summarized the parliamentarians' sense of grievances, they comprised 'acts of power not warranted by law' and 'a judgement given under form of law, by which the law that protects the subjects is threatened to be violated and ruined.' On the question of religion, the House of Commons had not been especially active, a fact of which members seemed acutely aware when the Parliament reassembled on 20 January 1629. As Sir Walter Earle explained it, he had felt that the previous session was best spent 'in vindicating those rights and liberties of the subject which had formerly been impeached and were then in most imminent danger.' By late January 1629, however, Earle believed religion must take precedence over all other matters. 'What good will those rights and liberties do me,' he asked rhetorically, 'if religion remains unsettled?' Earle's plea was obviously addressed to a sympathetic audience because the king's expressed wish that the Tonnage and Poundage Bill be passed was swept aside by a House of Commons which shared Earle's determination to fall upon 'points of religion.' Not only did they reject Secretary Coke's request that the bill be read on the morning of 26 January, but, two days later, the House agreed that 'the matter of religion shall have precedence of all other business' and immediately sat as a Committee of the Whole 'to take consideration of Popery and Arminianism.' Thereafter, until Parliament was adjourned on 2 March, and subsequently dissolved, the attention of the members of the House of Commons was focused almost exclusively on the religious problem which was, of course, the subject of the first of the three resolutions passed by that House in its last hour.[40]

This second and very brief session of Charles' third Parliament thus provides us with an excellent opportunity to investigate the way in which members perceived the religious problem. Public statements to the House of Commons do not, of course, provide us with an especially sensitive guide to the private and personal religious piety of the members themselves, let alone the broader social group whom they represent. Yet the private consciences of the most public men in England in the seventeenth century – or any other century for that matter – are for the most part inaccessible even to their biographers. In recent years, for example, the biographers of the noted 'Puritans' John Eliot, Bulstrode White-locke, William Prynne, Denzil Holles, and the third Earl of Essex have had little to say about the private faith of their subjects.[41] Hence, often when 'Puritan' has been applied to these men, it has served to confuse rather than to clarify the sources of their behaviour. Furthermore, historians for whom 'Puritanism' provides a major component of their explanation necessarily rely on the kinds of public expressions of fervour as occurred in the House of Commons in the winter of 1629. A close examination of such evidence serves at least two purposes. It provides us with a sense of the way religious forces might legitimately be said to have impinged upon the broader political relationships within the increasingly polarized society of the late 1620s. And it permits us to enquire to what extent 'Puritan' or 'Puritanism,' as we have defined them, provide an appropriate label for these religious forces.

We have seen that when parliamentarians talked about religion in 1621, they tended to concentrate on two areas. First, they described what they saw to be the very obvious increase in the numbers of recusants and papists, both lay and clerical, and the public way in which they conducted themselves, especially at court and in the precincts of the houses of certain foreign ambassadors. This, they believed, was largely due to James' failure to enforce the anti-recusant legislation. Second, they were deeply conscious of the situation confronting the reformed churches abroad, and especially that of the Elector Frederick and his wife.

Seven years later, the gaze of the parliamentarians was focused much more closely on England, and the alarm was yet more urgently expressed. Whereas previously the monarch had been the victim of his own benign gullibility, and of his determination to distinguish between kinds of papists, by 1629 the threat to the church appeared to be much more serious. No longer was it just a matter of papists growing like weeds untended in a basically healthy and properly-run garden, but now the church itself was being undermined in a much more dangerous and insidious way. Even were the anti-recusant laws to be enforced, members were justified in wondering how disaster could be averted when popery was being steadily introduced into the church by those charged with its preservation.

By 1629, the threat to England's religion appeared to many contemporaries to come from two developments that were separable, though closely related. One was the greatly increased toleration being extended by the central government to England's apparently expanding Catholic community. The second, and to many they were scarcely to be distinguished, was the rise to power within the Established Church of the Arminian faction.[42]

Since 1621 there had been a number of events which made a mockery of the seriousness of the intricate network of anti-recusant legislation enacted between 1580 and 1610 and, by implication, of the authority of the legislation itself. In October 1623 nearly one hundred Catholics were accidentally killed when the floor of a room in which Mass was being said by a Jesuit priest, Robert Drury, gave way, plunging the worshippers to their deaths. Significantly, the room was located 'in a tenement two storeys above the [French] ambassador's wardrobe.' The gap between the political, religious and cultural assumptions of the aging monarch, James I, and those of many of his subjects had never been more apparent than in their respective responses to the accident at Blackfriars. To James' expressions of regret and to his wishes that the French ambassador might enjoy a 'speedy recovery' can be compared the reaction of the populace of London as described by the Venetian ambassador. While a few brave relatives came to mourn their dead, 'the wisest restrained their tears, as it is a dangerous crime to weep for those innocents who are considered guilty even in death by the rabid opinion of the heretical multitude.' One young girl, pulled half dead from the wreckage, was attacked by the crowd and her rescue 'provided the unhappy occasion for a general and bloody riot.'[43]

A few months later, a man, who claimed to have been a member of Dr Drury's congregation on the afternoon of the fatal accident, published a book which he dedicated to the members of James' fourth Parliament that was about to meet. In *The Foot out of the Snare*, John Gee, allegedly having been brought to his religious senses by the persuasive tongue of Archbishop Abbott, presented an attack on Catholicism, a list of some 155 or so titles of Catholic publications that he knew to have been in recent circulation, together with a list of the names of 255 'Romish Priests and Jesuits now resident about the City of London.' So precise was Gee's intelligence that he was able to provide not only names, but also frequently addresses and physical descriptions. Thus, for instance, he described Dr Townsend, alias Ruckwood, 'brother to that Ruckwood who was executed at the Gun-powder-treason' as 'a Jesuit, a little black fellow, very compt and gallant, lodging about the midst of Drury Lane, acquainted with collapsed ladies.' Leaving no stone unturned in his relentless pursuit of papists, Gee also included lists of popish physicians, apothecaries, and even the names of several 'rasor-chirurgions.'[44]

The year 1625 had seen the marriage of the young king to Henrietta Maria, sister of Louis XIII, goddaughter of Pope Urban VIII, a condition of which marriage was the guarantee of improved conditions for England's Catholics. While considerable disagreement developed between the two governments in their interpretations of the treaty, and deteriorating relations between them led to outright war in 1627, nonetheless by 1628 Catholics were clearly living under conditions of much less tension than at any time since the 1570s. No Catholic, priest or layman, had been executed under the provisions of the anti-recusant legislation since 1618. Moreover, fines paid by recusants into the Exchequer in 1628 amounted to £2132, the second lowest annual figure since the financial provisions of the anti-recusant legislation were put into effect in the late 1580s.[45]

Nor was this almost complete disregard for the anti-recusant legislation halted in 1628. It is true that on 15 March of that year the Privy Council ordered the arrest of seven Jesuits found living in a house in Clerkenwell and that by December all had been incarcerated, along with another three priests subsequently discovered, and that three had been tried and one sentenced to death. Nevertheless, on the eve of the execution all ten were released from prison. The arrest of the Jesuits was obviously timed to coincide with the opening of Charles' third Parliament two days later in an attempt by the government to counteract the predictable attack by the members for its failure to enforce the anti-recusant legislation. If so, it was only partially successful, for on the first day of regular business the House of Commons had given first reading to a bill 'to restrain the passing or sending of any to be popishly bred beyond the seas,' and ordered all members to supply the committee on religion with the names of all suspected recusants. If the existence of the Jesuit seminary was profoundly threatening to the members of the House of Commons in the first session of this Parliament which was, as Russell has pointed out, yet more preoccupied with 'vindicating English liberties,' the fact that the prisoners had been freed to continue their mission proved to be intolerable when Parliament reassembled in January 1629. The investigation by the House of Commons into the circumstances surrounding the release from prison of the ten Catholic priests, an investigation that went all the way to the king, was an important element in the proceedings of that body in its last days.[46]

Associated with this almost complete toleration of Catholicism by the central government in the late 1620s was the growing ascendancy within the church of the Arminian party. In the most recent twelve months, two bishops who had been accused in the first session of the Parliament of holding unsound opinions, William Laud and Richard Neile, had become members of the Privy Council. The controversial Arminian divine, Richard Montagu, author of *A New Gag for an Old Goose* and *Appello Caesarem*, who had been repeatedly criticized by successive Caroline Parliaments, was rewarded with the bishopric of Chichester. Other promotions as well made the trend unmistakeable. Not surprisingly, then, Arminianism was the other major preoccupation of members of the House of Commons in 1629. We are thus in a position to probe the importance of religion to these members of the governing classes by focusing upon their responses to what they believed to be a systematic policy to impose Laudian Arminianism uniformly on the entire Church of England. The problem with this policy was, as every student of seventeenth-century English history has long known, that an Arminian was seen to be neither more nor less than a papist in the thinnest of disguises. As Francis Rous expressed it so vividly:

an Arminian is the spawn of a Papist; and if there come the warmth of favour upon him, you shall see him turn into one of those frogs that rise out of the bottomless pit. And if you mark it well, you shall see an Arminian reaching out his hand to a Papist, a Papist to a Jesuit, a Jesuit gives one hand to the Pope and the other to the King of Spain; these men having kindled a fire in our neighbour country, now they have brought over some of it hither, to set on flame this Kingdom also.[47]

When the parliamentarians came to itemize the specific ways in which they saw their religion being eroded, there was some repetition from earlier years, although the general fear was felt more intensely. The prognosis for Protestants on the Continent was no more favourable in 1629 than it had been seven years before. As a result of the successes of the 'mighty and prevalent party,' the Protestant churches of Germany, France, and elsewhere were either 'already ruined,' or in the 'most weak and miserable condition.' But by far the heavier emphasis of the 'heads and Articles' accepted by the House of Commons on 23 February – and of the debates from which they stemmed – was upon the situation at home. Few doubted that there had been an 'extraordinary growth of Popery.' So conspicuous was this in some counties that, from one or two recusants in Queen Elizabeth's time, there had grown up more than two thousand and 'all the rest generally apt to revolt.' The presence of a Catholic queen raised a new set of problems, as the public resorted 'in multitudes without control' to the Masses celebrated in her court. Sir William Bulstrode was outraged by the freedom with which popery was practised. In addition to the queen's Mass, he pointed out, there were at least two others celebrated at the court each day, 'so that it is grown ordinary with the out-facing Jesuits, and common in discourse, Will you go to Mass, or have you been at Mass at Somerset-house? there coming five hundred at a time from Mass.' As always, Sir Robert Phelips could produce a statistic with which to document popish power. He said he could prove that 'there are nine hundred and forty persons in houses of religion being English, Scotch and Irish, in the Netherlands, maintained by the Papists of England.' In general, however, the threat posed by popery in 1629 was similar, albeit on a larger scale, to that earlier in the decade. As recently as the previous March, the two Houses had joined to submit the now quite familiar petition to the king concerning the recusants, but Charles had been no more responsive than his father even though now, with the discovery and the subsequent arrest of the Jesuits at Clerkenwell, there was even evidence of a Jesuit college flourishing within England.[48]

The increase in the number of papists and in their influence was serious but not new. As Sir Robert Phelips said, 'two sects are dangerously crept in to undermine King and Kingdom ... the one ancient Popery, the other new Arminianism,' and it was the new threat to which even more attention was given in February 1629. What made Arminianism such a problem was that by its novelty and its professed Protestant character its effect was divisive upon the reformed churches. By 'casting doubts upon the religion professed and established,' the effect of the Arminian success was to separate the English church from the 'Reformed Churches abroad,' but it also tended to sow the seeds of division internally. What was particularly troubling to members of the House of Commons was that the Arminians had managed to throw doubt on the theological base of the church in a way that would have been quite impossible for the papists. This was the problem to which John Pym was addressing himself in his speech to the House of 27 January in which he laid down what he conceived to be the major sources wherein were to be found the 'established and fundamental truths.' Leaving aside the interesting questions raised by his assertion of the constitutional function of Parliament in the establishment of the doctrinal base of the church, Pym's acceptance of the five pillars of church doctrine is conspicuous for its implied rejection of any zeal for theological reform. To Pym, the 'truth professed here' [in England] rested upon the 1552 Articles and Catechism; the writings of Martyr, Bucer, Wycliffe; the profession of the Marian martyrs such as Cranmer and Ridley; the 39 Articles; and the Lambeth articles sent by James to Synod of Dort. As Russell has observed, Pym was omitting even Calvin and Beza in the interests of church unity. Pym's religious ambition in 1629 appears not to have been a 'Puritan' zeal to reform an imperfect church, but a grim determination to preserve a quite satisfactorally reformed church from the threat of popery in both its old and its new guises.[49]

Stemming from the Arminian disposition to reject certain of the more Calvinist theological bases of the English church were the innovations they introduced into the dioceses and individual churches under their control. Theology was, after all, a complex subject not often discussed in any detail in the House of Commons. Liturgy, however, was a more everyday matter and changes in the arrangements within a church or in the manner of conducting a service were readily apparent and apt to be highly symbolic and immediately painful. The Arminian liturgical innovations represented the most conspicuous and most emotionally charged way that the Protestant, God-fearing gentry of England could see 'new paintings [being] laid upon the old face of the whore of Babylon to make her seem more lovely.' In the *Heads and Articles Agreed upon by the House of Commons*, much attention was paid to the 'bold and unwarranted introducing, practising, and defending of sundry new ceremonies ... in conformity to the Church of Rome.' In particular, what members objected to was the conversion of the communion table into an altar often adorned with candle-sticks and bowed to by the minister, the 'setting up of pictures, lights and images in churches,' and so on. Compounding the problem of the Arminians' insidious nature was the obvious ease with which they controlled the sources of patronage. Montagu's consecration as Bishop of Chichester was merely the most blatant instance of a clear trend whereby 'these persons who have published and maintained such Popish, Arminian and superstitious opinions and practices and who are known to be unsound in Religion, are countenanced, favoured and preferred.'[50]

The principle objection to Arminianism lay in the fact that it was believed to be a form of Catholicism. Were the Arminians such as Laud and Montagu to succeed in imposing their views uniformly on the whole English church, then it was widely believed that reunion with the Roman church would inevitably result, thus leading inexorably to the fundamental erosion of English culture. None of our subjects ever took the time to present a calm and rational analysis of precisely what they feared most in popery. The language in which popery and Arminianism were discussed in February 1629 was highly emotional, not notably rational, and remarkable for its rich and highly symbolic imagery. Close analysis of their highly inflamed rhetoric, however, does permit us to see some of the real fears that informed the stereotyped responses.

Francis Rous, from whom we have already heard on the Arminian-papist, tadpole-frog analogy, made a couple of references in that speech which provide an interesting clue to several of the associations that popery had for him. 'Yea I desire that we may look into the belly and bowels of this Trojan horse to see if there be not men in it ready to open the gates to Romish tyranny and Spanish monarchy,' he said, and continued, 'Yea let us further search and consider whether these be not the men that break-in upon the goods and liberties of this Commonwealth.'[51] For him, popery carried with it at least two direct implications: it involved foreign-Spanish domination, and it was a synonym for political tyranny. A Catholic England would be an England controlled by Spain in which the absolute rights to property and to personal freedom, believed inviolate under English monarchy, would be totally and permanently suspended.

There were, however, several other ingredients to the fear of popery in 1629 which added to its potent intensity. To Edward Kirton, the introduction of the 'Romish Religion' stemmed from 'the ambition of some of the clergy that are near his Majesty,' a development he explained in historical terms. Hundreds of years ago, he reminded members, 'the church of Rome and that which we now profess were all one,' a happy state of affairs destroyed by 'the ambition of the clergy.' In the English church now, he said, 'the highest dignity' available to a clergyman was an archbishopric, a title 'too mean for those who affect too well a Cardinal's cap.' John Eliot picked up this theme in his long speech to the House on 29 January. In this address, Eliot recalled the judgment rendered by the young King Edward VI on the bishops and clergy of whom he had written that 'some for sloth, some for age, some for ignorance, some for luxury, some for Popery were unfit for discipline and government.' Eliot feared that in 1629 similar generalizations could be made. While there were some amongst Charles' bishops who were 'fit to be made examples for all ages,' there were others who most decidedly were not. Of Montagu and others he said, 'I reverence the order, I honour not the man.' It is worth noting that six days after Eliot's address a bill was introduced into the House of Commons removing all clergy from the Commission for the Peace with the exception of bishops, deans, and vice-chancellors of universities within their jurisdiction.[52]

While members of the House of Commons showed some awareness of the history of the church before the Reformation, it is clear that the experience since the break with the Rome was more clearly etched in their memories. Foxe's *Acts and Monuments* provided a version of the history of the English church since its earliest times, but one suspects that for most gentry the story became truly compelling when he came to detail the persecution of the godly during the reign of Queen Mary. Since then, of course, 'eighty-eight' and the 'powder-plot' provided two more graphic illustrations of God's continuing care for his 'elect Nation,' a favour that now showed signs of being withdrawn.[53] They could not expect God to continue to 'fight our battles' in the face of 'our defect in religion and the sins of idolatry and popery.' Sherland expressed this sense of an immediate threat to the nation's faith in the broader context of the traditional historical conflict between the forces of popery and those of reform when he said: 'We have a Religion that is worth loving with all our hearts. It was sealed with the blood of martyrs and kept by miracles.'[54]

What gave the proceedings of the House of Commons in early 1629 their urgency was the widespread and almost apocalyptic conviction that the last days of true religion in England were at hand. Jeremiad followed jeremiad as the merchants of doom and gloom justified the need for immediate action. By allowing error and schism to flourish amongst them, Englishmen had driven God away, a fact that Phelips could easily demonstrate. 'I am afraid,' he said, 'that God sitteth in the council of our enemies against us ... We are become the most contemptible nation in the world.' With this in mind, the House of Commons petitioned the king to nominate a Fast Day, for they said, 'we have just come to conceive that the divine Majesty is for our sins exceeding offended with us.' Sir Richard Grosvenor, in his lengthy report to the House on 13 February, in which he summarized the results of their proceedings against popery in the last session, struck a similar posture: 'For whilst we are thus careless in standing for God that we dare scarce own our own Religion, it is no marvel that God estrangeth himself from us, and will not own us, as by too woeful experience we have cause to suspect.'[55]

This, then, is the context in which the Three Resolutions of 2 March 1629 must be read. The refusal of the House of Commons to consider the Tonnage and Poundage Bill not surprisingly caused the king quickly to decide on an end to parliaments for a while. The dissolution of the Parliament in turn caused the members to feel threatened as never before and thus to take the unprecedented step of declaring as a 'capital enemy to this Kingdom and Commonwealth' anyone who shall 'bring in innovation in Religion, or by favour or countenance, seek to extend or introduce Popery or Arminianism or other opinion disagreeing from the true and orthodox Church.'[56]

There can be little doubt that the majority of the members of the House of Commons in early 1629 believed themselves to be deeply concerned about the question of religion. The only other subject discussed for any significant period of time was tonnage and poundage, the collection of which in the absence of parliamentary sanction was taken very seriously by the members. As we saw in our discussion of the 1621 Parliament, this perception of religion was negative, pessimistic, and utterly defensive. The old enemy, popery, had now been joined by its more dangerous ally, Arminianism, which through its control of the avenues of power and patronage within the church was seeking 'to eat into our Religion and fret into the banks and walls of it.'[57] The zeal for reform, usually a hallmark of the 'Puritan' movement, was clearly conceived by the parliamentarians to be an essential trait of the Arminians. As far as the parliamentarians were concerned, while some of the old enemies of 1621 had vanished, to be replaced by a more formidable set eight years later, their religion does not appear to have changed substantially. Again, 'Puritanism' appears not to be the most telling label to apply to the religious persuasion of Sir Richard Grosvenor, John Pym, Sir Robert Phelips, and Edward Kirton because what seems to unite them and sustain their militancy is not any kind of desire to perfect the church, but a desire to protect it from the threat, at home and abroad, of the papists' conspiracy. It was not these men who wished to reform the church, but their enemies, the popish Arminians.

Finally in our consideration of the part played by religious forces in English national politics during the two decades prior to the civil wars, we come to the Long Parliament, about whose discussions so much has been written that it might reasonably be asked what more can possibly be said.[58] Once again we will make no attempt here to consider more than one small part of the proceedings of this body. Let us consider the way in which religious forces appear to have been a factor in the deliberations of the Long Parliament during its first twelve months or so, culminating in the adoption by the House of Commons of the Grand Remonstrance.

The religious views of the bulk of the members of the Long Parliament during the first year of its existence seem to have been more militant, more specifically focused, but not qualitatively different from those of members in the 1620s. In the earlier period, we have observed, while the specific political issues changed – from the Spanish match to the influence of the Arminians, for instance – the root cause remained constant. Concentrating upon the defence of the old Protestant church rather than upon its reformation, the set of religious attitudes shared by the majority of parliamentarians seems more aptly described as aggressively Protestant and as 'anti-Catholic' than as 'Puritan.' When we shift our attention to the early years of the Long Parliament, there seems no reason to believe the situation had much changed.

Broadly, the religious preoccupations of the members of the Long Parliament can be fitted into three categories. First, there was the time-honoured concern about the ever-increasing numbers of recusants and papists who were not adequately restrained by the anti-recusant legislation and who were even encouraged by certain powerful officials within the church. By 1640, this anxiety about the number of papists was usually animated by a fear that not only were their numbers increasing, but also that their activities had become much more conspiratorial, with the conspiracy involving those at the very centre of the councils of the nation in a bid to introduce popery and to undermine the country's laws and liberties.[59] The second concern related to the way in which the governing structure within the church had changed. Episcopacy, as the most convenient way of managing the Elizabethan and Jacobean church, had given way to *jure divino* prelacy which threatened to restore all the evils of the pre-reformed church. Finally, there were specific concerns about the innovations that had been introduced into many churches throughout the country. It was widely believed that these largely liturgical novelties were concrete proof of the success enjoyed so far by the popish and prelatical conspiracies.

The 'religious' conviction that seems to have been shared by the largest number of members of the House of Commons in 1640-1 was the belief that the phenomenon observed through the 1620s was now an even more serious problem. On almost the very first day's full debate in the Long Parliament, on 7 November, this familiar tale was repeated, as indeed it was throughout the entire first session, as increasingly wild tales of popish plots and conspiracies were entertained by an insatiable House. On 7 November, Sir Francis Seymour, who had sounded the alarm frequently throughout the 1620s, was almost the first on his feet to take up where he had left off in 1629 as he spelled out just how England was 'groaning under great burdens.' They, the king's counsellors, were obviously not trustworthy. 'One may see what dangers we are in for religion Jesuits and Priests openly to walk abroad and particularly ... What encouragement is this to our papists. No laws in execution. For papists often to goe to Mass.' Two days later when Sir John Holland summarized the Commons' grievances that he believed to be in need of redress, high on his list was the 'suffering of Priests and Jesuits.' The besieged court obviously realized that *de facto* toleration of the Catholics constituted a major problem, because the king attempted to buy favour from the House by announcing through Sir Henry Vane, Sr, that it was his intention to order the 'departing and disarming of papists from London and Westminster.' English kings had been promising this kind of action since 1605, however, so the House of Commons was scarcely reassured. Pym moved that a committee be appointed 'to see that the papists depart out of town.' The committee chosen on 9 November was empowered not only to supervise the enforcement of the king's proclamation, but also to subpoena any documents telling of any 'dispensations, discharges or immunities granted to recusants.' This committee reported back to the House on 28 November that the proclamation could not be effective for a variety of reasons, including the fact that many papists owned dwellings in or near London and many others were protected by 'letters of grace.' The committee was then instructed to frame a bill and a petition to the king to plug the enormous gaps left by the proclamation. In addition, there was a strong feeling that the anti-recusant laws should be applied not only to convicted recusants but to papists in general.[60]

It was this same committee whose report to the House on 1 December 1640 contained the information that in the space of one year, '64 Priests and Jesuits' had been discharged from prison, often on the authority of a warrant signed by Secretary Windebank. Many examples were also cited of Windebank's having written letters to instruct officials to 'stay proceedings against Papists.' As a result of this committee's report, Windebank was ordered to appear before the House and John Pym and Sir Ralph Hopton moved that 'some course might be taken to suppress the growth of popery.' Two days later the House of Commons ordered all JPs in Westminster, London, and Middlesex – later extended to the whole country – to instruct church wardens to compile lists of recusants within each parish 'that they may be proceeded against with effect, according to law, at the next session, notwithstanding any inhibition or restraint.'[61]

But in the early 1640s there was a new element added to the widespread contemporary consciousness of papists and recusants. Not only did they seem to be more numerous, and to behave more freely than they had in the past, but they were using this freedom to organize a massive conspiracy, as Pym described it, 'to alter the Kingdom both in religion and government.' Examples of what appear to have been a widespread and genuine belief that the whole country was mined by knots of papists and recusants conspiring to bring down the government, usually by force, abound throughout the records of the early Long Parliament. On 11 November, for instance, Alexander Rigby, member for Wigan in Lancs, alleged that he had seen a letter from the vice-principal of the English College of Douai, Anthony Champney, requiring all papists to fast for the 'Queen's pious intentions.' This would not have been quite so inflammatory had Rigby not gone on to describe how the papists in his county had 'prepared all this summer more arms than the Protestants' and that they were fasting 'every Saturday.' On the same day the House also heard a report that the Earl of Worcester had '500 arms and his commission' and also that 'another papist had many other shovels and spades and other provision for arms.' A few days later Sir John Wray informed the House that he had learned that a man who had been brought before the attorney general had informed him that 'there was a great plot, that within fourteen days would be attempted against this Kingdom.' Then on the afternoon of Saturday, 21 November, the House of Commons's committee on religion was informed that a JP in Westminster, Peter Haywood, Esq., had been stabbed by one John James, 'a popish priest.' Anticipating 1678 in more ways than one, the account went on to reveal that the papists had committed this crime just as the unfortunate magistrate 'was showing to a friend of his a schedule of such suspected and notorious Papists as were about Westminster.' When the House resumed sitting, it approved two recommendations of the committee. First they resolved 'that the Lord Mayor and Court of Aldermen should have knowledge of the names, and of the security offered by this House.' Second, the House agreed 'that a committee should be appointed, to consider of the state of the King's army; and what commanders, or other inferior officers, are Papists.'[62]

There was fear of the strength of the papists in both the English and Irish armies. When Sir John Clotworthy reported on the state of affairs in Ireland, he said that eight of the ten thousand soldiers in that country were papists 'ready to march where I know not. The old Protestant army have not their pay but the popish army are paid.' Fear of the Irish papists was constant through 1641 and helps explain the dramatic response to the rebellion later in the year. This can be seen most clearly in the debate that occurred on 4 January 1641 after Sir Walter Earle pointed out that all of Ireland was fearful of the 'New Irish army' who, he said, 'have seized on London Derry and said Mass in the church.' D'Ewes' response to this was especially interesting. This danger was, he claimed, 'not imaginary but real.' In addition to their naturally 'turbulent natures,' the Irish were 'wholly guided by their popish priests and Jesuits.' It seemed distinctly likely to D'Ewes that 'they being fallen from their late hopes, they would speedily break into some desperate action and set all on fire.' Just as worrying, however, were the papists in the English army in the north. The question was discussed several times during the early weeks of the session until, on 24 November, the House resolved 'to send to the Lord General to remand all popish commanders and officers of horse or foot as are papists or justly suspected be removed and out of garrison also be removed and Protestants placed in their room.'[63]

Thus when the Long Parliament met, and throughout its first year, its deliberations were conducted in a tense and highly emotional atmosphere that provided fertile conditions for the nurture and spread of rumours of popish plots. As Robin Clifton has pointed out, in the first month of the Long Parliament alone there were 'at least five different varieties of popish plots against Parliament and Protestantism' discussed.[64] On 11 February the House heard a lengthy report from Robert Reynolds which revealed in great detail the strength and plans of the papist armies in Ireland and South Wales. Fear of popish power reached its first climax, however, in early May 1641 when Pym informed the House of the first army plot. Immediately this widely shared emotion, never far from the surface of English politics, became the dominant force. Far-reaching anti-Catholic security measures were proposed, objections to the attainder of Strafford were swept aside, and the protestation of 3 May was subscribed to by the majority of the House of Commons. It was at this point in the proceedings of the early Long Parliament, suggests Fletcher, that Pym's belief in the conspiracy came to be more widely shared within Parliament and that the leader no longer had to 'make the running.' Continuing the essentially negative and defensive tone of the ostensibly religious statements of the House of Commons in the 1620s, the 3 May protestation pledged every member – future Royalists and Parliamentarians alike – to 'maintain and defend ... the true reformed Protestant religion expressed in the doctrine of the Church of England against all Popery and Popish innovations.'[65]

The presence of papists in large numbers, actively conspiring to pull down the church and state, was sufficiently horrifying to the Protestant members of the House of Commons to justify in their minds taking the strongest steps possible to see that the anti-recusant legislation was enforced. The situation was aggravated by the presence in high places of countless crypto-papists who made the threat from outside the church much more serious by their policy of popish reform from within. And here the focus was directly on the bishops. As Alexander Rigby put it, 'there was a popish ecclesiastical hierarchy and government over the whole government of this kingdom.' The danger in 1641 was much greater than it had been twelve years before because what had then been the Arminian potential for trouble had been realized. The canons of 1640, combined with the ecclesiastical innovations that were everywhere enforced by the courts, testified both to the power exercised by the bishops and to the ultimately Catholic nature of their ambitions. It is a conspicuous feature of the proceedings against the bishops in the early Long Parliament that the term 'Arminianism' was much less frequently used than in 1629. In 1641, English political society preferred to call an Arminian by what they believed was his real name – a papist.[66]

When Pym made his major speech to the House on 7 November and, incidentally, established the guidelines for many of the reforms attempted in the next twelve months, he made it clear that he believed the seriousness of the situation derived from the combination of the out-and-out papists and the 'corrupt part of our clergy that make things for their own ends and with an union between us and Rome.' Bishops would have to be reduced in 1640-1, less, it would seem, because there was no scriptural warrant for the office than because as holders of major secular employment and principal councillors to the king they were responsible for the treasonable attack on the lives, liberties, and properties of the subject as well as for introducing the popish doctrinal and liturgical innovations into the church.[67]

There can be little doubt that a major part of the time spent by the House of Commons in its first year on the question of religion dealt with what Sir John Holland referred to as the 'usurping of the Prelates.' Initially the anti-episcopal sentiment took the form of a concerted onslaught on the canons of 1640. These had been first raised in the House on 20 November and were formally discussed, and almost unanimously condemned, in the middle of December. The argument against the canons, passed after the Short Parliament had been dissolved, concentrated on three main points. First, the 'etcetera' oath was condemned as John Whistler, member for Oxford, put it, for being a 'most wicked oath ... not patterned [even] in the oaths of Jews, Turks or heathens.' Second, the right of Convocation to pass legislation 'to bind the subjects of England' without receiving parliamentary approval was rejected by all. Again as Whistler put it, 'had they power to make what canons they would, it were in vain for us to make any statutes here.' The canons, he said, were contrary to the Elizabethan Act of Supremacy, which had given to the crown 'what the Pope had usurped from it.'

Sir Thomas Widdington added the argument that not only were they procedurally wrong – passed in the absence of Parliament, which alone could legitimize the convocation – and passed contrary to Statutes, but they were also substantively repugnant. In the first canon, for instance, that dealing with regal power, 'they have medled with our liberties, Courts and laws, and taught new doctrine concerning the prerogative, and with matters they have nothing to intermedle in.'[68]

Underlying all of these arguments, however, and transcending whatever barriers there might have then been between future Royalists and Parliamentarians, was a deep and abiding mistrust of clerical power and an ineradicable tendency to associate clericalism in its prelatical form with popery. As John Maynard, member for Totnes, trenchantly stated in his case against the canons, those 'who would bind us by the canons of the clergy never cease striving to enlarge their power, but that ambitious design was ever opposed.' The future Royalist, Geoffrey Palmer, was no less adamant that to accept the canons would be 'like the setting up another Pope again.'[69]

It did not take the Commons more than two days to agree, *nullo contradicente*, that the clergy of England in any convocation or synod were powerless to make any canons regarding doctrine or discipline without the consent of Parliament, and that, as a consequence, the canons of 1640 were void. This, however, was only the first statement of the erastian sentiment that united the House. Not only were those canons void, but they were actually seditious and dangerous to, *inter alia*, the 'statutes of the Realm' and the 'property and liberty of the subjects.' Following this vote, the House then established a committee to investigate the 'promoters of the new canons,' which quickly advised the House to impeach Laud on a charge of high treason.[70]

To dispose of the canons and to impeach the archbishop of Canterbury, however, was not to solve what most members agreed was the serious problem of church government. The Root and Branch Petition that was presented to the House of Commons by Alderman Pennington on 11 December 1640 was only one of a large number of petitions on ecclesiastical matters, usually signed by many, submitted during the first few months of the sitting. Most of these petitions, some presented by radicals like Penington, but others by future Royalists like Edward Dering and Arthur Capel, called for the surgical solution to the problem, namely, 'that the government of Archbishops, Bishops, deans and Archdeacons, with all its dependancies, root and branch, may be abolished.'[71]

It has long been a matter of some controversy among historians as to the amount of support for these petitions there was inside the House of Commons in 1641. Clarendon took the view in his *History* that there were only a few inside the House at this time who opposed episcopacy. Gardiner believed that the Royalist party largely took its origins from the determination to protect bishops from the 'Puritan' and 'anti-episcopal' ambitions of the future Parliamentarians. In assessing the relative merit of these two views of opinion within the House of Commons concerning episcopacy, however, several factors are pertinent. First, it is worth remembering that the ordinance abolishing the office of bishop was not actually passed until 1646, until which time, as Morrill has pointed out, they retained the sole right to ordain candidates for the ministry. Second, it must be noted that many of those opposed to prelacy made a sharp distinction between the abolition of the institution of episcopacy and restoration to its original character. Finally, a distinction has to be drawn between an erastian jealousy of clericalism, either of the Laudian or the Presbyterian type, and a 'Puritan' determination to refashion the church along scriptural and reformed lines.[72]

Resentment of the bishops was a constant refrain running through the first years' proceedings of the Long Parliament, and was apt to surface whether episcopacy was formally the subject for debate or not. Early in the session just after Strafford had been accused of treason, Oliver St John raised the question of whether or not the prelates would have a voice in the trial. He believed they should be excluded from the trial: 'Bishops are to depart in cause of blood *ratione ordinis*, and they ought not to meddle in things of this world.' The same kind of anti-clericalism, whose roots seem distinctly secular and old-fashioned, emerged several months later when a subsidy bill was being considered by the Committee of the Whole and lists of commissioners were being reviewed. When the commissioners for Cambridge were named, it was observed that several doctors of divinity were included. Robert Reynolds, member for Hindon in Wiltshire, moved that they be excluded and thereby provoked a short debate. D'Ewes' contribution to the discussion, which appears to have been favourably received by the House, placed the current anti-clericalism in its historical perspective. He observed that 'it had been the old grievance of England that clergymen did intermeddle with secular affairs. It was a great grievance now to be remedied, and therefore we should much prejudice ourselves now to admit it.' Following the debate, the committee resolved that 'no clergy shall be commissioners in the subsidy in any county or place whatsoever.'[73]

Scarcely a single member of the House of Commons in 1641 was prepared to say a kind word about the bishops. This much is clear. Yet it does not seem constructive to see the roots of this anti-episcopal attitude lying in a 'Puritan' zeal for reform so much as in the kind of anti-clericalism that historians have traced back to Chaucer and beyond, and that Henry VIII harnessed in 1529. Sir Benjamin Rudyard illustrates the point. In a speech about the canons of 1640, he described his attitude to the bishops. He denied any desire to 'overthrow their government in the plural' and urged 'their reformation than their ruin.' Many bishops, he said, like Cranmer, Latimer, or Ridley, 'I would esteem and prize,' but 'if we shall find among them any proud Becket, or Wolsey-Prelates, who stick not to write *Ego* and *Rex Meus*; or if there shall be found any Bonners, such, I profess, I would not spare, for they will spare none.' As for Rudyard, opposition to those bishops he referred to as needing a 'specious, pompous, sumptuous religion, with additionals of temporal greatness, authority and negotiation' derived in part from his erastian dislike of clerical interference in secular affairs and partly from his fear that 'this Roman ambition will at length bring in the Roman religion.' Consciousness of the parallels between 1641 and the 1530s is also apparent in Sir John Wray's remark that 'we might as well meddle with bishops now as Henry VIII did with Abbeys in his time.'[74]

Similarly, Simonds D'Ewes' attitude to the bishops seems to have derived less from his 'Puritanism' than from his erastian anti-Catholicism. To the diarist a clear distinction was to be drawn between two meanings of the term 'episcopacy.' If by the word was meant 'their vain aerial titles of Lordship, the spoils of the crown with which they are loaden, and their vast and tyrannical power which they execute,' then he was wholly for the abolition of the office. If, however, by episcopacy is meant 'their spiritual function as it stood in the primitive and purest times,' then he would oppose any effort to abolish the office 'for I should highly prize a godly preaching Bishop.' D'Ewes believed that the secular and political overlay to episcopacy had been 'added to them in a most corrupt age,' although he conceded that even 'some of the Popish Bishops' had abhorred 'the addition of Baronies to their Bishoprics,' The relevant question to him in 1641 was not the abolition of episcopacy but the removal from that institution of 'those adulterations and intermixtures which we all disliked.' For D'Ewes and, as we have seen, for Rudyard, at least part of the problem with Laudian episcopacy resided in its popish associations. Were not cardinals, archbishops, and deans, after all, 'merely created by the Pope'? D'Ewes' rejection of outright abolition of episcopacy did not cause him to see the question as unimportant. The reduction of episcopacy was of major importance, he said, pointing out that in the past fifteen years 'a few wicked instruments amongst us at home have ... more weakened and undermined the truth than all the whole papists and Antichristian party by their conspirations and machinations could do in sixty years before.' D'Ewes was also conscious of the fact that the measures being attempted against the bishops in 1641 could be regarded as simply an extension of the anti-clericalism inherent in the original Reformation. Later in the year, when the bill to remove bishops from secular employment was being discussed, the diarist challenged Hyde's contention that such a bill constituted an interference with the rights of the House of Lords. In doing so he asked, 'what greater breech of privilege could this be than the taking away the votes in Henry VIII's time of all the Abbots and Priors?'[75]

It is quite clear that there was, during the first twelve months of the Long Parliament, widespread hostility to bishops exercising the kind of power that had become normal since the 1620s. This can most readily be seen in the ease with which the various measures limiting the power of bishops were passed by the House of Commons in March 1641. While 'Puritanism' may have caused a few members, such as Cromwell, Fiennes, and Vane, for instance, to support these measures, old-fashioned erastian and anti-clerical forces seem to provide a more plausible explanation for most. It is equally clear that by the summer of 1641 there was widespread sympathy in the House of Commons for the bill to abolish episcopacy 'root and branch.' Evidence for this may be seen in the progress achieved by the Root and Branch Bill in committee during the ten weeks after it had been introduced into the House of Commons on 27 May. Before interpreting support for the abolition of episcopacy as evidence of the extent of a 'Puritan' zeal for reform of the church, however, several factors ought to be borne in mind. First, there seems to have been too little opposition to the bill for it to be seen as anything more radical than another expression of anti-clericalism. If, as Anthony Fletcher has observed, there were so few still defending episcopalianism by July 1641, then there must have been a more widely-held persuasion than 'Puritanism' that was agitating the bill's supporters. It was, after all, a future Royalist, Sir Edward Dering, who introduced it originally into the House. Second, it is worth noting that the bill was introduced only when the rejection by the House of Lords of the Bishops' Exclusion Bill seemed certain. Support for the Root and Branch Bill thus formed part of a campaign to put further pressure on the Upper House to curtail the power of its episcopal members, and did not necessarily have anything at all to do with a 'Puritan' desire to complete the reformation of the church. Further evidence for this view would seem to lie in the facts that the bill did not proceed beyond the committee stage before the September adjournment; there was no reference to abolition of episcopacy in the Grand Remonstrance; and episcopacy was not, as we have noted, actually abolished by the two Houses until 1646. It seems helpful to recognize that in 1641 many perceived that episcopacy had been transformed into prelacy as part of the widespread conspiracy to undermine all of England's traditional institutions and, just as the drastic measures summarized in the Ten Propositions were needed to control the king's councillors, so equally drastic measures were necessary to control those who had distorted the traditional ecclesiastical institution of episcopacy. Thus the bill to abolish episcopacy was just another part of the campaign to eradicate the popish conspiracy throughout the land.[76]

The third form taken by the religious preoccupations of the members of the Long Parliament in the course of its first year's proceedings can be observed in the response of members to the large number of petitions submitted by individuals and groups of individuals concerning ecclesiastical innovations in general, and against delinquent clergymen in particular. The petitions themselves are not a legitimate source for us, given the way in which the study has been limited, but the reaction of the House of Commons to them is relevant.

The investigations conducted by committees of the House of Commons into the ministries of clergymen, ranging all the way from Archbishop Laud to scandalous ministers like Mr Jonathan Skynner, testify alike to the anxiety widely expressed by members concerning the way old forms of worship had in recent years been replaced by new. In the parish of Wolverstone, for example, in the diocese of Norwich, Mr Timothy Dalton had been a 'godly honest man and [had] preached laboriously' in the parish for twenty years until he was driven out by the Court of High Commission 'with his wife and children to fly into New England.' Dalton was succeeded by Skynner who was both 'wicked' and 'scandalous.' In addition to pursuing a way of life not befitting a clergyman, Skynner used to 'adore to and towards the Communion table and to and towards the sacrament after consecration, wherein he used also to cross the bread and cup before consecration and to elevate the bread.' For these offenses, Skynner was rebuked by the House and removed from his parish.[77]

On Friday, 8 January 1641, the House of Commons heard a petition against Samuel Utie, vicar of Chigwell in Essex. According to the petition, Utie was in the habit of praying with his back to the congregation, of kissing the altar, of denying the king's headship of the church, of refusing to admit that the pope was the Antichrist and, finally, of denying the authority of Parliament 'to treat of matters of religion.' D'Ewes was scandalized by the reports and wanted him sent for as a delinquent 'for he had practised a new part of idolatry in kissing the altar which was an old practice of the heathen.' D'Ewes concluded his remarks with a rare witticism, wishing that 'as he had kissed the altar so might he come and kiss the bar here,' with which judgment the House concurred.[78]

The committee struck to deal with the allegations against Dr Cosens, dean at Durham, found itself dealing with the same kind of material. The 'superstitious idolatries' of which he was accused included £2000 'in adorning unnecessarily the church and altar,' setting up 'many images,' bringing new services into the church, and preaching 'false and popish doctrine.' The final allegation against Cosens, according to D'Ewes, was that he denied the king's headship of the church and said that the king had 'no more power in ecclesiastical matters than his horse.'[79]

Throughout the first ten months of the Long Parliament, the broad question of the theological and liturgical innovations introduced into the church by the

Arminians thus received a considerable amount of attention from the House as a whole and from numerous committees. The attitude of the majority of members of the House of Commons to the vexed problem of liturgical innovation is best seen in the Declaration of the House of 9 September 1641. In recent years, stated the declaration, 'some matters concerning religion which are, in their nature, indifferent,' along with others that were illegal, had been enforced. As 'a full reformation cannot be made in this straight of time,' the House insisted, against opposition from the House of Lords, on an interim policy. As a result of the declaration, the communion table in every church was to be moved from the east end, crucifixes and the like were to be removed, bowing at the name of Jesus was to cease, and the Lord's Day was to be observed. On the subject of the status of the Book of Common Prayer, the House of Commons finally said nothing, despite pressure from the Lords to incorporate into the Declaration an endorsement of the established order of worship.[80]

Here too, though there is a consistency between some of the 'religious' thrusts of the declaration and that which is traditionally described as 'Puritanism,' it seems just as plausible to view the statement as part of the campaign to purge the church of Laudian accretions. Consistent with the removal of popish counsellors from the king, and the elimination of popish influences in high ecclesiastical places by placing restrictions on bishops even to the point of abolishing the institution, was this endeavour to purge the church of popish influences at the parish level.

With the passage of the declaration of 9 September, Parliament adjourned for six weeks, leaving the conduct of English affairs in the charge of a joint committee of the two Houses. The session resumed on 20 October and it is upon events during the following month that historians have traditionally focused in groping for their immediate explanation of the Civil War, for this period saw the decisive vote in the House of Commons on the Grand Remonstrance and the clear emergence of a Royalist party. In concentrating our gaze upon this time and place our problem is this: Recalling the various forms taken by religious anxiety in the earlier part of the session, how do we best characterize the religious atmosphere in which the Grand Remonstrance was debated? What form does religious zeal take in the manifesto itself? To what extent may the religious piety of those members of the House of Commons who supported the Remonstrance be described as 'Puritan'?

In assessing the frame of mind of the parliamentarians in November 1641, 'crisis' seems the most apt label. However contrived the 'Incident,' or exaggerated the horrors of the Irish rebellion might seem to us, to many contemporaries, in the House of Commons and in the streets of London, Norwich, Colchester, and elsewhere in the kingdom, they were real. When the news of the

'Incident' broke on 20 October, the House seemed to divide between a majority who took the conspiracy seriously and a group who did not. D'Ewes, although far from being a fanatic, was clearly in the former category. He believed that not only was it imperative to trace the 'true roote and spring whence all these conspiracies do arise,' but also to look to the safety of Parliament itself. Those 'black and evil spirits which plotted this in Scotland' were obviously in correspondence with 'those wicked Lynsey Woolsey clergymen amongst us.' The papists and prelates insidiously allied, argued D'Ewes, were clearly worried by the achievements of the previous session and in their desperate 'desire to subvert the true religion ... venture their lives, estates, fortunes and all.' Future Royalists, Falkland and Hyde, adopted a more sceptical stance and urged taking no specific action 'without very certain and undoubted grounds.' The alarmist persuasion carried the day and led to a conference with the Lords, touching 'this conspiracy discovered in Scotland,' to take steps to defend the kingdom and Parliament.[81]

Concerned about the turn of events in Scotland, members were utterly distraught upon hearing of the Irish rebellion. Fear of the popish army in Ireland, worry about the thousands of known papists in England and possibly even more who were unknown, alarm at the power still wielded by the prelates – all played a part in stimulating the unprecedented, unconstitutional assertions of November 1641 which culminated in the Grand Remonstrance. On 30 October Pym reported to the House the results of the examination of one Captain O'Neill which revealed that there was a 'new design now lately again to make use of the army against us.' The news of events in Ireland that arrived the next day was simply confirmation of the parliamentarians' worst fears and caused them to take the most drastic steps yet attempted to neutralize the papists and to rescue the king from his advisers. Lists were to be prepared of the most dangerous papists so that they could be secured and the king was asked to make no further appointments to his Council 'without the approbation of Parliament.' Protection from popish conspirators and a veto over the appointment of councillors were, to most, two aspects of the one policy. Simonds D'Ewes called for the removal of 'those evil councillors who have been the causes of all our miseries, there being I dare boldly say two Prelates in this Kingdom who have more shaken and endangered true religion amongst us within a matter of twelve or fourteen years last past than all the Popes and Cardinals have done before from the very time of the first reformation of religion here.'[82]

On 15 November a new conspiracy was reported. Thomas Beale related how he had heard two men in a field discuss a plot to 'take away the lives of some members of this House and to disturb the peace of the Kingdom.' The details of the plot are fascinating. One hundred and eight conspirators were to kill an equal number of members of both Houses, 'all Puritans.' Their reward was to be reception of the sacrament and – as even papists could not live by bread alone – money, ten pounds for a lord and forty shillings for a commoner. This may seem a ludicrous story, but within twenty-four hours of its being told, the lists were being presented of the leading papists in four counties and an ordinance was proposed to set the trained bands commanded by the Earl of Essex into a posture of defence. When the House met the following morning, Sir Walter Earle, member for Weymouth, moved that the prayer after the thanksgiving be supplemented. He proposed that in addition to giving thanks for the deliverances in 1588 and from the gunpowder treason, members should be thankful 'for our deliverances since the beginning of this Parliament.' Then, just two days later, on 17 November, after hearing the results of the examination by the Lords of a number of witnesses, the House of Commons declared that 'there is sufficient evidence for this House to believe that there was a second design to bring up the army against the Parliament; and intention to make the Scotch army stand as neutral.'[83]

In this atmosphere of fear and panic the Grand Remonstrance was debated clause by clause. Given this context, it is hardly surprising that the tone of the document should border on the paranoiac. There is little doubt that the authors of the document believed that religion was at the centre of their concerns and, furthermore, that what they understood by religion coincided with what we have seen in our consideration of the first twelve months of the Long Parliament. According to the document, there had been and continued to be a 'pernicious design of subverting the fundamental laws ... of this kingdom,' promoted by an unholy alliance of 'Jesuited Papists,' 'Bishops and the corrupt part of the clergy who cherish formality and superstition,' and self-serving courtiers. This triple alliance controlled all access to the king and was responsible, so it was said, for every aspect of government policy from the premature dissolution of the Oxford Parliament in 1625 to the most recent plot against the laws of the kingdom. However unlikely this view of England's recent past and present might seem to us, nonetheless we have to accept that this is how it appeared to those who approved the Grand Remonstrance, as well as to a large number, like D'Ewes, who did not.[84]

To describe the religious sentiment animating the Grand Remonstrance as 'Puritan' is to exaggerate the extent of a positive, programmatic zeal to reform the church along the lines of the best-reformed models. That some, inside the House as well as outside, believed the collapse of ecclesiastical discipline in 1641 to be literally true, a God-send, is certain. Such was the spirit, for instance, of a letter to Edward Dering in late 1641 rebuking him for his lukewarm position on ecclesiastical matters. The writer went on to remind Dering of his chance to participate in the 'thorough reformation of the church and kingdom so the church of England may, by your blessed means, become that which it never was yet, the glory of the reformed religion.' Such a 'Puritan' zeal for reform was not often expressed in the House of Commons in 1641, nor indeed can it be read in the Grand Remonstrance, even though it was not for want of trying by the preachers whose influence in these early years is sometimes assumed rather than demonstrated.[85] Religion, broadly defined, was of the greatest importance to most of the members. Yet there were not many who provide evidence of having experienced much zeal to make the church what 'it never was yet,' and the overwhelming sentiment amongst members was to protect or restore the church to that which it had once been so gloriously.[86] There were, of course, some members for whom such a judgment is unjust. To judge from their behaviour before or after 1641, and from the unmistakeable evidence of their strongly held theological opinions or of their distictive personal piety, it is surely true to say that individuals who exhibited a self-conscious godliness, such as Cromwell, Vane, Fiennes, and others, might legitimately be described as 'Puritan.' Among such as them lay the support for the proposed clause in the Remonstrance dealing with the disposal of episcopal lands and the opposition to the clause endorsing the Book of Common Prayer. In fact, of course, neither of these clauses was included in the final version. Instead, there are several vague statements of intent regarding church reform that would do a modern-day minority government, scrambling for its survival, credit. The actual content of those few paragraphs dealing with the proposed reforms of the church is minimal. After reducing 'within bounds that exorbitant power' of the prelates, keeping a tight rein on discipline, and calling a 'general synod,' which they fully intended to control, their sole remaining ambition was 'to reform and purge' Oxford and Cambridge universities, then, as now, a sure winner in certain circles.[87]

This suggestion that the religious content of the Grand Remonstrance was slight does not make an enormous contribution to the problem of explaining the essential difference between the 159 who approved it and the 148 who rejected it. It may, however, be suggested that there is no reason to think that the solution to that problem lies in the broad area of religion at all, let alone in specific kinds of religion. There seems to be nothing in the Grand Remonstrance to make one believe either that it was composed by 'Puritans' or that one would have to have been a 'Puritan' to support it.

There is no doubt that most members of the House of Commons between 1621 and 1641 believed themselves to be motivated by forces that they would have described as religious. Certainly there were more committees and sub-commitees established to deal with 'religion' than with any other subject. Nor is there any reason why we should not accept the parliamentarians' judgment of themselves and agree that not only was 'religion' prominent in their rhetoric, but also that it was a serious part of any explanation of their political behaviour. It is not, however, true that what historians have commonly called their religion, namely 'Puritanism,' constitutes the most apt description of their piety or of their beliefs. In the 1620s, we have seen, it makes no sense to deal with their political actions without considering their religion. But what they meant by the term, and what we should mean, was their genuine and awful conviction that, at home and abroad, their Protestant kingdom was being systematically under-mined by careless monarchs manipulated by open and disguised papists. In 1641, we have seen, the parliamentarians were even more anxious about their religion. This anxiety expressed itself in three distinct forms. The first was the now familiar awareness of the presence in ever-increasing numbers of recusants, other papists, Jesuits, and other priests, conspiring to employ force to bring down the government and the whole culture with it. The second was the less familiar – at least in the past hundred years or so – fear of prelatical power which was working in happy conjunction with the papists. The third was the only form of expression that might actually have something to do with religion: the shock and horror that accompanied the revelations that in many English churches there were being performed pagan and popish rituals which God-fearing Pro-testants had been obliged to attend.

To describe any of these religious expressions as 'Puritan' seems either to misconstrue the term 'Puritan,' misunderstand contemporaries, or both. There is no reason to think that Sir Robert Phelips, Sir Richard Grosvenor, John Eliot, or John Pym were conspicuous among their fellows either for their godly self-consciousness or their burning zeal to reform the church along the lines of the best-reformed models. Instead, one is struck by their resistance to the notion of church reform, their incomprehension of the 'godly society' and the 'new Jerusalem,' their resentment of Arminian innovations, and their determination to preserve or restore the Elizabethan church. Their motives for wanting so desperately to preserve the true reformed religion, of course, vary, and only some of them derive from what is strictly speaking religion – that is, a belief in their relationship with God. Doubtless, religion in this sense played a part in causing some members to go to such lengths to protect their church during the period, but it is likely that there were other equally basic forces besides. They cherished their reformed Protestant church between 1621 and 1641 – and at other times too – not solely or perhaps even largely because they preferred its theology and its liturgy, but because to them Protestantism was synonymous with putting down the over-mighty clergymen, with keeping the realm of England as an empire free of Roman-Spanish control, and, best of all, they thought, with preserving the freedom of men of property from the interference of a centralizing government.

5

The Religious Factor in English
Politics, 1666-88

Thus far this study has attempted to establish two main propositions. First, it has suggested that the approach of historians to pre-1642 England has been very different from that of scholars to the same society after the restoration of Charles II. We have seen that religious forces in general, and Puritanism in particular, have been viewed as crucially important in rendering intelligible the events of the 1640s. By contrast, historians of the Restoration period are usually content to leave Dissent to the denominational scholars and to see religious forces as little more than the anachronistic reflexes of an aging minority or as the genuinely-held beliefs of only a small group outside the mainstream of English political life. Second, we have seen that even though the relatively simple lines of Gardiner's 'Puritan Revolution' have been modified extensively in recent years, nevertheless historians are still wont to characterize large groups of pre-Civil War Englishmen as 'Puritan' – albeit variously defined – on the basis of little evidence. Insofar as Messrs Pym, Eliot, Holles, and Phelips were all moved to act by forces that might be described as 'religious,' it has been suggested that it makes more sense to view them as sharing a deep and strongly-felt fear of popery, for reasons that were only partly 'religious.' than as self-conscious members of the godly community united in their zeal to erect the new Jerusalem.

The case for continuity rather than revolutionary discontinuity as the dominant model governing our perception of England's religious-political history between 1620 and 1690 is reinforced if we look more closely at the phenomenon of anti-Catholicism in the period in which historians have analysed it most systematically – from the fall of Clarendon to the Revolution of 1688. For what is most striking about the 'religious' fears and preoccupations of Sir Thomas Meres, the Earl of Shaftesbury, and Bishop Compton is the extraordinary resonance between their rhetoric and that of Sir John Eliot, John Pym, Sir

Robert Phelips, and Edward Kirton, to name just four politicians in the pre-Civil War period.

Historians of later seventeenth-century English political history have long been aware of the significance of the fact that most English Protestants were profoundly mistrustful of Catholics. One would be hard-pressed to find any narrative of either the Exclusion Crisis or of the Revolution of 1688 that does not assign this anti-Catholic phobia its due. Yet, despite this consensus, most historians have not fully appreciated the importance of anti-Catholicism. For, while recognizing the tradition of anti-Catholic fervour that had been such a marked feature of English culture since at least the Marian period, they none-theless have accepted the implications of seventeenth-century discontinuity. 'Anti-Catholic' labels well enough the latent prejudices of political society yet, they imply, as an historical force it can scarcely be compared with pre-1640 Puritanism. As a consequence, anti-Catholicism as a phenomenon has scarcely attracted the degree of analysis that its ubiquity in narratives would seem to demand and that has been accorded similar national phobias in other cultures – for example – anti-Semitism in modern European history or Nativism in American history.[1]

J.R. Jones, whose work on the Exclusion Crisis and on the revolution a decade later has significantly altered modern appreciation of later seventeenth-century political history, illustrates the problem confronting Restoration historians.[2] He pays anti-Catholicism its due as a force for change when he writes that 'anti-popery was the strongest, most widespread and most persistent ideology in the life and thought of seventeenth century Britain.' Yet, notwithstanding his rejection of the view that perceives 1688 as merely a postscript to the 'real revolution,' even he sees a profound difference between the secularism of most of the Whigs and the religious motivation informing the politicians of 1640-2. Thus, in his analysis of the composition of the first Whigs, he distinguishes between the 'old Presbyterians' and the bulk of the party: the former, he writes, were characterized by a 'genuine and positive zeal for religious reform.' For the same reasons, Jones has also drawn a distinction between the causes of the Exclusion Crisis and those of the Civil War. They were not identical, he says, because 'few of the younger Whigs were absorbed by religious questions, many reacting strongly against a puritanical upbringing.'[3] J.R. Western has taken to his study of England in the 1680s the same assumption of a major discontinuity characterizing the century. 'In the seventeenth century,' he writes, 'the defeat and execution of Charles I was a breach with the past after which nothing was ever the same again,' adding that 'taxation, the armed forces, municipal government and the religious situation were all transformed.'[4]

The most important exception to this trend among Restoration historians to base their analyses on the assumption that English society after 1660 had fundamentally changed since 1640 is John Miller's study of the Catholic factor in English politics between 1660 and 1688. Miller has obviously focused his attention on post-1660 politics but he has given some attention to the historical origins of anti-Catholicism. In the course of his brief historical overview from the Tudor period to 1660 it is noteworthy that the concept 'Puritanism' is never mentioned and that his entire narrative is couched in terms both of the essential Protestantism of most Englishmen and the response of Protestants to a variety of Catholic threats. Rarely, if ever, does Miller find it useful to label anyone as 'Puritan.' He appears to be more conscious of the similarities running through England's history in the seventeenth century than of revolutionary change. Thus, for instance, he analyses the early history of the Long Parliament in 1640-2 in terms of its anti-Catholicism. The behaviour of the members of the Long Parliament was, he writes, 'a normal seventeenth century reaction to a crisis in which the Catholic question was involved,' adding that the pattern in the early 1640s was 'similar [to that in] the Popish Plot crisis.'[5]

Notwithstanding Miller's work, however, it is clear that a characteristic feature of the historiography of Stuart England has been the tendency of historians to view the Interregnum as a chasm separating two fundamentally contrasting cultures. Furthermore, it can be demonstrated that a principal area in which this discontinuity has been seen to exist is the penumbra where the religious motivation shades into the secular. Before 1640, Puritanism, an essentially 'religious' entity, is invariably called upon to carry a substantial part of the explanation of the Civil War. After 1660, neither Puritanism nor what historians perceive as its pale successor, Dissent, has the same importance. Most historians seem to assume that between 1640 and 1660 religious forces came to be dissociated from secular ones. Even Douglas Lacey, the historian of Restoration parliamentary Dissent, subscribed to this view. In his study of the Dissenting members of Parliament between 1660 and 1689, Lacey has demonstrated that they were far less numerous than were the 'Puritans' generally believed to have been in the Parliaments between 1621 and 1642. Rarely did their numbers approach even 10 per cent of the entire membership. More important than his analysis of their numbers in Parliament, however, is Lacey's assessment of the mainsprings of the Dissenters' political behaviour, which contrasts sharply with the way pre-Civil War historians treat the parliamentary 'Puritans.' For, as Lacey writes, while the thirty or so Dissenting MPs, who were necessarily occasional conformists, were 'active on religious matters yet these men were at their most aggressive when the source of their political power and their constitutional principle were under attack.' In the end, it was their parliamentarianism rather than their religious principles which moved them to action, a judgment which contrasts markedly with the prevailing treatment of Puritans who are generally seen to compose far more than 10 per cent of the House of Commons between 1621 and 1642 and to whom church reform is, by definition, generally believed to be of central importance.[6]

There is good reason to believe that Restoration historians are probably quite right to play down the importance of religious forces in their narratives and explanations of political events. Lacey's analysis of Restoration Dissent and his criteria for defining a Dissenter are impressive; it seems unlikely that many more will be discovered among the parliamentary classes. Similarly, historians of the Restoration are quite right to distinguish Dissent from anti-Catholicism and to attribute the latter force to quite diverse groups within the political community, not all of which can properly be described as Dissenting. Nonetheless, the general assumption that political men after 1660 were somehow different creatures from their fathers is a constant source of misunderstanding and tends to cast a shadow of implausibility over the best political analysis. For the anti-Catholicism which is indispensable to an understanding of events between 1660 and 1689 is 'religious' and not essentially different from the anti-Catholicism which obsessed most of the parliamentary classes during the twenty years prior to 1642.

In considering the character of English anti-Catholicism, we are dealing with a kind of prejudice of which there have been many historical examples. Of them all, however, the best known and the most systematically studied is anti-Semitism. Both are all-pervasive, albeit irrational, movements that have experienced an ebb and flow over time, at least since the beginning of Christianity, if not before, in the case of anti-Semitism, and since the Reformation, in the case of English anti-Catholicism. Both are 'religious' movements in the sense that they frequently justify themselves with the rhetoric and 'logic' of religion – the Jews as Christ-killers and the papists as Antichrist. Furthermore, underlying the superficially 'religious' character of each is a complex set of political, social, economic, and psychological factors which in turn mask the essentially emotional nature of the phenomena themselves. As I.S. Wechsler has written of anti-Semitism, 'in essence it is both an individual and a group neurosis ... [which] ... becomes understandable as we realise that culture and civilization are but thin veneers and that the human animal is still considerably blind and emotional in his behaviour.'[7] Similarly, both Jews and papists have long been regarded in highly conspiratorial terms: it mattered no more that Jews were often identified simultaneously with the forces of Bolshevism and international finance than it bothered anti-Catholics to believe that Charles I had been supported most enthusiastically by papists who were also guilty of regicide.

Inevitably, of course, there are important differences between anti-Semitism and English anti-Catholicism. Perhaps the most important is the way in which the two phenomena were affected by the secularization of society that followed industrialization in the nineteenth century. Whereas the Christian form of anti-Semitism underwent a metamorphosis emerging as the yet more virulent and potent form of secular and racial anti-Semitism whose end result was Nazism and the Final Solution, anti-Catholicism experienced no comparable transformation. Whereas the Jews were identified by their host societies in cultural and racial as well as religious terms, this was not so with the Catholics. As religion lost its potency – Orange Lodges notwithstanding – Catholics were much less readily identifiable and tended to be assimilated more evenly by the surrounding culture.[8] There was, furthermore, in England by the nineteenth century a liberal political and cultural tradition that was quite different from that in Germany and which deprived the forces of anti-Catholicism of the same opportunities exploited by German anti-Semitism.

The failure of English anti-Catholicism to culminate in a modern totalitarian party reinforced by its Buchenwald and by its Auschwitz ought not to distract us from the fact that, in late seventeenth-century England, it provided a more all-encompassing framework than any other idea or set of attitudes and that only by coming to grips with it can we hope to grasp the role of 'religious' forces in the political crises of Exclusion and the revolution.

For almost an entire generation after the Great Fire, but especially through-out the period of political crisis, from the publication of Titus Oates' revelations in the summer of 1678 until the partial easing of tensions signified by the compromises reached in the Convention of 1689, the Catholic Question was central to English politics and in the forefront of the consciousness of most members of political society who wrote or spoke on contemporary issues. For all of the Lockean and contractual implications of the Exclusion Bills, the 'vacant throne,' and subsequent Bill of Rights, what contemporaries *thought* they were trying to do was to protect themselves from the evils of a popish successor. And here, of course, we are immediately confronted with a central question: What were the principal ingredients of the anti-popish phobia? How did Englishmen of various social strata perceive the role of popery in their nation's history, and precisely how did they see themselves threatened by the papists around them? How realistic was the fear and, to the extent that it was not realistic, how is its pervasiveness to be explained?

Fundamentally, the fear that most Protestants in the 1670s and 1680s expe-rienced in relation to papists, although couched in the language of religion, was not simply a 'religious' phenomenon as the Catholic stereotype most commonly reviled embraced a number of mutually reinforcing components. The first of these involved the conspiratorial role played by papists in England's history at least since the Reformation. Viewing the past in essentially dialectical terms, English Protestants saw their cause as having been engaged in an unrelenting struggle with the forces of international popery which, notwithstanding defeats in individual battles, appeared to have the resources to win the ultimate war. Partly stemming from this view of history, contemporaries feared the political threat represented by popery whose victory in England would, it was widely assumed, assuredly result in foreign domination, domestic tyranny, and clerical privilege. Then, there was the economic dimension. While perhaps there were still some who truly feared for their formerly monastic lands in the event of a papist king, much more widespread was the assumption that the inevitable consequence of popish absolutism was the certain loss of economic freedom. Animating these components was a commitment to the Protestant doctrine and worship of the Established Church. There were many to whom a religion whose adherents ate the body and blood of their God after an elaborate ritual conducted in a foreign tongue was repugnant and inimical to their spiritual wellbeing.

The character of much of the political controversy during the Exclusion Crisis was historical. And notwithstanding the work of J.G.A. Pocock on Brady, Spelman, and the development of constitutional historiography in seventeenth-century England, the history in which contemporaries were most involved, and about which they were most intensely partisan, was England's history since the Reformation. As the Tory scholar, Robert Brady, was preparing the historical argument against the 'common-law interpretation of history' that had been most recently propounded by William Petyt, less learned contemporaries, active in the political arena, were revealing their dependance upon a rather more primitive version of English history and were looting their recent past for horror stories with which they hoped to embarrass their opponents into silence.[9] Inside Parliament and outside, in ballads, polemical broadsides, and learned treatises, the evidence is overwhelming that the reformation of the church in King Harry's time was seen to mark the beginning of a distinct and recognizably modern phase in the history of England. Furthermore, what was distinctive about this approach to recent history was its conspiratorial and dialectical quality. While the Reformation had dealt a body blow to the forces of popery in England, Rome had not given up without a struggle. As John Trenchard, member of the House of Commons for Taunton, expressed his sense of recent history in the course of the debates on the Exclusion Bill, 'consider how restless the spirit of Popery has been ever since the Reformation.'[10] While not every Restoration Englishman subscribed to this conspiratorial view of England's history during the past 150 years, and while there were variations in the degree of commitment to the element of conspiracy, nevertheless this view seems to have received widespread assent.

A classic statement of the conspiratorial anti-papal view of England's relatively recent history can be found in a tract written by a 'Sober Protestant,' *Friendly Advice to Protestants*. Since the accession of Queen Elizabeth, the author wrote, 'how many hundred plots and conspiracies have been set on foot by the papists against the lives of our Kings and Princes and the peace of this nation.'[11] Charles Blount had an even longer historical perspective when he saw the plot revealed by Titus Oates as just one more in a tradition of conspiracy extending back to the 1550s. 'The Catholic Cause, like the chestnut in the fable hath ever since Queen Mary's reign been in the fire ... the Papists make us of the Episcopal and Court parties claw, to take it out.'[12]

Some of the historical examples used to support this conspiratorial view of England's history do not strike the modern reader as surprising. In this way, for example. Sir Henry Capel, prominent Whig member of the Exclusion Parliaments, reminded his audience that 'in Queen Elizabeth's time there were conspiracies against her when Mary, Queen of Scots was taken off [and] in King James's time, the Gunpowder Treason.' This was the historical tradition which caused November 5th and 17th, the anniversaries, respectively, of Guy Fawkes and Elizabeth's accession, to 'stand in our calendar in red letters' as days when all Englishmen celebrated the 'wonderful series of Divine Providence' which had permitted them to continue to triumph against the 'old Dragon ... [and his] flood of fire.'[13]

A less familiar component of this view of England's history as the story, most fully articulated by John Foxe a century before, of the continuing struggle between Protestant Christianity and Popery is the role ascribed to the papists in the English Civil War. For it was a view widely expressed by historians, preachers, politicians, and propagandists that not only were the papists to be held responsible for the Armada, the Gunpowder Plot, the Fire of London, and the Plague, but, greatest crime of all, their machinations resulted in the civil wars and in the subsequent regicide.

At one end of the political spectrum in 1678, occupied by the likes of Charles Blount, Robert Ferguson, Gilbert Burnet, and many of the most passionate exclusionists, the role ascribed to the papists in the 1640s, as in 1678, was unambiguous and clear-cut. They had been responsible not only for embroiling England in civil war, but also – wonder of wonders – for the actual execution of the king. Blount in 1679 fully admitted the Tory argument that there was 'some coherence between the beginning of the late Civil Wars, and this our present age' but, unlike his opponents, asserted that 'then, as now, the ambitious Papists and French faction were the chief, nay the only incendiaries which set us all in a flame.'[14]

The intrinsic connection between popery and king-killing was a theme developed at length by the historian and future Williamite bishop, Gilbert

Burnet. In his initial response to the news of the Popish Plot in 1678, Burnet proclaimed that he was 'not surprised' because even though he conceded there were 'some loyal papists' they were the exceptions to the general rule that 'loyalty is fundamentally inconsistent with the principles of popery,' and that furthermore 'regicide is inherent in popery.' At every step in the movement of England's history during the 1640s, he wrote, the papists were to be seen conspiring against the king. The 'horrid rebellion in Ireland,' for instance, had been 'so far set on by Rome, that a nuncio came publicly to direct their councils.'[15]

Nearly three years later, in a sermon to London's aldermen commemorating the martyrdom of the king's father, Burnet resumed his elaboration of this theme. Distinguishing between the church, the reformed religion, fanaticism, and popery, he denied that the reformed religion could in any way be held responsible for Charles' death, though he ridiculed the weak and irreligious behaviour of some of the sectaries. Many of the 'most considerable Dissenters' in 1648, as in the late 1670s, had written against regicide and had been 'industrious in the bringing home of his Majesty that now reigns.' Such men, urged Burnet, were clearly innocent of regicide. In contrast, the fanatics were little more than puppets of the papists, for those of them who 'justified the shedding of this blood' used maxims that 'have been chiefly borrowed from Popish writers.' In 1681, Burnet bemoaned the way in which the fanatics had given 'the Protestant religion [and] the English nation a bad name,' first by their involvement in regicide and secondly by 'their unintelligible way of talking about religion [and] their crumbling into so many sects.' Three years later, in his famous Guy Fawkes Day sermon at the Chapel of the Rolls, soon after which he was dismissed from his chaplaincy, he again insisted upon the popish origins of the civil wars, of which he said 'the later rebellion, as it was managed with a Popish, that is, a bloody spirit, so many of the arguments that were used to defend it, were taken from Popish Authors.'[16] Not that Burnet, the ideological anti-papist, was not at times somewhat abashed by the instincts of Burnet, the historian, who was less clear in his mind as to the precise sense in which Henry Vane, Oliver Cromwell, Henry Marten, and others could have been described as papists: 'What hand they [the papists] had in this execrable crime, and how far they disguised themselves into all the forms and divisions about Religion that were among us, I shall not positively assert: it has been done with very much assurance by persons of great worth and credit: and there are many probabilities to induce us to believe it.'[17]

It is, of course, a problem inherent in the study of attitudes and ideas, popular or deeply learned, that we can never know the extent to which they were attractive to any but the authors of the tracts, speeches, or sermons in which the ideas have been passed down to us. What is striking about Burnet's assumption that the papists were ultimately responsible for the evils of the 1640s is the variety of people who appear to have subscribed to that view. Thomas Barlow, for instance, who managed to obtain preferment under Cromwell, James II, and William, and who was Bishop of Lincoln in 1679, in his violently anti-papal publications read the whole history of Charles I's reign in terms of the Catholic conspiracy. Not only did he see the 'doctrines and principles of Popery' as 'pernicious to Kings [and] prejudicial to the just rights of monarchy' but he also appears to have believed that the papists had made an attempt to murder Charles I and Archbishop Laud before 1642. The climax of the conspiracy occurred, however, in 1648 when the popish conspirators held a council of priests and Jesuits which, sitting in London, submitted the case to Rome who determined that 'it was for the interest of the Catholic cause that the King should die.'[18]

Nor was this preoccupation with the Civil War as part of the Catholic conspiracy confined to the politically prominent, the well born, and the literate. At the height of the panic that followed the publication of Oates' revelations, one Richard Parker was brought before the Leicester magistrates on a charge of sedition. He had been overheard to say that the death of the late king was quite 'just,' for Charles had, after all, been a papist and 'his hand and seal was [sic] at the rebellion in Ireland.'[19]

From a different point on the religious spectrum, Richard Baxter appears to have shared at least this conspiracy theory with Barlow. Baxter's explanation for the Civil War had to reconcile his personal support for the parliamentary side in 1642 with his profound respect for the magistrate, and this was possible only by his having identified Charles I (and later James II) with popery. In his account of the origins of the Civil War, Baxter wrote:

[the Irish rebellion] filled all England with a fear both of the Irish and of the papists at home; for they supposed that the Priests and the interest of their religion were the cause: in so much, that when the rumour of a plot was occasioned at London, the poor people, all the countries over, were ready either to run to arms, or hide themselves, thinking that the papists were ready to rise and cut their throats: and when they saw the English papists join with the King against the Parliament it was the greatest thing that ever alienated them from the King.[20]

A similar perception of the civil wars seems to have informed – or justified – the political militancy of at least some of the Exclusionist members of the House of Commons. Sir Henry Capel, for instance, son of one of a handful of peers executed in 1649, denied that it was violation of laws, liberties, or property which 'brought that disaster in ... but it was the unhappy hand of Popery which brought that discord in, and possibly shed the blood I came of.' In the same vein another Exclusionist member of the Commons, John Dubois, a Huguenot merchant prominent in the East India Company, described how Sir Kenelm Digby had gone to the College of Sorbonne to ask 'Whether, for the good of the Catholic cause, the King might not be taken away?' The college affirmed their right, with which judgment Rome concurred. Summarizing this part of his argument, Dubois concluded simply, 'Pursuant to this, the King's head was cut off.'[21]

Although the precise way in which the papists fomented the troubles and brought about Charles' execution could not be delineated, this in no way diminished the seriousness with which the view was held. On the contrary, the fact that the papists appeared in different guises, 'riding another sort of men,' was a tribute to their cunning and the cause of their effectiveness. This, then, was how the 'Puritans' were explained and, in the end, justified. As one anonymous writer put it, the Puritans would never have 'separated from the Church of England' had not popish 'engines ployed amongst us.' Until the late 1630s all the 'sober, godly party, and Puritans too,' were 'conformable to the decent and orderly government of the Church of England.' Then, however, 'was a bird hatched at Rome, sent to be nursed in England, knowing well it would bring to pass their infallible design to divide us; and from the same counsels came into our Churches those crowds of trumperies, Tapers, and Crucifixes, Cringings and Bowings that the Service of God was turned to a Popish Article ... to bring us as near as possible to a union with Rome.'[22]

According to this view, therefore, the English civil wars were yet one more illustration of the way in which the nation's history for 130 years or more had been essentially the story of the conflict between the forces of light and those of popish darkness. In this story, the role of religious dissent in the 1640s – what historians have, for the last hundred years, referred to as Puritanism – was a minor theme, just one means used by the papists to divide the Protestant church the better to re-establish the Roman religion throughout England. According to this view, many of the Anabaptists, Quakers, Fifth Monarchists, and even some Presbyterians and Independents were actually Jesuits. As the author of *Friendly Advice* wrote, 'all this while the Knave [papists] lurked under the shape of an Anabaptist, of a Quaker, of a Fifth-Monarchy man, and sometimes for his interest he would appear amongst the Presbyterians and Independents.'[23]

Although the anti-Catholic phobia was to be seen in its starkest and most irrational light amongst the most extreme supporters of Exclusion, this view of England's recent history was by no means confined to their ranks. Even among those who abhorred the activities of the petitioners and who supported most strongly James' right to succeed his brother, there was a marked preoccupation with the recent activities of papist conspirators and a tendency to interpret England's history in the 1640s in terms of their machinations. A major difference between the two perceptions, however, can be seen in their differing attitudes to religious nonconformity. Whereas Charles Blount and Gilbert Burnet distinguished between a moderate, responsible, and godly critique of the church and the fanatical excesses of the late 1640s, to the Tories of the Exclusion period Dissent and Popery had been and still were separate but equally insidious and subversive influences.

At the other end of the spectrum from that occupied by Blount and Ferguson were Tories, such as Edmund Bohun and John Nalson, who, despite their resistance to the notion that constitutionally extreme measures were necessary to counter the perils revealed by Titus Oates, were far from assured that popery represented no real threat to their world. Amongst the propagandists, politicians, and clergymen who opposed Exclusion between 1678 and 1682 it is possible to distinguish between two broad positions. On the one hand were those whose position is exemplified by the following piece of doggerel:

Then I began to think which was the worse,
Fanatic blessing, or a Popish curse.
I put them in two scales to try their weight
And found the balance equiponderate.[24]

On the other hand was the view that while the papists did indeed represent a threat to the wellbeing of England and had played a part in the civil wars, they were no worse – and often less dangerous – than the dissenting sects who had deliberately exploited anti-popish fear for their own political purposes.

For more than thirty years after the Restoration Roger L'Estrange, surveyor of the press for much of this whole period, was one of the most prolific propagandists to write in defence of the church and state of the restored Stuarts. And never was his pen busier than in the years of crisis that followed 1678 when, more than any other writer, he was determined to remind the new generation of the horrors of civil war. What he wrote in concluding one tract he may as well have said of most that he wrote: 'The principal scope of it was to lay open the misery and method of the late rebellion; and so to expose it, that the same project, and a model may not be made use of for another.' Or, as he wrote elsewhere, 'Let us enquire into the springs and reasons for their fortunes and fall: as well as gaze upon the issues of them: a timely search into the grounds of one rebellion may prevent another.' Where he differed from the Whigs in his view of the civil wars, however, was in his perception of the part played in them by the papists and Dissenters. Without denying the seriousness of the popish threat, either in his own time or in the past, L'Estrange thought that the Dissenters were even worse. Originally, he wrote, the rebellion had been a 'conspiracy against the Government,' the beginning of which lay in 'a cabal of Scotch and English Presbyterians.' Relying for support on the 'corrupted interests of both Kingdoms,' this cabal used 'the fear of popery [as] the leading jealousy.'

L'Estrange's objective in all of his Exclusion Crisis writings seems to have been to establish the closeness of the analogy between the Whig alliance of 1678-82 and the rebels of the 1640s. On both occasions, he insists, popery was a device used for political purposes rather than a principal threat to law and order. Thus he compared the declaration of the Lords and Commons of 1642, calculated to demonstrate that the king was 'popishly affected,' with the stories that were circulated in 1677. In one tract L'Estrange specifically addressed himself to the charges levelled by Charles Blount in his *Appeal from the Country to the City*. Without wishing to defend popery, L'Estrange was determined to assign responsibility for the Civil War more appropriately. 'Never was any papacy so tyrannical and so ridiculous together as that persecuting and nonsensical Presbytery, which we had in exchange for the best-tempered ecclesiastical government upon the face of the earth.' Of the Presbyterians he wrote, 'they began with a cry against Popery, but they concluded in the murder of the King.' Blount's notion that responsibility for the king's execution should some how be laid at the papists' door he dismissed with commonsensical contempt, since he could not 'find one papist on the whole list of regicides.' In fact, he rejected Blount's whole vision of England's history since the Reformation as 'so notorious a mistake.' The Catholics had not been manipulating the court since the Marian period; on the contrary, all English monarchs since Mary 'have opposed papal errors,' and, furthermore, the 'late King lost his life in the defence of the reformed religion.' A more fruitful way to look at the recent history of England, suggested L'Estrange, would be to focus upon the 'history of the schismatics.' And instead of recoiling from Blount's image of 'papists ravishing wives and daughters,' he said, 'remember December 1659 [when] whole droves of cobblers, dray-men, ostlers [insisted] upon free quarters with you till some of your wives and daughters are forced to prostitute themselves for bread.'[25]

Lest L'Estrange's determination to assign the reformers their fair share of guilt for the atrocities of rebellion might seem to have made him 'soft on popery,' it is worth noting the *Compendious History* he published in 1680. In this survey he was concerned to trace the development of the treason that culminated in the revelations of the late 1670s. The 'chief actors' in this conspiracy had been 'the Roman Catholic clergy,' and his history began in 1666, for it was in that year, he wrote, that 'the greatest fire broke forth ... which sacrificed to the fury and ambition of the Jesuits and popish priests the fairest and largest part of one of the richest and most populous cities in the world.' The conflagration of September 1666 was the result of a plot over which the Jesuits 'had been many years brooding.' Two years before, alleged L'Estrange, the conspirators had duped a group of Fifth Monarchy Men into co-operating with them to bring about their grand design 'both for firing the city, and murdering the King.' Plans had failed the first time, but their second attempt had been successful. With the help of 'fifty or sixty Irish to ply the work,' the Jesuits arranged for Hubert and a companion to convey 'at the end of two long poles, three fire-balls, first lighted with matches, through a hole in the wall, into Farriner's House, not stirring till the room was in a flame.' This, wrote L'Estrange, the former Cavalier and ultra-Tory propagandist in 1680, was how the Great Fire began.[26]

The theme massively developed in thousands of pages by L'Estrange was frequently expressed more tersely, yet as effectively, in innumerable ballads widely distributed on broadsheets. As one of them put it:

From sawing the Crown 'twixt Phanaticks and Fryers;
From Whitehall Scaffold and Smithfield fires;
From the Jesuits' morals, outdone by the Tryers,
Libera nos Domine.[27]

At the Tory end of the political spectrum, the end which attracted the majority of propagandists and, by the early 1680s, the bulk of English political society, it was generally assumed that law and order – that is, the political and ecclesiastical establishment – were threatened equally by the forces of popery and of Dissent and that the crisis of the late 1670s was simply the inevitable outcome of the past century's history. History was, after all, the prime weapon of the Tories in the propaganda battle. Like L'Estrange, most of the Tories were principally concerned to establish the proposition that the Whigs in 1678 were the direct descendants of the rebels of the 1640s, and thus they all became 'historians' of the civil wars. Some, of course, like John Nalson, whose collection of Civil War documents has been a major source for historians, were serious scholars. Others, like the Earl of Halifax, were politicians and pamphleteers who used history for narrow didactic political purposes. In either case, however, their views were not dissimilar.

To Nalson, the papists and the Presbyterians were equally obnoxious, although he was careful to distinguish between them. Of the Church of Rome, he wrote, it was obvious that 'this doctrine of absolute papal supremacy ... is absolutely inconsistent with the very being, security and succession of monarchy, the liberty, happiness and property of the people.' He did not, however, blindly accept the Whig argument which automatically blamed the papists for the atrocities of the 1640s. Nalson conceded the fact that the papists were basically loyal to Charles I during the war and later were even of assistance to his son. He took this position despite the fact that it would lead the Presbyterians to label him 'a favourer of papists, which censure I know none that can escape who is not a schismatic.' And for all of Nalson's hostility to the papists, he was yet more passionate in his denunciation of the Presbyterians. After presenting a brief analysis of Calvin's political ideas, he asserted that 'these words of Calvin, interpreted by the Presbyterian faction, did contribute to the late horrid rebellion,' for it was obvious that 'Presbytery aims secretly at supremacy.' In the end, he concluded, there is clearly 'no great difference between those of the foundations of Loyola and Geneva, but that the latter have by their horrible actions brought that infamy upon the Protestant cause and Reformation, which the others had in vain attempted.'[28]

Writing more polemically, yet with the same purpose, were many Tory propagandists such as the anonymous author of *The Cloak in its Colours, or the Presbyterian Unmasked*: 'Tis true many wicked Papists, by their plots and conspiracies have often attempted, in a most inhumane manner, to destroy our King and subvert our Government: but the brave Presbyterian, scorning to trust always to such pitiful contrivances underhand, have at several times publicly raised whole armies in open rebellion against their Prince.' The two examples of such Presbyterian infamy were the Scottish rebellion against Mary, Queen of Scots, and 'their unparalleled cruelty in the tragical and never-to-be-forgotten murder, not only of a Protestant Prince, but also of King Charles I.' It was the same view of the Presbyterians' role in England's history that informed the Earl of Halifax's observations when he wrote: 'the poison of presbytery, formerly known by the name of puritanism, hatched at Frankfort and Geneva, grown to a head in Scotland with the reformation, has infected the generality of the kingdom ... with hatred against monarchy and the church of England. This was certainly the invention of Rome to overthrow us, by thus sowing divisions.'[29]

Common to this essentially conspiratorial Tory view of England's recent history was the conviction that papists and Presbyterians had, for more than a century, represented equally dangerous threats to the country's traditional order and that indeed so similar were the ends of the two parties that there must surely be some kind of connection between them. As Edward Pelling expressed it in his 30 January sermon in 1679, 'we shall never want occasion of informing the world of the bloody attempts of the Romist and Reformed Jesuit, the Devil with a crucifix and a legend, and the devil with a bible and Samuel's mantle.' Pelling believed the two to be linked inextricably, he said, because 'they set all on fire though they are turned tail to tail, and their faces look contrary ways.' The anonymous author of *An Impartial Survey* made the same connection when he wrote that just as 'Christ was cricified between two thieves, so was Charles I between the Jesuits and the phanaticks.' The popular Tory vision of the civil wars was clearly less single-minded than the Whigs' but no less conspiratorial. Essentially, the Presbyterians were held responsible for events in the 1640s, although few doubted that the papists were either responsible for sowing the seeds of disloyalty or were actually involved in stirring the embers. As another 30 January preacher put it in 1678, the condition of the king was jeopardized as it had been thirty years before and in these constant machinations 'the most distant parties and factions conspire and accord perfectly.'[30]

Finally, it is worth noting that not everyone whose position on the Exclusion issue was couched in terms of his version of the civil wars accepted the conspiratorial role of the papists without question. William Dugdale, the historian, for instance, referred to the way those 'of the Puritan party,' after 'reducing the King to Necessities,' then persuaded the people that his ultimate intention had been 'to bring upon them no less a vassalage than that of the French peasant and to endanger their souls by enthralling them to the superstitions of the church of Rome.' The effect of this bias was to alienate many from the Established Church, 'pretending it to savour of Popery.' The moderate member of Parliament, Daniel Finch, made the same point when he pleaded with the Whig majority of the House of Commons that 'we have had one Prince cut off on pretence that he was given to Popery. I would not disinherit another on suspicion of Popery.'[31]

What is noteworthy about this point of view is not that it disdained the conspiratorial approach to England's past, but rather that it replaced one set of conspirators with another. The author of a *Letter to the Earl of Shaftesbury* accused the Whig leader of imitating the men of 1641 and of playing 'the same game over again.' In 1678, as in the earlier period of crisis, the conspirators introduced the plot so that in subsequently discovering it they became 'the blessed instruments to save us at this time from the paw of anti-Christ.' Both in 1641 and again in the late 1670s, wrote the author, 'Tom Tell-Truth,' 'have there not been many of a higher form, who through discontent, or love of faction, and change of argument, or for not being continued or preferred to the highest and most honourable places therein, have endeavoured all they can to breed difference...' The Tory preacher Edmond Hickeringill, in a sermon whose text 'Curse ye Meroz' was a repetition of that used by Stephen Marshall in his first sermon to the Long Parliament in 1640, blamed the preachers of 1640/1 for setting the people 'agog,' frightening them 'out of their wits with fears and jealousies of Popery and arbitrary government and know not what forgeries of their own making.' Hickeringill concluded that 'if there were not a Papist in England (and I wish there were not) yet they would fright the people with fears of popery.' This view of the Popish Plot was not especially attractive to the Whig-dominated House of Commons which sent Sir Robert Cann to the Tower for suggesting that 'There was no Popish Plot, but a Presbyterian Plot.'[32]

It seems fairly clear, then, that a central component of the widespread and obsessive fear of popery which informed political attitudes at most points on the spectrum in the late 1670s was historical. Whigs and Tories alike were deeply conscious of the striking resemblance that 1678 bore to 1640/1, and to a large extent they agreed that the similarities derived from the menace represented by the machinations of the popish conspiracy. Not that 1641 presented the only instance of the plot. Rather, it was simply the most dramatic example of what had been a continuing conspiracy that derived its origins in the aftermath of the Reformation, if not before.

The view of history that informed the virulent anti-popery of so many Englishmen during the Exclusion Crisis – the tendency to see England's past in terms of the conflict between the Protestant forces of light and the popish forces of darkness – was not unique to this period. At least since John Bale wrote in the 1530s and 1540s, there had been an apocalyptic strain in English Protestant thought intrinsic to which had been a conspiratorial and dialectical historicism. Recent research has shown that from the very beginnings of the Reformation in England until at least the middle of the seventeenth century there developed a body of ideas that revolved around the prophetical scriptural texts and that formulated a distinct view of the past which, applied to the prophecies, led to the development of various views of the future.'[33]

Drawing upon an historicist tradition that stretched back to Saint Augustine and relying more immediately upon the work of European theologians Heinrich Bullinger and Richard Gualter, Reformation scholars developed an apocalyptic outlook which was, as Richard Bauckham writes, 'primarily a theology of persecution and a theology of history.' For what England provided the European prophetic tradition was persecution in abundance, first by Henry and then, in spades, by Mary. It was this relentless persecution by the popish Antichrist that heightened contemporary awareness of history as the ceaselessly accelerating conflict between good and evil and that made contemporaries gloomily aware that their generation must surely witness Christ's coming and the world's final days. A sense of the past as consisting essentially of the story of the persecution of God's church by the Antichrist, increasingly certainly identified with the pope, combined with a sense of the future as being very short indeed, provide two distinguishing features of what Bauckham has described as the 'Tudor Apocalyptic.'[34]

By the middle of the seventeenth century, however, this tradition was significantly transformed and in the process may well have been given a much wider audience. In the first place, men's expectations of the immediate future changed as the belief in the imminent second coming of Christ, which would signify the end of the world, gave way to the more secularly optimistic notion that before Christ would come there had to be the Millenium. This development was complex because under the relatively straightforward label 'millenarian' were a number of varieties of belief. The fundamental distinction historians have drawn within millenarianism is between pre-millenial and post-millenial belief. To John Foxe's view that the Millennium had already happened was opposed the contrary notion that either the Millenium was already in progress or that its onset was imminent. Those in this latter category were in turn split between those who shared a feeling of 'excited but passive expectation' and those who felt obliged 'to translate their vision of the future into concrete revolutionary activity now – namely, the politically active Fifth Monarchy men.[35]

The second development within the apocalyptic tradition resulted from the rise of millenarianism accompanied by a loss of faith in the spiritual integrity of the prince. John Foxe's dependence upon the godly prince was modified by writers like Joseph Mede and William Prynne to allow for the authority of the godly parliament.

Third, the international or continental Protestant assumptions that were fundamental to the makers of the Tudor apocalyptic tradition, and especially to John Foxe, were nationalized. With the writings of Thomas Brightman, for instance, men came to see that when their millenarian vision came to pass, England could then become God's elect nation and, as such, a model for the world.[36]

While there is a modicum of agreement amongst scholars concerning the rudiments of the apocalyptic tradition in English Protestant thought in the century or so before the English Civil War, there are sufficient areas of disagreement or uncertainty that leave open to speculation the precise connection between the apocalyptic tradition on the one hand and the development of widespread anti-popery on the other. For example, there is the question of how widespread was this preoccupation with the prophetic tradition. It is not always the case that what is of absorbing interest to scholars affects the perspective of society at large. While belief in the apocalyptic tradition was more common than scholars believed a decade ago, it is not clear how generally the non-scholarly world, and particularly the political world, participated in this sense of expectation. Bauckham, for instance, has observed that his sixteenth-century apocalyptics 'tended to be martyrs rather than men of the world, for the apocalypticism of the sixteenth century belonged predominantly to the unworldly strain of sixteenth century religion.' Similarly, Katharine Firth has commented that 'as the popularity of apocalypticism increased among some sections of the community, it was on the wane among the more educated,' largely as a result of 'too many theories attempting to cover too much material.' Conversely, William Lamont, who has done as much as anyone else to kindle interest in seventeenth-century millenarianism, would seem to disagree sharply with this evaluation. In the first volume of his trilogy, Lamont wrote that John Foxe, the man who 'domesticated the Apocalypse ... had made the pursuit of the Millennium respectable and orthodox.' It is not clear whether Lamont would now agree with his earlier judgment because he later wrote that his own efforts to include the Laudians within the 'millenarian framework' were ill-advised.[37]

Another area of disagreement relevant to the present study is the fate of the apocalyptic tradition in the Restoration period. Some historians, such as Keith Thomas and Christopher Hill, take the view that after the Interregnum the ubiquity of the prophetic tradition or, in Hill's case, the manifestations of belief in the Antichrist, diminish markedly. As Thomas writes, 'the spate of prophecy was sharply checked by the Restoration, the return of the Anglican Church, and the persecution of the Dissenting sects.' Christianson seems to share this view when he writes that after the work of Joseph Mede in the 1620s, 'the creative force of the apocalyptic tradition slowly evaporated.' Lamont, however, is not so sure. Whereas in 1969 he devoted part of his study to the proposition that 'implicit millenarianism ceases to be a formative influence on English Protestantism by the time of the Protectorate,' a decade later he had been persuaded by his work on Richard Baxter's prophetic papers from 1685 to change his mind. Earlier he wrote that 'interest in the Millennium tailed off after the Restoration.' More recently, following his study of Baxter and noting also Isaac Newton's well-known interest in prophetic literature, he has commented: 'What has sometimes been taken to be a diminution of interest in the Apocalypse after the Restoration may simply have been a more effective concealment of interests which had perforce to be driven underground.' Miller agrees, arguing that the 'language of antichrist abounds after 1660.'[38]

In seeking to understand seventeenth-century anti-popery, however, it is not necessary to resolve these scholarly differences. Regardless of how widespread this apocalyptic tradition was, whether it was passionately held by a majority of the population or by a tiny handful of scholars, there are marked similarities between its historicism and that expressed so generally during the Exclusion Crisis and indeed during the political crises a generation or two before. As Christianson has written, 'the apocalyptic interpretation of the reformation between 1540 and 1640 ... 'made events seem to fit together as parts of a pattern,' whereby 'Popery' in any of its forms merged into a whole chain of cosmic evil and formed a part of the age-old struggle between the minions of antichrist and the saints of Christ.' While those who participated in the great debates of Exclusion show few signs of having shared the apocalyptic enthusiasms of Bale, Foxe, Brightman, or Baxter, they did share their historicism. Though Shaftesbury, Meres, and the like were disinclined to quote from Revelation, they shared the apocalyptic view of the past as witnessing a continuous struggle in which the popish conspirators were constantly seeking to destroy God's church and the whole array of political and social institutions so closely associated with it.[39]

There was more to Restoration anti-Catholicism, of course, than an historical framework. To contemporaries, profoundly disturbed by Oates' revelations, the past was merely the storehouse of examples that confirmed their fears for the future in the event of a popish takeover. And the fears that animated the Whigs so strongly in 1678, and the Tories as well ten years later, were political, economic, religious, and, ultimately, personal.

The stereotype most commonly associated with the papists, by publicists ranging all the way from Edmund Bohun to Gilbert Burnet, was political.[40] It was widely assumed that the principal reason for striving to avoid a Catholic succession was that it would inevitably bring with it arbitrary government on the model of France, Spain, or, worse still, Turkey. Sir Francis Winnington expressed the universality of the view when he remarked to the House of Commons: 'I am sorry that heats should arise amongst ourselves, when against Popery and Arbitrary Government we are all of a mind.' Sir John Hotham had expressed the same assumption the day before when he complained that 'we do not only labour under Popery but desperate arbitrary power.' To these men, as to Halifax and Bohun, popery, arbitrary government, and French government were synonyms. Of them all, perhaps no one put it more graphically than the Earl of Shaftesbury when he said that 'popery and slavery, like two little sisters, go hand in hand, and sometimes one goes first, sometimes the other but wheresoever the one enters, the other is always following close at hand.'[41]

Arbitrariness and slavery are, of course, themselves stereotypes and simply mask more basic and more primitive fears which the historian's discipline scarcely permits him to explore. But in the case of such a pervasive and widespread obsession as anti-popery, it might be useful to consider what lies behind these various slogans. The fundamental fears that seem to have comprised the bedrock of anti-Catholicism were made fairly explicit in Blount's *An Appeal from the Country to the City*, a publication which ran through three editions between 1679 and 1681. In this pamphlet, the author begins with a self-conscious description of the general conditions that exist when 'popery prevails.' Under such circumstances, suggests Blount, one could normally expect to see whole towns in flames, 'as before,' [in 1666], 'Popish troops ravishing your wives and your daughters,' and the fires of Smithfield, which were, he reminds his readers who needed no such reminder, 'a frequent spectacle the last time Popery reigned amongst us.'[42]

At the most basic level it seems that large numbers of Englishmen of property truly believed that, were England to fall into the hands of a Catholic, their personal liberties, that of their families and their property would be immediately jeopardized. Gilbert Burnet, who was deeply conscious of this particular version of recent history, said of the papists, 'here is an enemy that if it prevails it must either swallow up our souls or ... it will devour our bodies.' The Roman church, said Burnet, 'has substituted this wildfire of rage and cruelty to their gentle flames of love and charity; and that, instead of making us love one another, makes us destroy and burn one another, is the most opposite thing possible to a society founded on the gospel.' To the Scot, preaching his last official sermon in England before 1688, what was most offensive about the papists, beside their insistence on burning heretics and overthrowing Protestant kings, was their imposition of a tyranny upon the 'tenderest part of our natures, our reason, which is the most jealous of its liberty, as well as the most desirous of it.'[43]

The full impact of the general image of a papist derived much of its strength from the stereotype of an Englishman. Emphasizing the horrors of popery was an image of Englishmen as 'naturally of a kind and loving heart of a merciful nature and pitiful disposition,' or as Sir Henry Capel put it, 'of a quiet nature.' These fine qualities, however, adhered to Englishmen only as long as they adhered to Protestantism, whose temper had been demonstrated at the time of the Fire of London. As William Lloyd said at Godfrey's funeral, despite the fact that 'so many believed and very few much doubted' the popish origins of the fire, the Protestants were not vengeful and exhibited great patience. 'Yet there was no tumult rose upon it; no violence done that extended to the life of any person.' Whenever they became infected by the 'principles of their corrupted religion the Englishmen ... became so unrelenting and hardhearted as to cut the throats of their friends, neighbours and acquaintances.' Indeed, the anti-Catholic mythology in the 1670s and 1680s was well supplied with historical examples of papist atrocities and propagandists did not hesitate to describe them in their bloody detail. Using Foxe's *Book of Martyrs*, for example, the author of *The Antichristian Principle* went as far back as 1200 when he wrote, 'this bloody beast of persecution began to show his fangs, and his sharp nails, and armed powers.' For 350 years hardly a decade passed without some divine or layman suffering the 'cruelty of persecution.' But, of course, 'all this was nothing, to the range and executions of bloody Bonner and wicked Gardiner, two notable agents of cruelty and tyranny, and who stoutly spurred on the raging beast of persecution in the days of Queen Mary.' During their five years' ascendancy, 'the land still is all in a flame, and blood and cruelty reigneth in every place.' Nor did his litany of atrocities end with the accession of Queen Elizabeth. The author went on to provide, in gruesome detail, an account of the Irish uprising in October 1641, instigated by 'the Priests and Jesuits' who told the papists that 'it was no more sin to kill [a Protestant] than to kill a dog' and that it was 'a meritorious act to kill' Protestants. Notwithstanding the author's protestation that 'it would be too tedious to give you a full relation of it,' he nonetheless goes on to provide the lurid details of how some of the 300,000 Protestants were murdered. 'Some being grievously wounded, they hung upon tenter hooks, some thrown into bogs, others hanged up by the arms whilst they slashed their bodies with their skenes, to know how many cuts an Englishman would endure ere he died.' In short, it was insisted, the papist religion 'alters the very nature of Englishmen and makes them like Turks, Infidels and Barbarians.' So frequently was the belief expressed, and so consistent with the course of English politics in the 1670s and 1680s was it, that we can hardly question Sir John Hotham's sincerity when he announced that 'I think there is not a Papist of Quality in England, but is guilty of cutting all your throats.'[44]

Restoration Englishmen of culture and education expressed such naked fear only under extreme provocation. Normally, these emotions were articulated in the conventional formulae of political society. It was widely alleged, for instance, that popery would jeopardize England's autonomy. What Burnet characterized as popery's 'blind dependence upon a foreign power' was a major ingredient of anti-Catholicism. Every English papist, up to and including James, was thought to owe his final allegiance to Rome and to be directly susceptible to French pressure and example. Sacheverel, reviewing the state of the nation in 1678, traced all the problems to the fact that upon Charles' restoration 'his Ministers knew nothing of the laws of England, but foreign government,' and that as in France affairs were 'managed by a premier Minister of State.'[45]

Equally common was the assumption that popery would necessitate the reintroduction of a standing army. Following Sir Henry Capel's perception of the civil wars as essentially the result of a papist plot was his assertion that 'from Popery came the notion of a standing Army and arbitrary power.' Charles Blount's propaganda carried the same message. A popish successor would surely govern with an army and then, he asked rhetorically, 'what will all your laws signify?' For then he 'will levy his arbitrary taxes and his army shall gather them for you.'[46]

A standing army was widely abhorred because its existence would both facilitate the burning of 'heretics' and would undermine the legendary property rights traditionally protected by Parliament and the common law. For no secret was made of the belief, cherished by many, that under a popish king property in general would be vulnerable, and former church lands in particular would be liable to immediate confiscation. Lord Russell was perhaps protesting a little too much when he said, 'I have Abbey-lands, but I protest before God and man, I could not be more against Popery than I am, had I none.' Henry Booth was expressing the same fear when he asked members of the House of Commons, 'shall we support a man whose principle it is to destroy the religion and gentry of England?' The Tory author of the *Weekly Discovery*, a series of broadsides that purported to be an account of the civil wars but which were obviously a comment on the crisis of the late 1670s, clearly saw the church-land question as an important constituent of anti-popery. In 1640, he wrote, implying as much for 1680, 'many who had no great concern for religion more than to preserve lands as had formerly belonged to the dissolved Monasteries, had yet a most violent passion for liberty and property, which they were made to believe were in danger to be swallowed by arbitrary prerogatives.' Thus, he said, 'the fear of popery combines with the fear of arbitrary government.' To his inflammatory and widely circulated pamphlet Charles Blount added a postscript: 'if any men (who have estates in abbey-lands) desire to beg their bread, and relinquish their habitations and fortunes to some old greasy bald-pated Abbot, Monk or Friar then let him vote for a Popish successor and Popery; for when once that religion is established amongst us ... the Pope will then tell you that his predecessor had no right to give away what belonged to the Church.' To the manic 'Sober Protestant,' whose tract *Friendly Advice to Protestants* has already been mentioned, there were two main reasons why the nation was generally averse to popery. To some, popery was an abomination 'out of interest, and for fear of losing their Impropriations and Abbey-Lands,' while others objected to popery 'out of a principle of Religion.'[47]

And this brings us to a factor the impact of which is difficult to evaluate, but which was never far from contemporary consciousness whenever the tide of anti-Catholic sentiment was running strongly. In the 1670s, as in the 1620s and 1630s, popery was resisted because it represented a massive threat to the country's Protestant religion. To some, such as Edward Pelling, in his 30 January sermon in 1679, it was sufficient simply to reiterate the traditional identification of popery with the Antichrist. To more, however, popery was wrong because it was idolatrous, 'a confederacy against God,' 'a bloody superstition.' Lord Russell expressed the broadly 'religious' case against popery, proclaiming 'I despise such a ridiculous and nonsensical religion – a piece of wafer broken betwixt a Priest's fingers to be our Saviour: And what becomes of it when eaten, and taken down, you know.' Few were quite as specific as Russell, yet it seems likely that he was stating the personal opinions of many. The rhetoric of virtually all anti-Catholics took for granted that popery represented a threat both to man's institutions and to God's. A fundamental feature of Restoration Englishmen's assumptions was their belief that their institutions were God's. England's Protestant religion since the Reformation was God-given and was a kind of 'natural religion,' the social implications of which corresponded precisely to the country's institutions and secular values. This was the English legend which sustained political society at those times of crisis when the forces of popery appeared to be poised for their ultimate victory.[48]

For the connection between popery and political crisis in the latter part of the seventeenth century was, as fifty years before, unmistakeable. The events of the 1660s and 1670s, culminating in the revelations of Titus Oates in 1678, seemed to a large number of Englishmen to constitute irrefutable evidence that the management of the country's affairs, and indeed the entire court, was under popish domination and that not even the appearance of a Protestant established religion would survive the death of Charles II, an event which could occur, naturally or unnaturally, at any time. For just as James I had seemed to abandon the Protestant cause in 1621 and as his son had similarly appeared to be making preparations for a Catholic takeover in 1640, so too in the 1670s and 1680s a similar alliance seemed to be in the making. The apparent identity of interest between popery and the court, which became increasingly scandalous after James, Duke of York's conversion to Catholicism became common knowledge in 1674, once again provoked and was the central issue in the two political crises. What drove the Whigs to support the policy of Exclusion was not so much a coherent political philosophy or a solidly based view of the historical roles of monarchy and parliament, but a sense of the imminent collapse of their entire way of life. Similarly, a decade later, what caused Whigs and Tories alike to unite for the few months that were necessary to exclude not only their reigning monarch from his rightful prerogatives but also all his heirs and successors was precisely the same fear.

In assessing the importance of the widespread and traditional antipathy to Catholics in the political crises of the late 1670s and 1680s, two problems need to be borne in mind. First, there is the extent to which anti-Catholic sentiment was present at various levels in society. How did the anti-Catholic attitudes articulated by the groups represented in Parliament compare with those forces that animated the thousands, in London and elsewhere, who participated in pope-burnings and the various other 'celebrations' that were a marked feature of November 5th and 17th? Second, there is the matter of the genuineness with which anti-Catholic sentiment was held. It might well be argued that anti-Catholicism was not so much an ideology sincerely held as a ploy useful for political manipulation. There is obvious reason for viewing anti-Catholic feeling in this light as it was such an effective political issue and one which for several centuries was guaranteed to elicit public response. Yet the fact that it was effective as a clarion call does not necessarily mean that it was only that or that it was self-consciously used as a device. Given the enthusiasm with which large numbers of people participated in anti-Catholic celebrations and riots in the 1670s and 1680s, and given the wide assent that many, though not all, members of England's political elite gave to rumours of popish conspiracy during the same period, it seems inconceivable that manipulation could have done more than add fuel to a fire already burning fiercely.[49]

Between the outbreak of the Great Fire in 1666, celebrated in Dryden's *Annus Mirabilis*, and the flight of James II to France in December 1688, the issue which dominated the political consciousness of most Englishmen at most levels of society was the popish plot. Never far below the surface of society since the days of the Marian persecutions, anti-popery re-emerged in the aftermath of the burning of London and was the one constant factor that fanned the flames of political controversy for the next twenty-two years.

The immediate response of the people of London to the sight of the centre of their vast city being destroyed by fire was that the only possible way it could be explained was by reference to popish conspirators. In 1700 William Taswell recalled that 'The ignorant and deluded mob, who upon the occasion were hurried away with a kind of frenzy, vented forth their rage against the Roman Catholics and Frenchmen; imagining these incendiaries (as they thought) had thrown red hot balls into the houses.' Similarly, Gilbert Burnet asserted in his *History* that 'the papists were generally charged with it' and the historian himself was not prepared to commit himself, even years later, on the crucial question as to 'whether it was casual, or raised on design.' Clarendon too, though just as resistant to the idea of a 'Popish Plot' in 1666 as he had been in 1641, nonetheless also testified to the generality of the belief. Within thirty-six hours of the outbreak of the conflagration, wrote Clarendon, 'a suspicion arose that the fire was the result of a conspiracy.' At first, he wrote, the suspicion focused upon only the Dutch and the French, but 'shortly after, the same conclusion comprehended all the Roman Catholics,' and though they kept within doors, 'some of them, and of quality, were taken by force out of their houses and carried to prison.' Supported by frequent assertions that 'the incendiaries had been seen throwing fire-balls into houses,' the belief in the conspiracy was so widespread 'that anyone controverting the suspicion was immediately suspected.' Clarendon himself, whose political career was a testament to his resistance to the national paranoia, never subscribed to the conspiratorial view and wrote: 'Notwithstanding the popular excitement and clamour, no just grounds for suspecting its existence could be detected ... [for] there was never any probable evidence (that poor creature [Hubert] excepted) that there was any other cause of that woful fire, than the displeasure of Almighty God.'

Nor was this popular response to the popish plot confined to the scene of the fire. In Warwick, for example, a boy claimed to have seen a man deposit in a ditch a 'blackish-brown ball.' Upon closer examination this ball was deemed to be an 'unfinished fire-ball.' Rioting ensued, at least one well-known Catholic was arrested, and order was ensured only after the militia was called in.[50]

Obsessively and confusedly linked with this broadly-based tendency to see fire-ball-hurling papists scattered throughout the kingdom was another fear that was also a persistent feature of post-Civil War English society – the fear of a popish army. In the midst of the Great Fire, Taswell remembered, 'a report of a sudden prevailed that four thousand French and Papists were in arms, intending to carry with them death and destruction and increase the conflagration.' This belief in the imminence of a popish coup lasted well beyond the five days of the fire itself. Samuel Pepys' entries in his *Diary* throughout the weeks after 5 November 1666 constantly record rumours and alarms of fires and apprehensions of the 'fatal day' when the papist massacre will be perpetrated. For example, Pepys records a conversation with Thomas Crew, member of parliament for Brackly, on 5 November in which Crew concludes it 'as a thing certain, that [the fire] was done by plot – it being proved by many witnesses that endeavours were made in several places to increase the fire, and that both in city and country, it was bragged by several popists that upon such a day or in such a time we should find the hottest weather that ever was in England.'[51]

And while some observers of the English scene in 1666, like Clarendon, Pepys, and Evelyn, took what would seem to the twentieth-century mind a dispassionate and commonsense view of the origins of the fire, many more in public life reacted hysterically. Members of the House of Commons, for example, responded almost unanimously and with rhetoric that bore a striking resemblance to that of 1641. As one observer put it, 'the Parliament itself did since the Fire manifest a greater zeal and hotter displeasure against the Papists than ever before.' The embers of London were not cold before the House of Commons voted to set up a committee to investigate the fire. The deliberations of this committee lasted almost a year and resulted in, first, the trial and execution of Robert Hubert for having set the fire; second, in the collection of a vast amount of literature that placed the fire in the context of the traditional popish conspiracy against the laws, lives, and liberties of Englishmen; and, finally, in parliamentary endorsement of the popular view that the Great Fire had indeed been set, if not by Hubert, then by a general conspiracy of papists. Thus, writing ten years after the parliamentary committee reported, Andrew

Marvell professed to take for granted the fact that 'the firing of London (acted by Hubert, hired by Pieddelou, two Frenchmen)' was merely one of the 'more visible effects' of popery thus far experienced in the reign of Charles II.[52]

It is worth observing that not only did members of the House of Commons react in 1666/7 in a manner and with rhetoric that was strikingly similar to that of the 1620s and 1640/1 but, furthermore, that many contemporaries were conscious of the analogies. The House of Commons in October 1666 resolved to ask the king for a proclamation banishing all priests and Jesuits and to implement the anti-recusant laws, thus re-enacting proceedings in every Parliament between 1603 and 1641, and many believed the kingdom to be in as serious jeopardy as it had been in on the eve of civil war. Lord Conway, for instance, wrote on 30 October 1666 that 'the temper of the House of Commons is strangely altered, and grown like to that in forty-one. Nothing but discontents in Parliament, court and kingdom. And now we are proceeding with as great severity against the Papists upon such like jealousies and apprehensions as in the beginning of the Long Parliament.' Samuel Pepys, too, was reminded of 1641 when he entered into his diary on 14 December 1666 that the courtiers were inclined to look upon their parliamentary critics 'as bad rebels as ever the last were.'[53]

This anxiety concerning the ubiquity of the popish peril, which became a national preoccupation in 1666 for the first time in a quarter-century, did not quickly or permanently recede. And when Charles II, acting upon the advice of Lord Ashley and John Locke and in broad accord with the terms of the secret clauses in the Treaty of Dover as well as his general instincts, issued his Declaration of Indulgence in March 1672, the cat really was set loose among the pigeons. For Charles' attempt to employ his prerogative power in ecclesiastical matters to suspend the penal laws so as to enable Dissenters to worship in licensed but public places, and Catholics to practise their religion freely in their homes, brought about a heightening of a kind of political tension that was not relaxed until after 1689.[54]

When we come to examine closely the character of the political tension which resulted from the 1672 Declaration of Indulgence and which was magnified, though not greatly altered, by Titus Oates' revelations six years later, two factors became apparent. First, it is clear that, insofar as one can know about the political consciousness of a period from the rhetoric of contemporaries, the political controversy of the 1670s had a great deal to do with religion. In the minds of politicians and pamphleteers alike in 1673, and this includes Ashley who was one of a handful who supported both the Declaration of 1672 and the Test Act a year later, while the issue was not solely religious, it was largely so. Second, it is worth noting that what most meant by religion in 1673 was not very dissimilar from what their fathers and grandfathers had meant during the generation before 1642: the preservation of the English church from the threat of popery.

Despite the best efforts of the government to soothe suspicions concerning the intentions of the declaration, hostility to it was widespread. And even though some expressed doubts as to its constitutionality, most fears centred on its religious implications. As Gilbert Burnet wrote, 'When the declaration for toleration was published, great endeavours were used, by the court, to persuade the nonconformists to make addresses and compliments upon it. But few were so blind as not to see what was aimed at by it.' Alexander Brodie wrote in his diary on 29 March that the declaration 'appears to have been a deep popish design to procure indulgence to Presbyterians, that they might make way for toleration of Popery. The popish books and all show the design.' John Evelyn too recorded in his *Diary* that the declaration was clearly perceived by contemporaries to be aimed at 'the extreme weakening the Church of England and its Episcopal Government.' Thus, while the legality of the declaration was an issue for some, the more general reaction appears to have been to its religious implications – to the fact that it appeared to represent a major step towards the introduction of the popish religion into England. Furthermore, what is particularly significant is the fact that it was John Locke whose memorandum persuaded the king that his prerogative entitled him to suspend statutes in this way. In view of the fact that both Shaftesbury, the architect of the Whig alliance of 1678-82, and Locke, the theorist of Bill of Rights, supported Charles II's 1672 Declaration of Indulgence, it becomes difficult to explain the reinvigoration of opposition to the court on constitutional or philosophical grounds.[55]

But, as was so often the case in the midst of the political crises of the 1670s, one has to go to the records of the proceedings of the two Houses of Parliament to witness the full intensity of the politicians' reaction to the royal Declaration of Indulgence. Desperately short of the money necessary to sustain his share in the Anglo-Dutch war, Charles reconvened Parliament at the beginning of February 1673. And notwithstanding the 'Revolution' that is alleged by most to have intervened since the 1620s, the scenario that was enacted at Westminster in the next two months bore a striking resemblance to those that had been frequently repeated five decades before. The Lord Chancellor, now the Earl of Shaftesbury, reminded his audience that the Dutch war was theirs. In authorizing the war of 1664 they had supported the present one. Thus could the Lord Chancellor say: 'This is your war. He [the king] took his measures from you, and they were just and right ones; and he expects a suitable assistance to so necessary and expensive an action, which he hath hitherto maintained at his own charge.'[56]

But much more familiar was the position adopted by the king and the response it elicited: Charles informed Parliament that he needed money to fight the Dutch and attempted to soft-pedal the significance of the Declaration of Indulgence. The toleration he had extended to papists was no compromise of his support for the Established Church, but, nevertheless, he went on to insist vigorously on his right to issue such a declaration. Nor, he maintained, was his standing army aimed at the 'law and property' of his subjects, but in any event must be increased in size.[57]

Most familiar of all, of course, was the reaction to the government's position that came from all sections of the House of Commons. Unaware of the hidden clauses in the Treaty of Dover, few members expressed opposition to the alliance with France or to the assumption that Holland was England's natural enemy – a position implied by Shaftesbury's memorable phrase 'delenda est Carthago.' Foreign policy was not, in the end, what moved most members of the parliamentary classes to action, unless it seemed to mask what was ultimately important, the Protestant church. The members of the House of Commons in February 1673 rejected the government's appeal for supplies in much the same way and for the same reasons their grandfathers had denied James' and Charles' requests in the 1620s. They would provide the crown with money, £1.26 million, if Charles would withdraw his declaration and give his assent to a statute that would effectively put an end to the popish inroads being made into the personnel of government. Supply would follow passage of the Test Act.

What is striking about the spring of 1673 session of Parliament is the fact that while questions of foreign policy and the constitutional propriety of the suspending power were involved in the political controversy, what seemed to animate the opposition to the policy of the court was a dogged determination to protect the Protestant church from the threat of popery. Within a few days of the opening of the session, the House of Commons agreed in principle to a generous vote of supply in support of the king's alliance with France and the war with the Dutch. However suspicious of a French compact they were to become in the future, it seemed clear that in early 1673 it did not constitute a problem. Moreover while a good deal of the parliamentarians' rhetoric was couched in constitutional terms, it is difficult to dispute Haley's judgment that during this parliamentary session 'there was in being a country party whose main preoccupation was fear that the King's religious policy would lead to Popery.' As Sir Thomas Meres put it, 'what is it that makes us now so zealous in this question, but our fears of popery?' It was this general suspicion of popery that inspired yet another address to the king 'for preventing the Growth of Popery.' In March 1673, as so many times before, the House of Commons declared that the members were 'very sensible of the great dangers and mischiefs that may arise ... by the increase of popish recusants amongst us.'[58]

Sir Thomas Meres had reintroduced into the language of English politics the court-country division when, on 22 February, he said he spoke for 'plain country men [who] ... could not speak so smoothly as the fine men about the town, but they meant as well to the King as they did.' What united these 'plain country men' in 1673 and gave them the strength to challenge the court was the belief that the king's policy would result in the re-establishment of popery and that there was clearly a large increase in the numbers of papists having access to the king. The unity of anti-popery was a prime source of strength to this country party as it had been to that in 1640 and before, and in March 1673 it resulted in two major victories. On the 7th of that month Charles personally revoked the declaration and three weeks later he gave his assent to the Test Act, the most effective measure yet devised to implement the constant objective of two generations of English Protestant gentlemen to combat the power exercised in public life by the seemingly irrepressible papists.[59]

Anti-Catholic sentiment was in a state of constant ferment throughout the 1670s and it seemed to be the case that frequently neither members of the House of Commons nor their constituents could worry about anything else. In January 1674, for instance, one of the members for the borough of Leicester, Sir John Pretyman, generally regarded as a 'Church-and-King country gentleman,' informed the local magistrates that the House of Commons had agreed that it should 'first proceed to relieve grievances effectually, to secure the protestant religion, liberties and properties, to remove all papists and evil councillors from about the King and all other persons obnoxious and dangerous to the government.' Three years later, John Gray, the man who succeeded to Pretyman's seat in the House upon his death and who was later to be a solid supporter of Exclusion through the Parliaments from 1678 to 1681, informed the mayor of the borough that the lower house had rejected the Lords' bill for 'the more effectual conviction and prosecution of Popish Recusants' because it was inadequate, and had substituted one that he hoped would more surely guarantee 'suppressing the growth of Popery.'[60]

Similarly, the letters of the member of the House of Commons for Hull, Andrew Marvell, to the town's mayor and corporation throughout the 1670s are filled with references to this central religious question. In April and May 1675, Marvell thought it of the utmost importance to inform his electors of how the House was proceeding against the papists and he was clearly relieved to write on 20 May 1675 of the two bills that had been introduced on that day: 'The first is a Test for the Members of both Houses containing a large renunciation of the most distinguishing doctrines of the Papists. The second a Generall Bill for the speedier conviction of all Papists.' A week later he reported that 'today hath been chiefly employed in reading and committing the bill for Conviction of

Papists and distinguishing and exempting Protestant Dissenters from this or any other law made against Papists.' The following week he juxtaposed to his report of the progress in committee of 'their Bill of Test' the following alarming piece of gossip: 'the Pope hath given a Cardinal's Hat to Father Howard, the Queen's Almoner.' The preoccupation with the popish peril was no less pervasive four months later when the House of Commons met as a Committee of the Whole upon religion. In addition to bills that were positively 'Puritan' in their reforming intent, the committee proceeded to propose bills 'to prevent the growth of Popery [and] that the children of the Royal family should be educated in the Protestant Religion and no Popish Priest to come near them.'[61]

Given the way Marvell reported on parliamentary developments during the 1670s, it should have come as no surprise to his contemporaries that he was the author of a long tract in 1678 that provides us with the classic expression of the conventional Protestant view of the highly conspiratorial role of the papists in contemporary English society. The central thesis of Marvell's tract was not significantly different from that which had informed the Grand Remonstrance in November 1641 or those many outbursts that had kept the political pot boiling through the 1620s. Marvell was quick to come to the point of his *Account of the Growth of Popery.* Its first sentence reads: 'There has now for divers years a design been carried on to change the lawful government of England into an absolute tyranny, and to convert the established Protestant Religion into downright Popery.'[62]

At this point in our study, there is little in Marvell's tract that is new. Almost every facet of the stereotypes that provided the essential context for English Protestant gentry self-perception was paraded before the reader. In contrast to the liberty which all Englishmen enjoyed was the tyranny implicit in the 'Romish yoak'; in contrast to the dignity of the Protestant church was popery, 'such a thing that cannot, but for want of a word to express it, be called a Religion, – this last and insolentest attempt upon the credulity of mankind.' Worse than 'either open Judaism, or plain Turkery, or honest paganism,' popery, by a 'new and antiscriptural belief, compiled of terrors to the fancy, contradictions to Sense, and Impositions on the understanding, their Laity have turned Tenants for their Souls, and in consequence tributary for their Estates to a more than omnipotent Priesthood.' To Marvell, England's history for over a hundred years could only be interpreted in terms of the popish conspiracy. During the reign of Queen Mary, no less than during that of Charles I, 'we may reckon the reigns of our late princes by a succession of the popish treasons against them.' In the past, Marvell believed, the papists had conspired, just as in his own day they continued to conspire, for religious, political, and economic ends, for 'even now the Romish clergy on the other side of the water snuff up the savour odour of so many rich abbies and monasteries that belonged to their predecessors.' Notwithstanding the demonstrable evil of popery, Marvell concluded, he held it to be true, and, to judge from the response to Titus Oates' revelations a few months later, his was not an isolated opinion, that 'there are those men among us, who have undertaken, and do make it their business, under so legal and so perfect a government, to introduce a French slavery, and instead of so pure a religion, to establish the Roman idolatry.' Given the popularity of this point of view among many members of his social class, it is scarcely surprising that Titus Oates' allegations should have provoked such alarm.[63]

The history of what is generally referred to as the 'Popish Plot' has been written and rewritten over the years – most recently by J.P. Kenyon. So comprehensive is this latest study that it is unlikely that a great deal can be added to our knowledge of the details of that complex series of events. The anti-Catholic tradition, the lives of Titus Oates and Israel Tonge, the response of the court to the allegation concerning the plot, and the hysterical reaction within large sections of English society to Oates' fabrications – these are all entirely familiar to us. Only the identity of Sir Edmund Bury Godfrey's murderer, if there was one, remains a secret.[64] Yet, despite the plethora of factual information on the subject, historians have not fully grasped the significance of the popish plot of 1678. For in their very labelling of these events as 'The Popish Plot,' thereby singling it out as unique and *sui generis* in the political history of England in the seventeenth century, historians miss the crucial point – that the response of English society to the stories of 1678 was not very different from its response to the publications of other evidence, in the decades before as well as after, of the imminence of the Catholic takeover. For not only is there a tradition of anti-Catholic sentiment in England during the century or so following the accession of Elizabeth that helps explain the otherwise aberrant reaction of 1678-9 but, more important, anti-Catholicism represents the crucial element in the context which renders intelligible the political program of every anti-court group between the accession of James I and that of William and Mary. Just as widespread anti-popery alone makes sense of the Whig program in 1679-81, no less is this true of the political behaviour of the anti-court alliances during the earlier but comparable political crises in the 1620s and in 1641.

The obsession with the popish peril that set in with Titus Oates' revelations and that was sustained at least until the spring of 1680 was not different in kind from that which had surfaced on countless occasions during the preceding century. However, because it involved the heir to the throne, it encouraged the adoption of the fundamentally radical constitutional theories inherent in Exclusion. As had been the case during earlier outbursts of anti-popery, the predominant force that animated even well-educated and sophisticated gentry was fear. The precise character of the thing feared was not, of course, clearly delineated, but this in no way detracted from its force. Maynard illustrated this in the course of debates during the final session of the Long Parliament in late 1678 when he said, somewhat plaintively, 'I do not know what changes may be hereafter should Popery be settled amongst us.' If Serjeant Maynard believed he was unable to foresee the future, Sir Edward Dering suffered from no such inhibition. 'I declare, if nothing be done this Session for the Protestant Religion we have nothing remains but to make our graves, and lie down in them.'[65]

Furthermore, it is apparent from a reading of the debates and minutes of the House of Commons between 1678 and 1680 that this profound fear of an unknown but ghastly future was widespread amongst members of that body. Perhaps not every member was privately convinced on 31 October 1678 by the evidence contained in Coleman's letters to the French cleric, La Chaise, but it is significant that no one opposed the motion that 'upon the evidence that has already appeared to this House, this House is of opinion that there has been, and still is, a damnable and hellish Plot contrived and carried on by the Popish Recusants, for the assassinating and murdering the King, and for subverting the Government, (and rooting out) and destroying the Protestant Religion.'[66]

In assessing the character of gentry anti-popery in the late 1670s it is worth distinguishing between that exhibited before and after the summer of 1678. Through the waning years of the 1670s and in the winter of 1677-8 in particular one can describe the atmosphere in the House of Commons as preoccupied but not obsessed with popery. The cause for anxiety was, furthermore, solidly based. As Sir Thomas Lee put it, 'No man but desires to reduce himself to any condition of living to suppress the growing greatness of the French King.' In the context of the secret provisions of the Treaty of Dover, it is scarcely surprising that contemporaries should have felt concern at the 'growing greatness of the French King.' Then, when one recognizes the presence of appreciable numbers of Catholics at the court of Charles II, together with the fact that the king's brother was a Catholic, it is understandable that concern became alarm and that the House of Commons before 1678 was distinctly nervous. The character of the anti-popery endemic to England's political gentry society before the summer of 1678 is typified by Powle's criticism of the king's message in February of that year: 'But these four years, addresses have been made to prevent the growing greatness of the French, and the Ministers declare against him, and yet France grows great against these Counsels. I fear some inclination is still amongst the Ministers to France, and they have brought us to the brink of ruin.'[67]

In the last session of this Parliament, however, and throughout most of the Exclusion Parliaments, what had been a preoccupation became an obsession, and what had been to some extent a reasonably based fear of a foreign enemy became an unreal and neurotic conviction that the fundamental laws and liberties of English society were being undermined by a largely invisible conspiracy which, notwithstanding French connections, was essentially domestic. No longer was the real threat of French power a paramount consideration; in its stead there reigned the conviction that every papist was conspiring against the king and that for every one known Catholic there was an indefinite number awaiting to declare themselves in the event of the successful coup.

The obsessive nature of anti-Catholic sentiment, both within political society and lower down the social scale, between 1678 and 1681 and again in 1688 is easily documented and widely known. Amongst the members of the Exclusion Parliaments, for example, credulity knew virtually no bounds. Speaking to the second Exclusion Parliament in October 1680, Russell put his conviction bluntly: 'This Parliament must either destroy Popery, or they destroy us; there is no middle way to be taken, no mincing the matter.' To Sir Henry Capel the crisis was the culmination of a century long struggle: 'In the descent of four Kings, still the Parliaments have been troubled with Popery. Laws have been made against it, and all fail. Sometimes Popery is in the Ministers of State, and in another state too, the Clergy; and now, to our misfortune, we find it in the Heir presumptive to the Crown, and the son of that father who died a Martyr for the Protestant Religion.' It was in the course of this debate, on 26 October 1680, that another former opponent of Exclusion, Sir Francis Winnington, articulated the classic conspiratorial view of the crisis and explained how he reconciled his view of the constitution with his conversion to Exclusion. His speech was largely devoted to demonstrating 'the progress the Papists have made, since the dissolution of the last Parliament by the Conspirators.' Recalling the Meal-Tub Plot, the abhorring of the petitioners' campaign, the protection of papists by the Court of King's Bench, he bewailed his country's fate. 'When we see such a coherence and conspiracy against us, we must be ruined.' As Winnington could best foresee, the only way to make the king and kingdom glorious, to protect 'our Civil Rights,' is by Parliament's proceeding 'to secure the nation against Popery and to prevent a Popish Successor.'[68]

It is only in the context of such an all-consuming and irrational paranoia that the proceedings against Sir Robert Cann make sense. For allegedly having stated publicly in October 1679 that 'there was no Popish Plot, but a Presbyterian Plot,' Cann was unceremoniously and quickly 'tried' by the House and immediately expelled. Cann's plaintive plea to the Speaker was to no avail: 'I ever did and ever shall believe this to be a Popish Plot, as sure as you are in the Chair.'[69]

Nor is it the case that the character of anti-popery changes profoundly in the course of the Exclusion Parliaments. Insofar as the rhetoric of members of the House of Commons provides an index to the prevailing state of mind, the anxiety level in the Oxford Parliament was as high as two years before. Perhaps the sense of panic that had followed Oates' revelations had receded somewhat by 1681, but the more basic conviction that fundamental English values could not survive a Catholic succession was unaffected. As Colonel Birch expressed this view, 'We cannot preserve the Protestant Religion with a Popish successor to the Crown, any more than water can be kept cold in a hot pot.'[70]

In assessing the character of anti-Catholicism in the three Exclusion Parliaments, two traits stand out. First, there is the obvious intensity with which anti-popish sentiment was experienced. Hampden was surely speaking for a large segment of the House of Commons when he said: 'If we fear nothing but Popery, we fear everything. There is nothing when Popery comes in, but to destroy your Souls, or lose all you have in the World.' In the apparent wave of fear which swept the House of Commons in the immediate aftermath of the defeat of Exclusion in the Lords in November 1680, Sir Henry Capel said: 'let every man consider, when he goes to bed, at this rate what may become of him before morning.' To Sir Richard Graham, 'the Papists are enemies to all mankind, but those of their own persuasion.' Capel agreed fully, for was it not evident that 'all our miseries are founded upon Popery?' To Sir Francis Russell, the threat posed by popery was of violence to the persons of all Protestants. A bill banishing papists from London would 'do no good,' he said: 'You will send them out of London into the Country, to cut our throats.'[71]

Second, there are the deep historical roots of anti-popery. What made anti-papal sentiment between 1678 and 1681 so powerful was that it was much more than just a panic-stricken response to the most recent plot. More important was the fact that Oates' story was simply one more illustration of the theme that dominated modern English history. What shaped the political consciousness of many who supported the policy of Exclusion was a sense of continuity with generations of post-Reformation Protestants. Colonel Titus obviously exaggerated the fragility of English Protestantism, yet he was deeply aware of the fact that in Tudor times the religious persuasion of the monarch prevailed. 'Henry VIII declared his supremacy of the Church; the Kingdom did so too, and threw the Pope out of the Kingdom. Queen Mary burnt the Protestants, and the Kingdom did so too.' To Trenchard, popery posed a grave threat not because of recent events so much as because the prospect in 1680 was no better than it had been 150 years before. As he said, 'Consider how restless the spirit of Popery has been ever since the Reformation.' But it was Sir Francis Winnington who expressed most clearly the sense that the central problem confronting Englishmen in 1680 was not essentially different from that which faced their forebears a century before. During Elizabeth's reign, he said, 'it was apprehended a Popish successor would undo her in her reign.' Even though 'the Protestant Religion was not yet well-grown, the People of England entered into an Association that if the Queen should fall, the Papists should make any attempt upon her, they would avenge it even unto death.' The essential difference between the predicament of his generation and that of his forebears was the quite different posture adopted by the government. Then, he said, 'there were good ministers of state,' whereas now, 'the whole frame of the government is out of order, and Popery [is] so publicly carried on by the Ministers.' Sir William Jones, speaking immediately following Winnington in the debate on the Bill of Association, made the same point about the difference between government in the 1580s and the 1680s. 'Those who were her Counsellors and Ministers, at that time, took great care to keep out Popery; so far was an Association from a crime, that the Privy-Councillors at that time joined with the people in it.' The present advisers to the king, he observed, 'are not of the same disposition now, as they were then.'[72]

Leaving aside the question of the validity of the comparative positions on popery of privy councillors in 1583 and 1680, it is clear that contemporaries in the later period *believed* there was an enormous contrast. While popery had been and would always be a threat to England's traditional institutions in 1678-81, there was a completely new threat in that the Catholics had, through the Duke of York, penetrated to the very heart of the court. This fear was, we have seen, widespread in the first two Exclusion Houses of Commons. Nor was it significantly diminished in the short-lived Oxford Parliament. The preoccupation with Oates and his reports had diminished over time, but the general fear of popery had not. The sense of imminent disaster which informed the debates in 1681 is inescapable to even the most casual reader of Grey's *Diary*.

Our discussion of the fear of popery during the Exclusion period has focused on the Parliament partly because Exclusion was essentially a parliamentary crisis, and partly because nowhere else can one relate so conveniently traces of contemporary anxiety. This is not to say, however, that fear of popery was found only in the House of Commons during those years.

Richard Baxter, for example, both remarked upon the widespread fear of popery, and simultaneously shared the fear. In 1679 he wrote, 'all London ... is in such fear of them [the Papists] that they are fain to keep up private watches in all streets (besides the common ones) to save their houses from firing.' Baxter's fear was compounded by his resentment of the fact that the papists were responsible for a renewed campaign against the Dissenters: 'If the Papists have not confidence in the French invasion, God leaveth them to utter madness to hasten their win. They were in full junctness through the land, and the noise of rage was by their design turned against the Nonconformists.' Sir John Reresby, while he himself never seemed to place much credence either in the plot or in Exclusion, nevertheless did not doubt that the fear itself was genuine. When in his *Memoirs* he came first to mention the plot, he wrote: 'it is not possible to imagine what a ferment the artifice of some, and the real belief and fear of others concerning this plot, put the two Houses of Parliament and the greatest part of the nation into.' Alexander Brodie first wrote of the plot on 17 October 1678. His entry reads: 'I heard of the Popish conspiracy against the King by Dr. Oates and others. I desire to consider this, and to be instructed. Lord: turn it to thy glory and thy church's. Lord: bring forth good out of this hellish plot.' A few months later, Brodie notes news he has had 'from the South.' What he heard was 'that the King of France was preparing armies and fleets, and intended to invade us, having made peace with all their neighbours except Brandenburg; The farther discovery of the plot, and Godfrey's murder.'[73]

One of the more notable characteristics of anti-Catholicism around the period of the Exclusion Crisis derives from the fact that its primitive quality does not seem to change much as one observes it in various social classes. The anti-popery which animated the Exclusionists in the House of Commons was not markedly different in character from that which inflamed the crowds who participated in the pope-burnings and bonfires on November 5th and 17th most years between 1673 and 1681, and again in 1688. Notwithstanding the fact that these annual expressions of popular culture were encouraged and subsidized by the politicians – there is evidence that the 17 November 1679 procession, for example, was organized by Elkanah Settle, who had been hired by Shaftesbury and was subsidized by Shaftesbury's Green Ribbon Club – these festivities provide evidence of the extent to which popular anti-Catholicism was deeply rooted in English society. Such is the nature of bonfires that one cannot always be certain precisely what motivates the participants. There is, however, at least a clue in the images honoured and the effigies burnt. In the great spectacle on 17 November 1679, attended, so it was said by 200,000, there was a statue of Queen Elizabeth with the Magna Carta and symbols of the Protestant religion. After bowing before the queen and her institutions, the pope, preceded by a parade of cardinals, bishops, and court chaplains, was consumed by flames. Every such celebration in the 1670s and 1680 was a variant of this: the queen was celebrated, court popery reviled, and the pope incinerated. One doubts that many at this level in society were concerned about the reclamation of abbey lands or the implications for local autonomy or absolutism. This does not, however, distinguish this popular fear of popery from that of the elites. Both feared idolatrous clericalists, foreign domination, and, above all, the essentially unknown consequences of popery.[74]

For two years or so after James succeeded to the throne, anti-popish sentiment was somewhat muted and ceased to be sharply focused on specific political objectives. The Parliament of 1685 made no secret of its anti-Catholic opinions but it was still astonishingly receptive to the monarch whose succession had been so vehemently opposed five years before. Nor is there much evidence of concerted resistance to the policies of the new king before 1687. The reasons for this decline in the level and intensity of anti-popery would seem to be two. The persecutions of the early 1680s must have taken the sting out of the Whig connection and introduced a note of caution into the proceedings of the activists. More important, however, was the fact that James had succeeded to the throne at the age of fifty-one and had had twelve years of childless marriage. In whatever ways the king modified the country's political or religious institutions, the changes would be temporary. In Mary and in Anne the succession was assuredly Protestant.

In 1687 two developments shattered these assumptions. First, in angling for an alliance with the Dissenters, in his systematic efforts to back Parliament, and in his deliberate rejection of anti-Catholic statutes, James seemed to be serving notice of his intention to change permanently the religion of England. But, simpler yet more profound, the queen became pregnant. The fear of a Catholic future, always present but politically focused only three times before – in 1628-9, 1640-2, and 1678-80 – was again experienced, this time with unprecedented urgency. For the first time it was not simply that the court was linked with popery, either through a wife, an archbishop and panoply of councillors, or the heir; in 1687-8 the threat took its most serious form. So serious indeed was the threat that even the majority of bishops was persuaded that if any kind of Protestant church were to remain, the king would have to be resisted and perhaps even his abdication would ultimately have to be accepted.

It is scarcely necessary to spend much time in demonstrating that anti-Catholic sentiment was an important factor in English politics in 1687-8. There has probably not been an historian since 1688 who would have needed to be convinced of the truth of that basic proposition.[75] Nor is it required to show that this anti-Catholic sentiment was not the sole prerogative of any one social or political alliance in 1687-8. The formal declarations that poured off the broadsheet presses in November 1688 are as one in the extent to which their authors saw the crisis in 'religious' terms. Those who subscribed to the declaration at Nottingham, for example, asserted their refusal 'to deliver our posterity over to such a condition of Popery and Slavery as their accusations had described,' and thus pledged to support the Prince of Orange and a 'freely elected Parliament.' This was the only possible response by a group to which it was all 'too apparent that the very fundamentals of our religion, liberties and properties, are about to be rooted out by our late theoretical Privy Council.' To the Whig, Lord Delamere, the choice in 1688 was simple and revolved around the question of 'religion': 'I am to choose whether I will be a slave and a Papist, or a Protestant, and a Freeman.' In the three Ridings of Yorkshire, the perception of the crisis was similar. As the ultra-loyal Sir John Reresby described the process by which support for James receded in late 1688, religion was clearly central to his colleagues' concerns. It was widely accepted that 'there having been a great endeavour by the government to bring in popery into this kingdom of late years, and to invade the laws many ways,' the only solution was a 'free Parliament.' Many, such as Lord Willoughby, were clearly uneasy to be thus 'engaged against the Crown ... but there was a necessity either to part with our religion and properties or do it.'[76]

Scarcely any contemporary observers were able to view the Catholic question dispassionately. Even John Evelyn was affected. His diary entry for 25 August, for example, referred to 'the popish Irish soldiers [who] commit many murders and insolences' and, he added, 'the whole nation disaffected and in apprehensions.' By the beginning of October, Evelyn recorded, the king's policy of removing Protestants, putting papists into 'places of trust,' and retaining Jesuits 'about him' gave 'no satisfaction to the nation, but increasing the universal discontent brought people to so desperate a pass as with utmost expression even passionately seem to long for and desire the landing of that Prince, whom they looked on as their deliverer from popish tyranny.'[77]

Amongst the gentry, churchmen, and nobility, anti-popery brought on a crisis of allegiance which expressed itself in the form of calls for a freely-elected Parliament, support for or acceptance of the invitation to William, and, ultimately, a willingness to give assent to James' abdication. Lower down the social scale, fear of popery was just as pronounced, but expressed itself in other ways. Reresby has described the form popular anti-Catholicism took after the king's flight from London in December 1688: 'The rabble, being sufficiently animated against the papists before, and more especially now (thinking, and reasonably, that the council given the King to withdraw himself came from them) rose in prodigious numbers, and dividing themselves pulled down the chapel of that worship and many houses of such as did profess it, taking and spoiling their goods, imprisoning such as they suspected to be priests.' On the following night, the level of violence and general anxiety had scarcely abated. Bands of Irish troops, numbering thousands, were believed to be 'burning Towns, massacring the people, and marching directly for London to put the like in execution here.' As the only serious study of popular anti-popery in 1688 has pointed out, the fear of Catholicism was widespread throughout England in the autumn and it represents a major part of the explanation of the speedy acceptance by the

Convention Parliament of the Revolution Settlement. A populace rendered tense and uneasy about popery represented a major threat to law and order, a threat which some saw could only be averted by acceptance of William. As one observer wrote on 13 December: 'All the Lords and city have invited the Prince of Orange, which we all pray may come quickly that a stop may be put to the fury of the rabble who have done great mischief.'[78]

Nor was this deeply-felt anti-Catholic anxiety experienced solely in the capital. Samuel Newton, alderman and former mayor of Cambridge, described similar scenes in his university town. On 13 December he wrote: 'and several nights before, there were up in arms a great many in this town some night two or three hundred (many scholars among them) of the rabble called the Mobile who, at first under a pretence to seek for papists and such who had favoured them and to ransack their houses for arms, at last came to be very insulting and wherever they pleased to enter men's houses and do them much mischief.' The next night, he noted, rumours spread that 'five or six thousand of the Irish lately disbanded had burnt Bedford and cut all their throats there' and were headed for Cambridge to attempt the same thing. This led to an uproar in the streets until, some hours later, 'it was considered how improbable such a thing should be so of a sudden.' It was during this same turbulent week in Cambridge that some of the College Fellows, suspected of 'being inclined to popery,' were attacked. Clement Scot, a Fellow of Corpus Christi College, for instance, was attacked in his rooms and forced to flee over the roof. Dr Thomas Watson, the Bishop of St David, who was staying nearby, was seized by an angry crowd and brought to Cambridge, a prisoner, again for his suspected popery.[79]

As everybody knows, James Stuart went away never to return. William of Orange came and stayed. The substitution, legitimized by the subsequent Revolution Settlement, put an end, once and for all, to the likelihood of English monarchy being identified with the popish religion. The immediate result was not the establishment of political stability for, as J.H. Plumb has explained, this was to require the resolution of more issues than that raised by popery in high places. The accession of William and Mary did, however, mean that for the first time in seventy years the court was unambiguously Protestant – as was the country. Popery did not cease being seen as a threat, as the pervasive fear of Jacobitism through much of the eighteenth century, and the Gordon Riots towards the end, demonstrate. Popery was, however, no longer an issue that divided the ruling classes, but rather became an issue that helps explain the consensus on which the eighteenth-century oligarchy was to be based. When one contrasts the essentially harmonious domestic politics of the Elizabethan and early Hanoverian periods with the turbulence of the Stuarts, it is hard to escape the conclusion that a crucial component of the difference lies in the fact that, at every level, English society radiated a profound aversion to popery.[80] It was this which facilitated political harmony under unequivocally Protestant courts, but which played a large part in causing the political turbulence of the seventeenth century when neither James I, his son, nor his grandsons could permanently establish the credibility of their regimes to the satisfaction of the profoundly anti-Catholic sentiments of their subjects.

6

Conclusion

In the course of this study we have moved through rugged terrain – it would perhaps be more accurate to describe it as a minefield – but the path we have followed has been kept deliberately narrow. Given our theme, we have inevitably had to refer to some of the major problems that have bedevilled scholars of seventeenth-century England for a hundred years, but we have not had the temerity to pretend to solve these problems. 'Puritanism' and 'revolution,' whether considered separately or conjointly, raise extremely complex questions and it would be absurd to think that in this brief study we have done more than pose a possible way of looking at a connection between the two. Thus it is more important than usual, when reviewing the conclusions which might be drawn, to separate what we might conclude from what we have clearly not said.

The first problem we confronted concerned the concept 'revolution' and it should be emphasized here that we did not argue that events in England between 1640 and 1660 either were or were not 'revolutionary.' Not only is that a difficult question but, more to the point, it is probably not worth arguing about for in the end it involves considerations that are semantic, not historical. It is, however, important to reflect upon the implications of labelling events during England's Interregnum as constituting a 'revolution.' In this connection we have made three observations.

First, we noted that as far as contemporaries were concerned, and indeed this view prevailed for almost two hundred years, events between 1640 and 1660 amounted to a catastrophe narrowly averted, not a revolution. The latter event occurred, gloriously, in 1688 and it was not until well over a generation after the French Revolution that events surrounding the civil wars came to be construed as the real revolution of seventeenth-century England, with 1688 representing little more than a 'postscript.'

Second, we noted that the consensus within the historical profession for the past hundred years has been unchanged. Despite the reluctance of most historians to attempt a definition of 'revolution,' and notwithstanding the fact that those who have made the attempt have failed to persuade others of their view, nevertheless few deny that what happened in England between 1640 and 1660 amounted to a 'revolution.'

It is our third observation, however, that is most important to the argument. What resulted from the application of the label 'revolution' to events between 1640 and 1660 was the development of a presupposition that there must be a huge gap between virtually all aspects of English culture and society before and after the Interregnum. Where before the mid-nineteenth century, historians had happily written about pre- and post-Civil War England in single studies, Gardiner and his successors were reluctant to do so. Whereas continuity had been the prevailing metaphor, for the past century or so it has been replaced by that of revolutionary discontinuity.

Now it may or may not be the case that England after 1660 was simply unrecognizably changed in many, or most, crucial respects from the early Stuart period. A study on a grander scale than the present one would be needed to answer the question. But in at least one area, where things religious impinged upon the broad political narrative at the national level, an area that has enjoyed more than its share of historiographical attention since 1860, it would seem that there were fewer differences than the revolutionary model implies.

Here we must focus our attention on 'Puritanism' and again we must distinguish carefully between the limited conclusions we might draw and the massive topics we skirted. It has not been our intention to prove or disprove the ubiquity of 'Puritans' in seventeenth-century English society or to challenge the usefulness of 'Puritanism' in summarizing certain aspects of religious thought. The terms were used by contemporaries and that alone legitimizes them. In saying this, however, we must recognize that 'Puritan' was used by contemporaries polemically and politically, not clinically or objectively. Hence, when we come to employ the concept three hundred years later we are obliged to sort out which of the contemporary senses we intend. If we intend the term to refer to something religious – to an individual's commitment to a body of doctrine pertaining to man's relationship with God – then we are under a considerable obligation to ensure that when we label a contemporary as a 'Puritan' we have good reason to do so.

It seems highly probable that there was a large number of men and women who flourished in England between 1600 and 1700 who may properly be labelled 'Puritan.' In other words, there were doubtless innumerable individuals – many but not all of them clergymen – who were characterized by a conspicuous preoccupation with their relationship with God, a reliance upon Scripture as the essential vehicle of communication between God and themselves, and a firm and unyielding belief in the unscriptural, and therefore sinful, nature of the established Church of England and a commitment to its further reform.

It might even be argued that there was a common 'core of doctrine,' or a set of values, to which all 'Puritans' subscribed, and to which no one subscribed who was not a 'Puritan.' The case for this, however, has yet to be made, and until it has, it seems preferable for historians to use the concept 'Puritanism' as sparingly as did contemporaries.

It has not been the purpose of the study, however, to describe the 'Puritan' phenomenon or to assess its extent. The concern here has been much more limited: to examine a relatively small number of politically prominent laymen who flourished between 1621 and 1641 and who have conventionally been described as 'Puritan,' and another group who flourished in the world of national politics between 1667 and 1688 but who have never been accounted 'Puritans,' in order to compare the ways in which they perceived and articulated their religious preoccupations in the context of their political lives. Here, two conclusions have emerged.

First, if one develops a reasonably rigorous concept of 'Puritan,' one which distinguishes a 'Puritan' from either a 'Protestant' or an 'Anglican,' then it is not possible or helpful to view many members of the English political establishment between 1621 and 1641 as 'Puritan.' (If one does not develop a reasonably rigorous concept of 'Puritan,' incidentally, then describing as 'Puritans' all or most members of the politically active gentry during those twenty years is even less helpful.) Insofar as the political origins of the civil wars may be traced to the activities of men like John Pym and John Eliot, it is not useful to describe these men, or many like them, as Puritans. So far from being 'Puritan,' so far from being driven by a passionate zeal to complete the reformation of the church begun by Elizabeth, it is much more accurate to say they were impelled by the opposite urge to protect it from subversive change.

Second, there is a remarkable similarity between what politically active gentry were saying about the 'religious' problem between 1621 and 1641 and what the next generation said about it. Not only was the problem of how to protect the Protestant church from popish subversion central to the concerns of both generations, but the political crises that are characteristic of both periods appeared to contemporaries to be the direct result of these subversive activities.

This is not to say necessarily that in most areas of human experience there was an essential similarity before and after the English civil wars. In one area, however, and one to which historians have paid a great deal of attention since the mid-nineteenth century – that where religious preoccupations impinge upon the secular political process – it is surprising how powerfully the anxieties of the pre-1642 period reverberate forty years later.

Nor is this to say that the political crises of the 1620s, or of 1641, were identical in all respects to those of 1678-81, or of 1688. The passage of fifty years had inevitably wrought changes. Yet it seems misleading for historians to approach the latter period as if it is unrecognizably different from the former. In the one area we have examined, and, one suspects, in many others, it is not necessary for the scholar to pass through a conceptual decontamination chamber to prevent a frame of reference appropriate to the pre-1642 period from being carried over into the Restoration period.

In reaching this conclusion, we finally return to a problem with which we began. 'What happened to Puritanism?' is not a question that urgently needs to be answered. Being a 'Puritan' in the 1660s was inevitably a different experience from being a 'Puritan' in the 1630s or in the 1570s, but nothing cataclysmic occurred to 'Puritanism' between the Interregnum and the Restoration period. Most members of England's political establishment before the civil wars were not 'Puritans,' so it is not surprising that their sons were not 'Puritans' after the Restoration. Far from there being revolutionary differences between the generations, there was remarkable agreement. In the face of an unending and almost continuous challenge to the entire political, social, and religious order, constitutional caution was thrown to the winds as a series of increasingly desperate measures, culminating in the enforced abdication of James II, were devised, all designed to put an end to the blandishments of their common enemy, the whore of Babylon.

Notes

CHAPTER 1

1 See William Haller, *Liberty and Reformation in the Puritan Revolution* (New York 1955); William Haller, *The Rise of Puritanism* (New York 1938); M.M. Knappen, *Tudor Puritanism* (Chicago 1939); Patrick Collinson, *The Elizabethan Puritan Movement* (London 1967); Christopher Hill, *Society and Puritanism in Pre-revolutionary England* (London 1964); Paul Seaver, *The Puritan Lectureships: the Politics of Political Dissent, 1560-1662* (Stanford 1970); George Yule, *The Independents in the English Civil War* (Melbourne 1958); George Yule, *Puritans in Politics* (Appleford 1981); J. Sears McGee, *The Godly Man in Stuart England* (New Haven 1976).
2 For an illuminating consideration of the variety of usages of 'Puritan' between 1560 and 1640 see Hill, *Society*, chap. 1.
3 For discussions which begin with the kinds of evidence used by Hill, but which reach different conclusions, see C.H. George, 'Puritanism as History and Historiography,' *Past and Present*, 41, Dec. 1968, 77-104; Michael G. Finlayson, 'Puritanism and Puritans: Labels or Libels?' *Canadian Journal of History*, VIII, 3, 1973, 201-23. See also R. Briggs, 'The Catholic-Puritans, Jansenists and Rigorists in France,' in Donald Pennington and Keith Thomas, eds., *Puritans and Revolutionaries: Essays in Seventeenth Century History presented to Christopher Hill* (Oxford 1978), 333.
4. J. Sears McGee, who clearly contends that there was a fundamental distinction between Anglicanism and Puritanism, recognizes the problem when he writes that 'it is curious that Puritanism has been more thoroughly studied than Puritans' (*The Godly Man*, 266).
5 A.S.P. Woodhouse, ed., *Puritanism and Liberty* (London 1951); Michael Walzer, *The Revolution of the Saints* (Cambridge, Mass. 1965). Though a gen-

eration apart in time, and much further removed in mentality, Woodhouse and Walzer share an attitude to the causal connection between Puritanism and modernity. It is instructive to compare Woodhouse's argument, that 'while operating within the prescribed bounds of "Christian" liberty, Puritanism further does a great deal to foster the notion of individuality, and an individualistic outlook, with results partially, though not wholly, favourable to democracy' (*Puritanism*, 81), with Walzer's, 'This, then, is the relation of Puritanism to the liberal world: it is perhaps one of historical preparation, but not at all of theoretical contribution' (*Revolution*, 303). Christopher Hill also assigns 'Puritanism' a major explanatory burden when he writes, 'Puritanism was perhaps the most important complex of ideas that prepared men's minds for revolution, but it was not the only one' (*Intellectual Origins of the English Revolution* [Oxford 1965], 6). The list of examples could be extended almost indefinitely. For Woodhouse see also A.S.P. Woodhouse, *The Heavenly Music: a Preface to Milton*, ed. Hugh MacCallum (Toronto 1972), 102.

6 See, for instance, R.H. Tawney, *Religion and the Rise of Capitalism* (London 1926). Brian Manning, in his contribution to the Hill Festschrift, though not citing Woodhouse's introduction to the Putney Debates, suggests a similar logical connection between 'Puritanism' and 'democracy' ('Puritanism and Democracy, 1640-42,' in Pennington and Thomas, eds., *Puritans and Revolutionaries*). Lawrence Stone indicates the ubiquity of 'Puritanism' in explanations of developments in seventeenth-century England and beyond when he writes that for the past fifty years some of the 'best minds in both history and the social sciences' have associated 'Puritanism' with 'the rising bourgeoisie, the spirit of capitalism, the scientific revolution and applied technology, political democracy, social egalitarianism, religious toleration, mass literacy and extensive higher education, the conjugal child-centred family, and institutionalised philanthropy for social betterment: in other words, with all the elements which together have been transforming human society over the last two hundred years' (*The Past and the Present* [London 1981], 150).

7 Lawrence Stone, *The Causes of the English Revolution* (London 1972), 98-9

8 The literature in the general area of 'metaphor' is vast and it would not be appropriate to attempt here a bibliography. One work that I have found helpful on the subject, however, and that has influenced my thinking is Colin Murray Turbayne, *The Myth of Metaphor* (Columbia, SC 1970). I am grateful to my colleague Michael Kirkham for this reference.

9 As Turbayne writes, the use of metaphors becomes risky when the author loses sight of the 'as if' quality of his image or model (*Myth*, 4, 6, 46-50). At a symposium held in 1962 to enable philosophers of history and historians to improve communication, the historians tended to be critical of their more speculative colleagues. Bernard Bailyn, however, admitted that there was one area where philo-

sophers might well help historians – in their 'reliance on metaphor' (see Bailyn in Sidney Hook, *Philosophy and History* [New York 1963], 100-1).

10 There are many definitions of 'Puritanism' and few historians shrink from attempting their own, or at least from providing a comprehensive description. What is lacking, however, is a significant agreement on the precise content of this 'Puritanism' over the hundred-year period. This problem is addressed more systematically in chapter 3.

11 Mary F. Keeler, *The Long Parliament, 1640-1* (Philadelphia 1954), 35, 159-60. Compare, for instance, Keeler's treatment of Buckinghamshire and two of its burgesses, the Drake brothers. She refers freely to the fact that 'Puritanism was strong in the shire' and notes that 'both of the Drakes were Puritans.' When she comes to write her brief biographies of the brothers, however, through want of evidence, she can say virtually nothing about the religion of either.

12 David Underdown, *Pride's Purge* (Oxford 1971), 69-71, 404. To label someone a 'Presbyterian' in 1648 is, arguably, to indicate as much about the individual's political views – his attitude to the army, to the Scots, to law and order, to a national church – as about the quality of his piety or of his theology.

13 John Morrill, 'The Church in England, 1642-9,' in John S. Morrill, ed., *Reactions to the English Civil War* (London 1982), 91 (I am grateful to Dr Morrill for giving me access to this article in proof). Elsewhere, Morrill has referred to the establishment of a 'narrow and intransigent anglicanism' as 'one of the most puzzling problems in the whole period.' To explain why the restored Church was so intolerant is, of course, to explain 'what happened to Puritanism' (*Seventeenth Century Britain, 1603-1714* [Folkestone 1980], 68, 75). J.P. Kenyon, not one given to hasty despair, has also confessed himself to be bewildered by this problem: 'But the failure of Parliament to assert itself in 1660 was just one aspect of a general trend which still defies analysis – the collapse of Puritanism' (*Stuart England* [London 1978], 182). Other historians too have addressed the problem of what happened to Puritanism, but their solutions ring with optimism rather than conviction. Lawrence Stone, for instance, in his recent survey of the 'century of upheaval, 1621-1721,' has suggested that 'the wave of religious enthusiasm generated among very wide sections of the population in the 1640's and early 1650's could not have lasted,' adding that 'the result of twenty years' zeal was the spread of worldly cynicism' ('The Results of the English Revolutions of the Seventeenth Century,' in J.G.A. Pocock, ed., *Three British Revolutions: 1641, 1688, 1776* [Princeton 1980], 58-9). William Lamont's preferred metaphor is anatomical rather than nautical but probably no more satisfactory when he observes 'how amputated Calvinism became when it lost its millenarian confidence, and when the Apocalypse was taken over by the political and social extremists of the mid-sevententh century' (*Godly Rule* [London 1969], 181).

14 Recent studies which deal with the problem of the connection between Purita-

nism and Interregnum politics include Blair Worden, *The Rump Parliament 1648-1653* (Cambridge 1974), and Austin Woolrych, *Commonwealth to Protectorate* (Oxford 1982).

15 John Morrill, 'The Diversity of Local History,' in *Historical Journal*, XXIV, 3, 1981, 718. See also Morrill, *Seventeenth Century Britain, 1603-1714*, 14. The scholarly careers of two of the leading historians of seventeenth-century England, who have also written general surveys of the period, illustrate the point. See Christopher Hill, *The Century of Revolution* (Edinburgh 1961) and Kenyon, *Stuart England*. Though both prolific writers, Hill has only occasionally ventured beyond 1660, while Kenyon's work has been largely confined to the period following Charles II's Restoration. Robert Ashton makes a similar point when he writes, 'For some time now it has become relatively unusual for those working in the period before 1660 to push their researches beyond that date, and for those working in the middle decades of the century to make investigations in depth of the period before the 1660s' (*The English Civil War: Conservatism and Revolution, 1603-1649* [London 1978], vii). *Three British Revolutions*, a volume of essays edited by Pocock which deals with the three British revolutions of 1641, 1688, and 1776, reflects a refreshing reaction against this discontinuous model. In particular, Lawrence Stone's interpretive essay, 'The Results,' on English politics in the years 1621 to 1721 illustrates how new meaning can be extracted from a familiar story when the perspective is altered.

16 It was François Guizot in 1826 who first used the expression in his *History of the English Revolution*, but it took Englishmen some time to learn to love the phrase. For a brief discussion see R.C. Richardson, *The Debate on the English Revolution* (London 1977), 64-7.

17 Elsewhere Hill writes, 'The Middle Ages in industry and internal trade also ended in 1641' (Christopher Hill, *Reformation to Industrial Revolution* [London 1967], 123, 135). Writing somewhat less categorically, but nonetheless in essential agreement with Hill, G.E. Aylmer states that '... the late seventeenth century can fairly be called a more modern age than the times of James and Charles I' (*The Struggle for the Constitution* [London 1963], 223). Pocock, ed., *Three British Revolutions*, 4

18 Cited in Melvin J. Lasky, *Utopia and Revolution* (London 1977), 295. J.R. Jones writes: 'At the time of the Restoration it was almost universally thought that now the wheel had turned full circle, bringing back the situation that had existed before the times of 1641-2 that had precipitated the civil war' ('Introduction: Main Trends in Restoration England,' in J.R. Jones, ed., *The Restored Monarchy* [London 1979], 9).

19 Paradoxically, Christopher Hill's recent essay addresses this point while reaching the opposite conclusion. Concerned to reconcile his notion of the 'bourgeois

revolution' with the awkward facts that there was neither a united bourgeois class supporting the revolution nor a 'revolutionary' intent manifested by the revolutionaries, Hill nevertheless cites contemporaries who, during the Interregnum, 'believed that they were passing through an unprecedented crisis.' The paradox lies in the fact that while the principal feature of Hill's historical method has always been his marvellous deployment of contemporary social comment, his central thesis concerning the nature of the English Revolution – its bourgeois character – rests less upon contemporary social self-consciousness than upon his assessment of the kinds of economic relationships that were unwittingly facilitated by the 'revolution.' Thus, Hill considers a class to be 'defined by the objective position of its members in relation to the productive process and to other classes.' Instead of simply asking how contemporaries perceived what were obviously stirring times during the Interregnum, Hill might also have enquired how these events were evaluated a decade or two later ('A Bourgeois Revolution?' in Pocock, ed., *Three British Revolutions*, 109–39).

20 Before our critical faculties are drowned by Stone's 'wave of passionate religious enthusiasm generated among very wide sections of the population in the 1640's and early 1650's,' we must ask precisely which English men and women shared this 'passionate religious enthusiasm,' precisely when did it manifest itself, and at what point did it affect political developments – 1641, 1642, or 1645/6? ('Results,' in Pocock, ed., *Three British Revolutions*, 58).

21 Royce MacGillivray, *Restoration Historians and the English Civil War* (The Hague 1974); Richardson, *The Debate*

22 Stone, 'Results,' in Pocock, ed., *Three British Revolutions*

CHAPTER 2

1 Edward Hyde, Earl of Clarendon, *The History of the Rebellion and Civil Wars in England* (3 vols., Oxford 1702–4; 6 vols., ed. W. Dunn Macray, Oxford 1888). Note that while Clarendon's history was not published until 1702 it was written during two earlier periods, between 1646 and 1648 and 1668 and 1674. George Macaulay Trevelyan, *England under the Stuarts* (1904; London 1928)

2 See, for example, Perez Zagorin, *The Court and the Country* (London 1969), for an account of England's history between 1603 and 1642 that has a great deal in common with Clarendon's or Trevelyan's.

3 Roland G. Usher, 'A Critical Study of the Historical Method of S.R. Gardiner with an Excursus on the Historical Conception of the Puritan Revolution from Clarendon to Gardiner,' in *Washington University Studies*, III, Pt II, 1, 1915, 125, 129, 157

4 H.R. Trevor Roper (now Lord Dacre) has suggested that David Hume relied

more heavily upon Clarendon than has always been thought, writing 'Hume himself was deeply indebted to Clarendon, in his general historical philosophy, in his particular application of it, and even in specific detail' ('Clarendon and the Practice of History,' in French R. Fogle and H.R. Trevor Roper, *Milton and Clarendon: Two Papers on 17th Century Historiography* [Los Angeles 1965], 48).

5 David Hume, *The History of England from the Invasion of Julius Caesar to the Revolution in 1688* (8 vols., London 1763), VI, 255. Trevelyan, *England under the Stuarts*, 159–66

6 Hume, *History*, VI, 358

7 Henry Hallam, *The Constitutional History of England from the Accession of Henry VII to the Death of George II*, (3rd ed., 3 vols., London 1832), II, 129

8 Trevelyan, *England under the Stuarts*, 196

9 Benedetto Croce, *History as the Story of Liberty* (London 1941), 60

10 Hume, *History*, V, 531–2; VII, 151

11 Hallam, *History*, II, 135, 139

12 Trevelyan, *England under the Stuarts*, 2

13 Hume, *History*, V, 531

14 Thomas Babington Macaulay, 'Hallam,' in *Edinburgh Review*, Sept. 1828, reprinted in Macaulay, *Critical and Historical Essays* (Everyman ed., 2 vols., London 1974), I, 3

15 Hallam, *History*, II, 371

16 R.C. Richardson, *The Debate on the English Revolution* (London, 1977), 69–75; Usher, 'Critical Study,' passim

17 Samuel R. Gardiner, *History of the Great Civil War, 1642-1649* (4 vols., London 1893-4), I, 9; Samuel R. Gardiner, *History of England from the Accession of James I to the Outbreak of the Civil War, 1603-42* (10 vols., London 1884), VIII, 246

18 For a stimulating analysis of Clarendon's views on the social character of the Civil War see Christopher Hill, 'Lord Clarendon and the Puritan Revolution,' in his book *Puritanism and Revolution* (London 1958), espec. 204-8.

19 Hume, *History*, VI, 429–30

20 John Lingard, *A History of England from the First Invasion by the Romans to the Revolution in 1688* (8 vols., London 1819-30), VI, 447. In the advertisement Lingard wrote of himself: 'with the exception of a few particular passages, to which his attention has been directed by his friends, he has not read a hundred pages in Hume's history during the last eight years. If the reason be asked, it was because he wished to preclude the possibility of imitation, and to stamp on his own work the features of originality' (viii).

21 Trevelyan, *England under the Stuarts*, 228–9

22 Trevor Roper, 'Clarendon and the Practice of History,' 48; Samuel Rawson Gardiner, *Cromwell's Place in History* (London 1897), 16-18
23 Hume, *History*, V, 531-2
24 Lingard, *History*, VI, 442
25 Ibid., 352
26 For example, see Hallam, *History*, II, 141
27 Ibid., 206
28 Macaulay, *Critical and Historical Essays*, I, 36-7
29 *Oxford English Dictionary*, 1914 ed., see 'revolution.' For a review of some of the literature on this subject see Zagorin, *Court and Country*, chap. 1. See also Vernon Snow, 'The Concept of Revolution in Seventeenth Century England,' *Historical Journal*, V, 2, 1962. For a fine account of the changing meaning of 'revolution' since the Renaissance see Felix Gilbert, 'Revolution,' in *Dictionary of the History of Ideas*, ed. P. Weinz (4 vols., New York 1973), IV, 152-67.
30 Gilbert Burnet, *Sermon* (London 1681), 30
31 Anon., *Considerations on the Nature of Parliaments and our Present Elections* (London 1689), 1
32 Declaration of Breda, printed in Carl Stephenson and Frederick George Marcham, *Sources of English Constitutional History* (New York and London 1937), 533
33 *Diurnal of Thomas Rugg, 1659-61*, ed. William L. Sachse, Camden Society, 3rd Ser., XCI, 1961, 1
34 *Seasonable and Healing Instructions* (London 1660)
35 William Cobbett, ed., *The Parliamentary History of England* (*1066-1803*) (36 vols., London 1806-20), IV, 22
36 Hume, *History*, V, 531
37 Ibid., VI, 309, 358
38 Ibid., 291, 300; VII, 156, 136
39 Ibid., VII, 357-8
40 Ibid., VI, 314, 358
41 Hallam, *History*, II, 515, 371-2
42 Ibid., 397, 133, 425, 138-40
43 Ibid., 206
44 F. Guizot, *History of the English Revolution of 1640*, trans. William Hazlitt (London 1846), preface to the first ed., ix, xii. For some interesting observations on the way in which nineteenth-century English historians changed their approach to the English Civil War see P.B.M. Blaas, *Continuity and Anachronism: Parliamentary and Constitutional Development in Whig Historiography and in the Anti-Whig Reaction between 1890 and 1930* (The Hague 1978), passim.

45 Cited in review by Douglas Johnson of Melvin J. Lasky, *Utopia and Revolution* (London 1977), in *New Statesman*, 11 Feb. 1977, 190

46 Gardiner, again like many modern scholars, was not totally at ease writing such works. In the preface to *The First Two Stuarts and the Puritan Revolution, 1602-60* (London 1876), when he had barely reached the mid-point of his work, he apologized for having to depend upon the researches of others for anything he had to say after 1634 (vi).

47 Gardiner, *History of England*, X. vii, viii; Samuel R. Gardiner, ed., *The Constitutional Documents of the Puritan Revolution, 1628-60* (Oxford 1889), xiv

48 Gardiner, ed., *Documents*, xxxiv, xiii

49 Gardiner, *First Two Stuarts*, 7

50 Gardiner, *Cromwell's Place in History*, 1-2

51 Samuel R. Gardiner and James B. Mullinger, *Introduction to the Study of English History* (London 1881), 129, 163

52 Gardiner, ed., *Documents*, xxxii, xli, lxvi, xiv

53 Gardiner, *Introduction to the Study of English History*, 165

54 Gardiner, ed., *Documents*, lxvi, xiii, xiv

55 What is implicit in Gardiner's scholarship is made quite explicit by J.R. Green. Green commenced his chapter on 1660-88 as follows: 'The entry of Charles the Second into Whitehall marked a deep and lasting change in the temper of the English people. With it modern England began' (*A Short History of the English People* [London 1893], III, 1286).

56 Christopher Hill, ed., *The English Revolution 1640* (London 1940; rev. ed. 1949)

57 Christopher Hill, *Change and Continuity in Seventeenth Century England* (London 1974), 279. For a more recent statement of Hill's view of the English Civil War see 'A Bourgeois Revolution?' in J.G.A. Pocock, ed., *Three British Revolutions: 1641, 1688, 1776* (Princeton 1980), 109-40.

58 Christopher Hill and Edmund Dell, eds., *The Good Old Cause* (London 1949), 19

59 Hill, *English Revolution*, 13, 14, 37

60 Hill, *Change and Continuity*, 279. Hill, 'A Bourgeois Revolution?' 111

61 Hill, *English Revolution*, 37

62 Hill wrote in the early 1970s that 'the historian in recognizing the existence of continuity is not, or should not be, denying the fact of change: he should rather emphasize its dialectical character' (*Change and Continuity*, 278).

63 Christopher Hill, *Economic Problems of the Church from Archbishop Whitgift to the Long Parliament* (Oxford 1956), 341, 344

64 Hill, *Puritanism and Revolution*, 24

65 Hill, *Economic Problems*, 352

66 Ibid., 345
67 Hill, *Change and Continuity*, 279-81
68 See above, n18.
69 Hill, *English Revolution*, 14
70 Hill, *Change and Continuity*, 278
71 C. Hill, *The Century of Revolution* (Edinburgh 1961), 222. Hill, 'A Bourgeois Revolution?' 126-7
72 Lawrence Stone, 'Theories of Revolution,' reprinted in his *The Causes of the English Revolution* (London 1972), 3-25. Perez Zagorin, 'Theories of Revolution in Contemporary Historiography,' *Political Science Quarterly*, LXXXVIII, 1, 1973
73 G.E. Aylmer, *The Struggle for the Constitution* (London 1963), 2
74 Ibid., 139, 167, 168, 165
75 Cited in Stone, *Causes of the English Revolution*, 48-9
76 Ibid., 49, 52-3. Elsewhere Stone has repeated his view that events from 1640 to 1660 constituted 'England's only "Great Revolution" and the first in the history of Western civilisation since the Fall of Rome,' adding that they were 'by any standards a major earthquake which brought crashing to the ground most of the key buildings of the old regime' ('The Results of the English Revolutions in the Seventeenth Century,' in Pocock, ed., *Three British Revolutions*, 24). The problems involved in locating precisely England's 'revolution' are addressed by both Professors Christianson and Hexter in their recent exchange (Paul Christianson, 'The Causes of the English Revolution: a Reappraisal,' *Journal of British Studies*, XV, 2, 1976, 46-9; Paul Christianson, 'The Peers, the People, and Parliamentary Management in the First Six Months of the Long Parliament,' *Journal of Modern History*, XLIX, 1977, esp. 575, 599; J.H. Hexter, 'Power Struggle, Parliament, and Liberty in Early Stuart England,' *Journal of Modern History*, L, 1, 1978, esp. 12-15).
77 L. Stone, *The Crisis of the Aristocracy* (Oxford 1965), 15; Stone, 'Results,' 23-4
78 Zagorin, *Court and Country*, 6
79 Perez Zagorin, 'Prolegomena to the Comparative History of Revolution in Early Modern Europe,' *Comparative Studies in Society and History*, XVIII, 2, 1976, 165, 172-3. Zagorin defines 'revolution' as 'any attempt by subordinate groups through the use of violence to bring about 1. a change of government or its policy, 2. a change of regime or 3. a change of society, whether this attempt is justified by reference to past conditions or to an as yet unattained future ideal.'
80 H.R. Trevor Roper, 'The General Crisis of the Seventeenth Century,' in Trevor Henry Aston, ed., *Crisis in Europe, 1560-1660* (London 1965), 62
81 J.H. Elliott, 'Revolution and Continuity in Early Modern Europe,' *Past and Present*, no 42, 1969, esp. 40-3
82 Guizot, *History of the English Revolution*, xx, xvii

83 G.R. Elton, 'A High Road to Civil War?' in Charles H. Carter, ed., *From the Renaissance to the Counter-Reformation: Essays in Honour of Garrett Mattingly* (London 1966); J.R. Jones, *The Revolution of 1688 in England* (London 1972)

84 Elton, 'A High Road to Civil War,' 341

85 Jones, *Revolution of 1688*, 10, 331; George Macaulay Trevelyan, *The English Revolution* (London 1938)

86 See, for example, Conrad Russell, *Parliaments and English Politics, 1621-29* (Oxford 1979); Kevin Sharpe, ed., *Faction and Parliament* (Oxford 1978); Christianson, 'The Causes of the English Revolution'; Christianson, 'The Peers, the People and Parliamentary Management,' 575; John Gruenfelder, 'The Electoral Patronage of Sir Thomas Wentworth, Earl of Strafford, 1614-40,' *Journal of Modern History*, XLIX, 4, 1977; Mark Kishlansky, 'The Emergence of Adversary Politics in the Long Parliament,' *Journal of Modern History*, XLIX, 4, 1977; Clayton Roberts, 'The Earl of Bedford and the Coming of the English Revolution,' *Journal of Modern History*, XLIX, 4, 1977; J.H. Hexter, 'Power Struggle,' 47

87 Alan Everitt, *Change in the Provinces: the Seventeenth Century* (Leicester 1969), 6

88 See, for instance, Alan Everitt, *The Community of Kent and the Great Rebellion, 1640-1690* (Leicester 1966); John S. Morrill, *Cheshire, 1630-1660: County Government and Society during the English Revolution* (Oxford 1974); Anthony Fletcher, *A County Community in Peace and War: Sussex 1600-1660* (London 1975).

89 Everitt, *Community of Kent*, 327

90 Morrill, *Cheshire, 1630-1660*, 330-2

91 Chalmers Johnson, *Revolutionary Change* (London 1968), 138

92 Stone, *Causes of the English Revolution*, 48

93 Everitt, *Community of Kent*, 326

94 Hill, *Change and Continuity*, 278

95 Thomas S. Kuhn, *The Structure of Scientific Revolutions* (Chicago 1962), 10

96 Ibid., 93, 24

97 G.R. Elton addressed precisely this point in his presidential remarks to the Royal Historical Society in 1977. Defending the proposition that the historian's 'social function' lies in his commitment to the idea of history as the most system-free of all disciplines, Elton argued that while 'developed interpretive frameworks are a dominant feature in practically every intellectual enterprise,' history, the discipline he himself practises with such distinction, is different, and therein lies its importance to the cause of freedom. 'Interpretive frameworks,' he insisted, 'are, or they should be, totally absent from history' ('The Historian's Social

Function,' *Transactions of the Royal Historical Society*, 5th ser., XXVII, 1977, 208).

98 Colin Murray Turbayne, *The Myth of Metaphor* (Columbia, SC 1970), 3. For an interesting analysis of the relevance of Kuhn to the study of political revolution see I. Kramnick, 'Reflections on Revolution: Definition and Explanation in Recent Scholarship,' *History and Theory*, XI, 1, 1972, esp. 32-3. For a discussion of the applicability of Kuhn's notion of the development of scientific paradigms to the work of historians of the United States see the review of Gene Wise, *American Historical Explanations* (2nd ed., Minneapolis 1980), by Paul F. Bourke in *History and Theory*, XXII, 1983, 64-74.

99 David Hackett Fischer, *Historians' Fallacies* (London 1971), 245

100 Everitt, *Change in the Provinces*, 6

CHAPTER 3

1 Christopher Hill, *The Century of Revolution* (Edinburgh 1961), 187, 190; Christopher Hill, *Some Intellectual Consequences of the English Revolution* (London 1980), 29

2 T.S. Eliot, 'The Metaphysical Poets,' in *Selected Essays, 1917-32* (London 1932), 247

3 S.L. Bethell, *The Cultural Revolution of the Seventeenth Century* (London 1951), 13, 99

4 For examples of historians to whom 'Puritanism' provides an essential element in the explanation of one or other of these modern phenomena see R.H. Tawney, *Religion and the Rise of Capitalism* (London 1926); Christopher Hill, *Society and Puritanism in Pre-Revolutionary England* (London 1964); Lawrence Stone, *The Family, Sex and Marriage in England, 1500-1800* (London 1977); for a useful discussion of the issue and for a review of some of the earlier literature see Leo F. Solt, 'Puritanism, Capitalism, Democracy and the New Science,' *American Historical Review*, LXXIII, 1967, 18-29. See also chap. 1, n6, above.

5 Lawrence Stone, 'The Results of the English Revolutions in the Seventeenth Century,' in J.G.A. Pocock, ed., *Three British Revolutions: 1641, 1688, 1776* (Princeton 1980), 58

6 See, for example, J.H. Plumb, *The Growth of Political Stability 1675-1725* (London 1967). It may be objected that the phenomenon of 'dissent' is invariably included in any historical explanation of the Industrial Revolution and that I am thus exaggerating the difference between pre- and post-Restoration historians. As I argue below, the way historians handle 'dissent' is fundamentally different from the way they handle 'Puritanism': the former constitutes the religious persuasion of a small and identifiable group whereas the latter is supposedly a

widely experienced phenomenon which, in a fundamental way, energized change. For the modest role of religious factors in modern explanations of the Industrial Revolution see, for example, R.M. Hartwell, ed., *The Causes of the Industrial Revolution in England* (London 1967).

7 One of the difficulties confronting the modern student of 'Puritanism' derives from the tendency by scholars to assume its existence and their inability to agree with each other on what 'Puritanism' is. For a sampling from the literature which illustrates the problem see Leonard J. Trinterud, 'The Origins of Puritanism,' in *Church History*, XX, 1951, 37-57; Basil Hall, 'Puritanism: the Problem of Definition,' *Studies in Church History*, II, 1965, 283-96; Christopher Hill, *Society and Puritanism in Pre-Revolutionary England* (London 1964), chap. 1; Charles H. and Katherine George, *The Protestant Mind of the English Reformation, 1570-1640* (Princeton 1961); John F.H. New, *Puritan and Anglican* (London 1964); 'Puritanism: a Panel,' *Church History*, XXIII, 1954, 99-129; J. Sears McGee, *The Godly Man in Stuart England* (New Haven 1976); T.H. Clancy, 'Papist – Protestant – Puritan: English Religious Taxonomy 1565-1665,' *Recusant History*, XIII, 4, 1976, 227-53. For an illuminating discussion of the problem of Puritanism in the religious history of England between 1560 and 1642 see Paul Christianson, 'Reformers and the Church of England under Elizabeth I and the Early Stuarts,' *Journal of Ecclesiastical History*, XXXI, 4, 1980, 463-82. For a criticism of Christianson and for a comment on what the author regards as a North American propensity to engage in 'exercises in orienteering' whereby taxonomy is elevated 'to a point where it almost replaces history' see Patrick Collinson, 'A Comment: Concerning the Name Puritan,' *Journal of Ecclesiastical History*, XXXI, 4, 1980, 486. See also Paul Seaver to whom it is incontestable that 'in the sermons preached from hundreds of Puritan pulpits that the Puritan ideology was set forth in its totality' (*The Puritan Lecturerships: the Politics of Religious Dissent, 1560-1662* [Stanford 1970], 5). See also chap. 4, n15, below.

8 David Underdown, *Pride's Purge* (Oxford 1971). J.R. Jones, *The First Whigs* (London 1970)

9 Underdown, *Pride's Purge*, 8, 15, 63, 233-4, 353

10 Ibid., 353

11 Jones, *First Whigs*, 10

12 What is true of Jones' study of the Exclusion Crisis is even more apparent in his later survey of late Stuart England (*Country and Court* [Cambridge, Mass. 1978], esp. chap. 1).

13 Underdown, *Pride's Purge*, 59; Jones, *The First Whigs*, 12, 35. In explaining why the moderate political group led by Holles lost its leadership role in the opposition, Jones writes that they represented 'the older generation and a pattern of politics which was rapidly becoming obsolete ... [because] ... they still placed

much greater emphasis on purely religious issues than [Shaftesbury] did.' For a recent biography of Holles see Patricia Crawford, *Denzil Holles, 1598-1680* (London 1979).

14 The assumption that underlies this discussion is that whenever 'Puritanism' is employed by historians, notwithstanding its political or socio-economic associations, it signifies something religious – it labels a set of beliefs that presupposed that men and women were dependent upon and ultimately required to obey and worship a higher being, and that their ultimate well-being depended upon the extent to which they succeeded in pleasing this higher being, that is, God.

15 In the seventeenth century scholars began to worry about defining a Puritan. It was not until a couple of centuries had passed that they focused upon the more difficult question concerning 'Puritanism.' See, for example, Henry Parker, *A Discourse Concerning Puritans* (London 1641), esp. 15-17; C. Hill, *Society and Puritanism*, chap. 1, which provides the best available survey of the contemporary usage of 'Puritan.'

16 See Patrick Collinson, *The Elizabethan Puritan Movement* (London 1967), 78 and Parts 1-3 generally.

17 Parker, *Discourse*, 13

18 Edward Hyde, Earl of Clarendon, *The History of the Rebellion and Civil Wars in England* (1702-4; 6 vols., ed. W. Dunn Macray, Oxford 1888); Thomas Hobbes, *Behemoth or the Long Parliament*, ed. Ferdinand Tönnies (2nd ed., with intro. by M.M. Goldsmith, London 1969); David Hume, *The History of England from the Invasion of Julius Caesar to the Revolution in 1688* (8 vols., London 1763)

19 Lucy Hutchinson, *Memoirs of the Life of Colonel Hutchinson* (Everyman edition, London 1908; reprinted in 1968); Richard Baxter, *Reliquiae Baxterianae* (London 1696); Daniel Neal, *The History of the Puritans or Protestant Nonconformists, from the Reformation to the Act of Toleration* (4 vols., London 1732-8)

20 John Lingard, *A History of England from the First Invasion by the Romans to the Revolution in 1688* (8 vols., London 1819-30); Henry Hallam, *The Constitutional History of England from the Accession of Henry VII to the Death of George II* (3rd ed., 3 vols., London 1832); Thomas Babington Macaulay, *History of England* (3 vols., London 1858)

21 Hobbes, *Behemoth*, 20, 23, 26, 46, 95

22 Ibid., 3-4, 88-9

23 Ibid., 116/17

24 Clarendon, *History*, II, 70

25 Ibid., I, 93, 122-3

26 Ibid., I, 244, 250

27 Ibid., I, 265-6
28 Ibid., I, 269; II, 319-20
29 Ibid., I, 308, 387; II, 70
30 Hobbes, *Behemoth*, 62
31 Clarendon, *History*, I, 401, 442; II, 250, 321-2; Hobbes, *Behemoth*, 55-6
32 Hume, *History*, VI, 325
33 There are exceptions, of course, as for instance when he describes the 'thorough-paced puritans.' These were 'distinguishable by the sourness and austerity of their manners, and by their aversion to all pleasure and society.' Ibid., V, 158, 161; VI, 211, 237, 301
34 Ibid,. VI, 421, 325n, 381, 430. See also R.C. Richardson, *The Debate on the English Revolution* (London 1977), 43ff.
35 Hume, *History*, VI, 140-1, 429, 433, 302, 421n
36 Hutchinson, *Memoirs*, 55, 6
37 Ibid., 4
38 Ibid., 4, 59
39 Ibid., 39-40, 61-71 passim
40 Ibid., 64-5, 31-2, 56, 63-5, 21
41 Ibid., 65, 233, 242
42 Ibid., 80, 269
43 The Test Act, he wrote, was a hardship both 'upon those gentlemen, whose manner of life hardly declares their unfitness for so sacred a solemnity' but are obliged politically to take the sacrament, and also for the dissenters. Neal, *History*, I, x; see also II, viii.
44 Thomas Fuller, *The Church History of Britain*, ed. J.S. Brewer (6 vols., Oxford 1845), IV, 327-31
45 Neal, *History*, I, vi, 230, 108, 240
46 Ibid., II, iv-vi
47 Ibid., II, 361-2, vi, 429
48 Ibid., II, 470-3, 434
49 Ibid., III, x; II, 595
50 Hume, *History*, VI, 213
51 Baxter, *Reliquiae Baxterianae*, 18. See also William M. Lamont, *Richard Baxter and the Millennium: Protestant Imperialism and the English Revolution* (London 1979), 24. Lamont writes 'like many Protestant Englishmen [Baxter] was more concerned about Popery than about the Petition of Right, and it was by reading Revelation right that the Popish Plot could be defeated.' For Lamont's views on Baxter's explanation for the Civil War see his *Baxter*, chap. 2 passim.
52 Lingard, *History*, VI, 237-8, 359, 380-1, 494
53 Hallam, *History*, II, 77-8, 228, 106, 270

54 Ibid., 75-6, 157-8, 163, 225, 237, 269
55 Macaulay, *History of England*, I, 60-1, 82, 103
56 Ibid., I, 117, 122, 124
57 See, generally, Thomas Carlyle, ed., *Oliver Cromwell's Letters and Speeches* (3rd ed., 4 vols., London 1897); Samuel R. Gardiner, *History of England from the Accession of James I to the Outbreak of the Civil War, 1603-42* (10 vols., London 1884); S.R. Gardiner, 'Introduction to English History,' in Samuel R. Gardiner and James B. Mullinger, *Introduction to the Study of English History* (London 1881); Samuel R. Gardiner, *Cromwell's Place in History* (London 1897); Samuel R. Gardiner, ed., *The Constitutional Documents of the Puritan Revolution 1628-60* (Oxford 1889); Samuel R. Gardiner, *History of the Great Civil War, 1642-1649* (4 vols., London 1893-4).
58 Carlyle, ed., *Cromwell's Letters and Speeches*, I, 6, 1, 39, 51. One historian has described Carlyle as having 'revolutionised the image of Cromwell for the nineteenth century.' See P.B.M. Blaas, *Continuity and Anachronism: Parliamentary and Constitutional Development in Whig Historiography and in the Whig Reaction between 1890 and 1930* (The Hague 1978), 145. See also the remarks on Carlyle and Macaulay in J.R. Hale, ed., *The Evolution of British Historiography* (Macmillan 1964). Hale describes Carlyle as 'the most passionately subjective of all English historians' (*Evolution*, 40). See also J.P.D. Dunbabin, 'Oliver Cromwell's Popular Image in Nineteenth-Century England,' in J.S. Bromley and E.H. Kossmann, eds, *Britain and the Netherlands*, V, 1975, 151, 153-5.
59 Gardiner, *Civil War*, I, 9-10
60 Gardiner, *History of England*, I, 178-9, 186
61 Gardiner, *History of England*, VII, 123, 128; *Civil War*, I, 256-7
62 Gardiner, *History of England*, I, 28-9, 31, 38; VII, 153
63 Ibid., VII, 11
64 Ibid., IX, 85, 79; Gardiner, *Civil War*, I, 9
65 Gardiner, *History of England*, VIII, 302; IX, 129
66 Ibid., IX, 121, 264, 409, 288, 157-8
67 Ibid., IX, 269; X, 141, 208
68 Ibid., VII, 36; in a note on Pym's religious views Gardiner writes: 'Pym is frequently spoken of as a statesman for whom religious questions had only a secondary interest. I believe this view of his character to be incompatible with his course in the early Parliaments.' See also chap. 4, n6, below.
69 Gardiner, *Civil War*, I, 1, 4 n2
70 See also J.W. Allen, *English Political Thought, 1603-60* (London 1938), esp. 143ff; George, *The Protestant Mind*, esp. 6-8, 363-72; C.H. George, 'Puritanism as History and Historiography,' *Past and Present*, 41, Dec. 1968, 77-104.
71 Hill, *Society and Puritanism*, chap. 1 passim, esp. 16-17, 24, 28-9; Hill, *Century*

of Revolution, 106. I am grateful to Dr J.K. Graham for drawing my attention to Widdowes' observation.

72 *The Works of Francis Bacon*, ed. James Spedding et al. (14 vols., London 1857-74), XIV, 448-9

73 Christianson, 'Reformers,' 481; Collinson, 'A Comment,' 487-8

74 Hill, *Society and Puritanism*, 9, 13, 14 n3

75 New, *Anglican*, 110. J. Sears McGee, concentrating on the period 1620-70, agrees fundamentally with New. Though Anglicans and Puritans 'thought of themselves as heirs of the orthodox Protestant tradition in England,' nevertheless they espoused 'distinct value systems' which provided important clues to our understanding 'the central conflict of seventeenth century England' (*The Godly Man*, 12, 14, 238); Hill, *Society and Puritanism*, 503

76 New, *Anglican*, 105; McGee, *The Godly Man*, 4. The logic of both historians here is fundamentally circular. To deny the importance of Puritanism, they argue, is to make nonsense of the Puritan Revolution, which concept is premised upon the importance of Puritanism. I. Breward seems to be making the same point when, in criticizing C.H. George for attempting to 'abolish Puritanism,' he writes that far from being abolished, Puritanism will be reinstated 'as an important factor in the causation of the civil war' (I. Breward, 'The Abolition of Puritanism,' *Journal of Religious History*, VII, 1, 1972, 34). For an interesting discussion of the logical problems involved in the use of metaphors like 'Puritanism' as heuristic devices see C. Mason Myers, 'The Circular Use of Metaphor,' *Philosophy and Phenomenological Research*, XXVI, 3, 1966, 391-402, esp. 391-3.

77 William Haller, *The Rise of Puritanism* (New York 1938), 17-18. William Haller, *Liberty and Reformation in the Puritan Revolution* (New York 1955), xiv

78 Seaver, *The Puritan Lectureships*, 4, 7. For another approach to the problem see Timothy Hall Breen, 'The Non-Existent Controversy: Puritan and Anglican Attitudes on Work and Wealth, 1600-1640,' *Church History*, XXXV, 1966, 273-87.

79 As Patrick Collinson has observed, to use 'Anglicanism' to label the position of the Established Church between 1560 and 1640 is anachronistic and the quotation marks used here and elsewhere in the work are designed to suggest as much. The term is used here, albeit in quotation marks, because many historians referred to persist in employing it. For the importance of Bullinger in the theological tradition of the Elizabethan and Jacobean Established Church see P. Christianson, 'Reformers,' passim; P. Collinson, 'A Comment,' passim.

80 A.S.P. Woodhouse, ed., *Puritanism and Liberty* (London 1951), [35, 37]

81 N. Tyacke, 'Puritanism, Arminianism and Counter-Revolution,' in C. Russell, *The Origins of the English Civil War* (London 1973), 119, 121

82 Hill, *Century of Revolution*, 83-4; Michael Walzer, *The Revolution of the Saints* (Cambridge, Mass. 1965), 211-12

83 In this connection note Woodhouse's celebrated distinction between Puritanism of the right, of the centre, and of the left (*Puritanism*, [16-17]). See also A.E. Barker, *Milton and the Puritan Dilemma 1641-60* (Toronto 1976), 19-24.

84 For a fuller discussion of this point see M.G. Finlayson, 'Puritanism and Puritans: Labels or Libels,' *Canadian Journal of History*, VIII, 3, 1973, 201-23.

85 Anthony Fletcher, *A County Community in Peace and War: Sussex 1600-1660* (London 1975), 124; Anthony Fletcher, *The Outbreak of the English Civil War* (London 1981), XXIV, 25, 26, 59, 38, 130. A similar acceptance of an 'essential dichotomy' between 'Puritanism' and 'Arminianism' underlines Fletcher's recent study of religious factionalism before the Civil War even though the author recognizes that 'the enforcement of Arminianism was provocative even where no more than a moderate protestantism was the established creed.' Thus Dr Fletcher describes the merchants of Chichester as 'Puritan' even though their resentment of 'Arminianism' would seem to be evidence less of a concern to 'erect the New Jerusalem' than an erastian concern to protect the old Protestant society and their place in it ('Factionalism in Town and Countryside: the Significance of Puritanism and Arminianism,' *Studies in Church History*, XVI, 1979, 294, 299, 300).

86 John S. Morrill, *The Revolt of the Provinces* (London 1976), 47

87 Ibid., 50

88 John S. Morrill, *Cheshire, 1630-1660: County Government and Society during the English Revolution* (Oxford 1974), 71

CHAPTER 4

1 Stone defines Puritanism as 'a generalized conviction of the need for independent judgement based on a conscience and Bible reading.' See Lawrence Stone, *The Causes of the English Revolution* (London 1972), 99, 103.

2 Ibid., 103, 116

3 Mary F. Keeler, *The Long Parliament, 1640-1* (Philadelphia 1954), 13

4 Ibid., 33, 122-3, 261-2, 330

5 Ibid., 12-13

6 J.H. Hexter, *The Reign of King Pym* (Camb., Mass. 1941), 97, 200-1. For an interesting analysis of Pym's consistent anti-popery see Conrad Russell, 'The Parliamentary Career of John Pym, 1621-9,' in P. Clark, A.G.R. Smith, N. Tyacke, eds., *The English Commonwealth, 1547-1640: Essays in Politics and Society presented to Joel Hurstfield* (Leicester 1979), 151-2. Russell writes: 'Pym was, from the beginning of his parliamentary career, one of those who believed the world was a perpetual struggle between the forces of good and evil, of Christ and Antichrist, a battle in which there was no resolution short of final victory.'

7 Anthony Fletcher, *The Outbreak of the English Civil War* (London 1981), 36, 38, 370, 374

8 Robert E. Ruigh, *The Parliament of 1624* (Camb., Mass. 1971), 3, 239, 241-2, 187

9 Ibid., 160-1, 177-8

10 Robert Zaller, *The Parliament of 1621* (Berkeley and Los Angeles 1971), 131

11 C. Russell, *Parliaments and English Politics, 1621-1629* (Oxford 1979), 26-32, 164

12 Kevin Sharpe, ed., *Faction and Parliament* (Oxford 1978), 23. See also chap. 2, n86.

13 G.S.S. Yule, 'The Puritan Piety of Members of the Long Parliament,' in G.J. Cuming and Derek Baker, eds., *Popular Belief and Practice* (Studies in Church History, vol. 8; Cambridge 1972), 187, 191-3; George Yule, *Puritans in Politics* (Appleford 1981), 106

14 Yule, 'The Puritan Piety,' 188-90. When Professor Yule cites Pym's and Holles' statements in 1640/1 indicating their concern for church reform as evidence of their 'Puritanism,' he is making too little of the distinction between contemporaries who wished to purge the Laudian church of its recent innovations and thus restore the church to its pre-Laudian, reformed state and those who wished to complete the task of Reformation aborted at the beginning of Elizabeth's reign. Furthermore, in his consideration of the Root and Branch Bill of 1641, Yule sees it as having been more divisive than it was. According to Fletcher, there was widespread support for the bill, partly to put pressure on the House of Lords to accept the Bishops' Exclusion Bill. This would imply that support for Root and Branch was not synonymous with 'Puritanism' unless the entire House of Commons was 'Puritan.' Yule, *Puritans in Politics*, esp. 16-17, 106-7, 111-14; Fletcher, *The Outbreak*, 102-3. With Yule's book compare John S. Morrill, 'The Church in England, 1642-9,' in John S. Morrill, ed., *Reactions to the English Civil War* (London 1982).

15 Patrick Collinson, *The Elizabethan Puritan Movement* (London 1967), 27; A.S.P. Woodhouse, ed., *Puritanism and Liberty* (London 1951), [37]. To William Lamont the 'common denominator' of revolutionary Puritanism lay 'in a chiliastic expectation of the downfall of Antichrist; in the identification of Antichrist with episcopacy; in the reforming zeal with which men set about the task of building a New Jerusalem' ('Puritanism as History and Historiography: Some Further Thoughts,' *Past and Present*, no 44, 1969, 144). Yule writes that 'Puritans saw themselves primarily in terms of reformers and the definition they gave themselves was in terms of reform' (*Puritans in Politics*, 16-17). Paul Christianson's definition of 'Puritan,' which includes only those reformers within the Established Church who wanted 'ministerial parity and a severely attenuated

liturgy,' seems arbitrary both for its exclusion of Separatists and for its concentration on two issues which, for all of their importance, fail to do justice to the diversity of the aims of would-be church reformers over eighty years. As soon as one proposes a definition of 'Puritanism' that moves from the genus to the species – that includes both the disposition to reform the church as well as specifying more precisely which particular reforms were intended – one becomes open to Collinson's strictures that such 'laboratory-bench taxonomy' risks oversimplifying an 'unstable and dynamic situation.' Paul Christianson, 'Reformers and the Church of England under Elizabeth I and the Early Stuarts,' *Journal of Ecclesiastical History*, XXXI, 4, 1980, 481; Patrick Collinson, 'A Comment: Concerning the Name Puritan,' *Journal of Ecclesiastical History*, XXXI, 4, 1980, 488.

16 See, for example, Richard Baxter, *Reliquiae Baxterianae* (London 1696), 2-3, 31; Lucy Hutchinson, *Memoirs of the Life of Colonel Hutchinson* (1908; London 1968), 56, 63, 242.

17 John Rushworth, *Historical Collection of Private Passages of State, Weighty Matters in Law, Remarkable Proceedings in Five Parliaments (1618-29)* (8 vols., London 1682-1701), I, 53; J.R. Tanner, *Constitutional Documents of the Reign of James I, 1603-25* (London 1960), 288-94. Conrad Russell, in challenging the milestones approach of constitutional historians to the history of Parliament from 1603 and earlier to 1642, has, I believe, underestimated both the magnitude of the confrontation in December 1621 and the significance of anti-Catholicism throughout the Parliament. In his desire to stress the propensity of parliamentarians to see the court not as the enemy, but as a route to political success, he has emphasized their essential timidity in the days before the dissolution of this Parliament, and, in so doing, has ignored the implications of the fact that the Petition and the subsequent Declaration were statements approved by the House. Furthermore, he pays too little attention to the implications of James' and Buckingham's reaction to these two statements. The fact that the statements were passed, that Parliament subsequently was dissolved without the second subsidy being approved, that those judged responsible were punished – none of this seems compatible with Russell's central proposition that, in general, 'the story of 1621 and 1624 suggests that not very much was wrong with relations between Crown and Parliament.' Russell, *Parliaments*, 4, 120, 132-44, 419. To Russell's judgment of the December Declaration that it was 'a powerless piece of paper, a last vain protest by a dying Parliament,' compare Zaller's remark that 'Parliament was attempting to create a new system,' and Stephen White's suggestion that the Protestation represented 'an extreme position on the issue of the Commons' privileges.' Russell, *Parliaments*, 142; Zaller, *The Parliament of 1621*, 180; Stephen D. White, *Sir Edward Coke and 'The Grievances of the Commonwealth,' 1621-1628* (Chapel Hill, NC 1979), 179

18 Wallace Notestein and Frances Helen Relf, eds., *Commons Debates for 1629* (Minneapolis 1921), 103 [hereafter *CD 1629*]

19 For an excellent and recent account of the politics of the early Long Parliament see Fletcher, *The Outbreak*.

20 Wallace Notestein, Frances Helen Relf, Hartley Simpson, eds., *Commons Debates, 1621* (7 vols., New Haven 1935), II, 10, 88 [hereafter *CD 1621*]

21 J.P. Cooper, ed., *Wentworth Papers, 1597-1628* (Camden Fourth Series, vol. 12; London [1973]), 153; *CD 1621*, II, 407. See also Russell, *Parliaments*, 21.

22 *CD 1621*, II, 17, 37-8

23 *Journals of the House of Commons* (17 vols., 1803), I, 519 [hereafter *CJ*]

24 Zaller, *Parliament of 1621*, 104

25 *CJ*, I, 600-1; *CD 1621*, II, 335

26 *Journals of the House of Lords* (18 vols., 1767), III, 134 [hereafter *LJ*]; *CD 1621*, II, 335. Zaller, *Parliament of 1621*, 104-15

27 *CD 1621*, II, 406-8, 428; V, 203-4

28 Ibid., 434-7

29 Ibid., 440-1, 447, 451 note g

30 Ibid., 446-8

31 See generally Margaret Atwood Judson, *The Crisis of the Constitution: an Essay in Constitutional and Political Thought in England, 1603-1645* (New Brunswick 1949). As they reject the fundamentally whiggish assumptions of Judson and many others, Conrad Russell and Kevin Sharpe have to be careful not to throw out the baby as well as the bath water. For a sharp statement of the conventional interpretation of the implications of the pre-1640 political conflicts in England see J.H. Hexter, 'Power Struggle, Parliament, and Liberty in Early Stuart England,' *Journal of Modern History*, L, 1, 1978, 1-50.

32 Rushworth, *Historical Collection*, I, 42-3

33 *CD 1621*, II, 488; VI, 332-9; V, 410-19. Rushworth, *Historical Collection*, I, 42

34 Rushworth, *Historical Collection*, I, 42. For a fuller discussion of the idea of the beleaguered nation see Carol Z. Wiener, 'The Beleaguered Isle: A Study of Elizabethan and Early Jacobean Anti-Catholicism,' *Past and Present*, no 51, May 1971, 27-62.

35 *CD 1621*, II, 448-9, 488-9, 491. This Thomas Wentworth is, of course, to be distinguished from the other cited above, who later achieved fame as the Earl of Strafford.

36 Rushworth, *Historical Collection*, I, 40-1

37 S.L. Adams has recently written: 'The debate was conducted between men who saw contemporary events as part of a pattern of Protestant apocalyptical history and men who, fearing the revolutionary implications of such an ideology, sought a policy more conducive to the stability of the political and social status quo'

('Foreign Policy and the Parliaments of 1621 and 1626,' in Sharpe, ed., *Faction and Parliament*, 140).

38 *CD 1621*, II, 456-7

39 See, for example, Frances H. Relf, *The Petition of Right* (University of Minnesota, Studies in the Social Sciences, no 8; Minneapolis 1917); George L. Mosse, *The Struggle for Sovereignty in England from the Reign of Queen Elizabeth to the Petition of Right* (East Lansing 1950); and also Sharpe, ed., *Faction and Parliament*; Russell, *Parliament*.

40 Robert C. Johnson et al., eds., *Commons Debates, 1628* (4 vols., New Haven 1977-8), II, 61-2 [hereafter *CD 1628*]; *CD 1629*, 18, 112, 247; *CJ*, I, 922

41 In his biography of William Prynne, for example, William L. Lamont writes: 'Prynne stands apart from his fellow Puritans by his lack of introspective curiosity. Less is known about Prynne's personal life than almost any other public figure of the time' (*Marginal Prynne – 1600-1669* [Toronto 1963], 12). See also Harold Hulme, *The Life of Sir John Eliot, 1592-1632: a Struggle for Parliamentary Freedom* (New York 1957), 355-8. The evidence that Hulme presents of Eliot's 'Puritanism' is quite slight. It suggests Eliot became religiously preoccupied at about the same time as he was first incarcerated. Nor is his 'piety' distinctive: 'Anglicans' too, in the 1630s, often believed themselves to live in the presence of God. Similarly Patricia Crawford, in her biography of Denzil Holles, though placing her subject squarely in the ranks of the 'Puritan' group in Parliament in the late 1620s, has virtually nothing to say about his personal religion (*Denzil Holles, 1598-1680* [London 1979], passim). Vernon Snow, in his biography of the 3rd Earl of Essex, has little to say about the rebel's religion. Snow writes: 'Essex's personal religious views remain extremely difficult to ascertain'; Essex was 'a militant Protestant, a staunch antipapist ... [with] a broad-minded attitude towards the religious differences of his day' (*Essex the Rebel* [Lincoln 1970], 253-4). See also Ruth Spalding, *The Improbable Puritan: a Life of Bulstrode Whitelocke, 1605-1675* (London 1975).

42 For the study which blazed the trail in its reassessment of the significance of the Arminian movement in England's religious and political history during the 1620s and 1630s see N.R.N. Tyacke, 'Arminianism in England: Religion and Politics 1604-1640' (D Phil thesis, Oxford University, 1969).

43 State Papers, Public Record Office [hereafter SP], 14/153/103, 106, 108; Calendar of State Papers, Venetian [hereafter CSP Ven.] 1623-5, 147; for a contemporary account of the Blackfriars accident see Samuel Clarke, *The Doleful Even-Song* (London 1623), reprinted in Henry Foley, *Records of the English Province of the Society of Jesus* (4 vols., London 1877), I, 78-86; see also Samuel R. Gardiner, *History of England from the Accession of James I to the Outbreak of the Civil War, 1603-42* (10 vols., London 1884), V, 142-3. For a systematic

review of the Elizabethan and Jacobean anti-recusant legislation, see J.A.
Williams, *Catholic Recusancy in Wiltshire, 1660-1791* (London 1968), 4-16.

44 J. Gee, *The Foot out of the Snare* (London 1624), passim.

45 SP, 16/2/1, 16/7/28; CSP Ven., 1625-6, 70, 96-9, 118, 129, 156, 177, 189, 190,
212, 221, 231, 236; Gardiner, *History of England*, V, 249ff; Russell, *Parliaments*,
204-19; Richard Challoner, *Memoirs of Missionary Priests* (London 1924), 359-
62; F.C. Dietz, 'The Receipts and Issues of the Exchequer during the Reigns of
James I and Charles I,' *Smith College Studies in History*, XIII, 4, 1928, 136-51;
F.C. Dietz, 'The Exchequer in Elizabeth's Reign,' *Smith College Studies in History*, VIII, 2, 1923, 80-9; Gordon Albion, *Charles I and the Court of Rome* (London 1938), 4

46 SP, 16/96/8; J.G. Nicholls, ed., 'The Discovery of the Jesuits' College at Clerkenwell,' *Camden Miscellany*, II, 1853; *CD 1628*, II, 41; Russell, *Parliaments*, 343;
CD 1629, 74-83, 98. On 23 February 1629, virtually the last day of 'normal' proceedings, in this the last Parliament before 1640, the House of Commons issued
its Heads and Articles which blamed the danger of religion in part on '1. the sus-
pension of negligent execution of the laws against Popery: instance, in the late
proceedings against the College of Jesuits. 2. Diverse letters sent by Mr. Attorney into the country for stay of proceedings against Recusants.' For a contemporary account of the response of the members of the House of Commons to the
freeing of the Clerkenwell Jesuits see Nethersole's Letters in *CD 1629*, 249-50.

47 *CD 1629*, 13

48 *CD 1629*, 96-7, 64, 70; *LJ*, III, 701, 703-4, 707. It is worth emphasizing that there
was a good deal of truth underlying many of these allegations concerning the
growth of popery in the 1620s. Recent estimates of the size of the English
Catholic community suggest that there were slightly fewer than 40,000 in 1603
and slightly fewer than 60,000 on the eve of the Civil War. Accompanying this
increase in the size of the English lay Catholic population was a remarkable
increase in the number of priests working in the English mission. Between 1603
and 1641 the number of priests in England rose from around 300 to around 725,
including a rise in the number of Jesuit missioners from around 20 at the death
of Elizabeth to around 175 in 1641. By the 1620s the number of Jesuits in England was deemed sufficient to justify the creation of an English province of the
Society of Jesus. Similarly, the secular priests were organized when William
Bishop was consecrated titular Bishop of Chalcedon and, in effect, the first English Catholic bishop since the Reformation. In addition, there were approxi-
mately 1100 English Catholics in seminaries, monasteries, and colleges in the
Spanish Low Countries. See generally John Bossy, *The English Catholic Community, 1570-1850* (London 1975), esp. 216-20, 419; J.C.H. Aveling, *The Handle
and the Axe* (London and Colchester, 1976), esp. chap. 3; Caroline M. Hibbard,

'Early Stuart Catholicism: Revisions and Re-Revisions,' *Journal of Modern History*, LII, 1, 1980, 1-34. As Hibbard observes, 'the "jesuit invasion" perceived by English Protestants was not an imagined phenomenon' (11). Bossy's estimate of the number of Catholics in England in the seventeenth century, 60,000 in 1640, which makes them slightly more than 1 per cent of the population, is much lower than that of some other historians. J.P. Kenyon, for instance, has suggested that there were 260,000 Catholics in 1670 and that the size of the Catholic community had been gradually declining. Some years earlier, Bryan Magee had estimated the number of Catholics at 400,000. Each of these estimates can be instructively compared with that of Nicolo Molin, Venetian ambassador to England, who wrote in 1607 that the Catholics were 'a third, or perhaps a little more, of the entire population,' which, as we now believe, would amount to around 1.3 million. John Kenyon, *The Popish Plot* (London 1972), 24; B. Magee, *The English Recusants* (London 1938), 111-12, 115-17. For a study of relations between the court of Charles I and that of Rome see Albion, *Charles I and the Court of Rome; CSP Ven.*, 1603-7, 571; Keith Wrightson, *English Society, 1580-1680* (London 1982), 122.

49 *CD 1629*, 12-17, 20-1. For a discussion of Pym's political life in the 1620s largely in terms of his anti-popery see Conrad Russell, 'The Parliamentary Career of John Pym,' in Clark, Smith, Tyacke, eds., *The English Commonwealth*; Russell, *Parliaments*, 410-11; Fletcher, *The Outbreak*, xxivff. Fletcher is quite right to emphasize Pym's deep sense of the conspiracy throughout the 1620s but he is less convincing when he claims that Pym 'had often been a one man band.'

50 *CD 1629*, 12, 66, 95-101

51 Ibid., 13; see also note 40.

52 *CD 1629*, 15, 27, 35-6; *CJ*, I, 926

53 William Haller's view of John Foxe's contribution to the formation of English self-consciousness has in recent years been significantly revised by a number of historians, most notably Richard Bauckham, Paul Christianson, Katherine Firth, Christopher Hill, William Lamont, and J. Sears McGee. For further discussion of the way Haller's interpretation of Foxe has been modified see chapter 5, 134-7. Notwithstanding the revision of Haller he was, I think, making an important observation when he wrote, 'Englishmen in general in the reign of Elizabeth accepted [the Book of Martyrs] as an expression of the national faith second in authority only to the Bible and as an unanswerable defence of England's ideological position in the contemporary struggle for national independence and power' (*Foxe's Book of Martyrs and the Elect Nation* [London 1963], 14).

54 *CD 1629*, 14-15

55 Ibid., 16, 67

56 Protestation of the House of Commons, reprinted in Samuel Rawson Gardiner, ed., *The Constitutional Documents of the Puritan Revolution, 1628-60* (Oxford 1889), 82-3

57 *CD 1629*, 12

58 See, for example, Perez Zagorin, *The Court and the County* (London 1969), chaps. 7-9; Keeler, *Long Parliament*, passim; Fletcher, *The Outbreak*; Hexter, *The Reign of King Pym*.

59 The interpretation of the history of the early Long Parliament primarily in terms of the conspiratorial preoccupations of the parliamentary leadership is most fully articulated in Fletcher, *The Outbreak*. The problem with Fletcher's approach, however, is that he attempts to reconcile this new recognition of the obsessive nature of the concerns of Pym and his associates with the old reliance on 'Puritanism' as the ultimate explanation. On the one hand he writes that for some, 'far-reaching reform of the Church remained paramount ... [while] ... belief in the imminence of the millennium inculcated a drastic and sharply depicted view of parliament's destiny,' yet at the same time he recognizes that 'there was a large spectrum of opinion between those who merely wanted to do away with the Arminian innovations and those who aimed to rid the country of the whole Elizabethan liturgy.' What he has not established, however, is the truth of Gardiner's belief that the 'core' of the parliamentary party, without which there would not have been war, was 'Puritan.' For all of his acute sensitivity to the almost pathological nature of anti-Catholic sentiment in the Long Parliament in 1641, Fletcher nonetheless has a disconcerting tendency to label individuals and groups as 'Puritans' even though they were not conspicuous for their zeal to complete the reform of the Elizabethan church (*The Outbreak*, esp. 122-4, 374, 417).

60 Wallace Notestein, ed., *The Journal of Sir Simonds D'Ewes from the Beginning of the Long Parliament to the Opening of the Trial of the Earl of Strafford* (New Haven 1923), 7, 15-17, 78; *CJ*, II, 24, 38, 39; Robin Clifton, 'Fear of Popery,' in Conrad Russell, ed., *The Origins of the English Civil War* (London 1973), 159

61 *CJ*, II, 41-2, 44; Notestein, *D'Ewes*, 89, 91, 101, 112. See also *Calendar of State Papers Domestic, 1640-41*, ed. William Douglas Hamilton (London 1882), 291-5.

62 Notestein, *D'Ewes*, 8, 24-5, 28, 36, 53; E. Hyde, Earl of Clarendon, *The History of the Rebellion and Civil Wars in England* (1702-4; 6 vols., ed. W.D. Macray, Oxford 1888), I, 328; *CJ*, II, 34

63 Notestein, *D'Ewes*, 14, 213, 229, 59

64 Robin Clifton, 'The Popular Fear of Catholics during the English Revolution,' *Past and Present*, no 52, 1971, 27-8

65 Notestein, *D'Ewes*, 348; *CJ*, II, 132; Fletcher, *The Outbreak*, 32. For a discussion

of the controversy in the House of Commons concerning the precise meaning of the religious clauses of the Protestation see Fletcher, *The Outbreak*, 113ff.

66 Notestein, *D'Ewes*, 24

67 Ibid., 8

68 Ibid., 15, 146-8

69 Ibid., 155; A.H.A. Hamilton, ed., *John Northcotes' Notebook* (London 1877), 71

70 *CJ*, II, 51-2

71 L.B. Larking, ed., *Proceedings, principally in the County of Kent* (Camden Society Publications 1862), 28-9. For a discussion of the Root and Branch Petitions and of the Root and Branch Bill see Fletcher, *The Outbreak*, 91ff.

72 Clarendon, *History*, I, 244-5, 308-10; Gardiner, *History of England*, X, 12-13. Gardiner would doubtless not take issue with Fletcher when the latter wrote that the hallmarks of the Royalist position in November 1641 included 'defence of the Church and the king's prerogative' (*The Outbreak*, 153). See also Yule, *Puritans in Politics*, 110ff; Morrill, 'The Church in England, 1642-9,' 93.

73 Notestein, *D'Ewes*, 29-30, 233

74 Rushworth, *Historical Collection*, IV, 111, 183; Notestein, *D'Ewes*, 336. Clifton makes a similar point when he suggests that 'in many respects Jacobean and Caroline anti-Catholicism perpetuated and re-directed pre-Reformation lay antagonism towards the clergy' ('Fear of Popery,' 148). See also James Fulton Maclear, 'Popular Anti-clericalism in the Puritan Revolution,' *Journal of the History of Ideas*, XVII, 4, 1956, 443-70.

75 Notestein, *D'Ewes*, 341-2, 140, 249; Willson Havelock Coates, ed., *The Journal of Sir Simonds D'Ewes from the First Recess of the Long Parliament to the Withdrawal of King Charles from London* (New Haven 1942), 30

76 Fletcher, *The Outbreak*, 98, 106. Elsewhere, Fletcher has argued that the debates over the Root and Branch Bill in 1641 demonstrated an attempt to legislate 'the authentic puritan programme of evangelical revival which had preoccupied gentry in many parts of England since the 1570's and 1580's.' Yet, at the same time, he shows that the bill was not divisive and enjoyed the support of almost the entire House of Commons. These two statements may be reconciled only by either assuming the entire House of Commons in June-July 1641 to be 'Puritan,' which no historian has ever said, or by regarding the bill as not a significant mark of 'Puritanism.' Anthony Fletcher, 'Concern for Renewal in the Root and Branch Debates of 1641,' in Derek Baker, ed., *Renaissance and Renewal in Christian History* (Studies in Church History, vol. 14; Oxford 1977), 284-6. Anthony Fletcher, 'Factionalism in Town and Countryside: the Significance of Puritanism and Arminianism,' in Derek Baker, ed., *The Church in Town and*

Countryside (Studies in Church History, vol. 16; Oxford 1979). See also Derek Hirst, 'The Defection of Sir Edward Dering, 1640-41,' *Historical Journal*, XV, 2, 1972, 193-208.

77 Notestein, *D'Ewes*, 200-1. See also A.G. Matthews, *Walker Revised* (Oxford and London 1948), 344.

78 Notestein, *D'Ewes*, 232-3; *CJ*, II, 65

79 Notestein, *D'Ewes*, 270

80 *CJ*, II, 287; *LJ*, IV, 391-6. For a discussion of the declaration see Fletcher, *The Outbreak*, 115ff.

81 Coates, *D'Ewes*, 14-15; *LJ*, IV, 398-9. See also Robin Clifton, 'The Fear of Catholics in England, 1637-1645' (D Phil. thesis, Oxford University, 1967), 155, 222-4.

82 Coates, *D'Ewes*, 58, 101, 104

83 *LJ* IV, 439-40; Coates, *D'Ewes*, 147; *CJ*, II, 318-19. For an account of the importance of anti-Catholic alarms in the politics of the early Long Parliament see R. Clifton, 'Fear of Popery.' Clifton writes: 'The alarms occurred in a very clear chronological pattern. Five distinct concentrations can be seen between April 1640 and August 1642, each coinciding with a period of major political crisis' (158). See also Fletcher, *The Outbreak*, passim.

84 The complete text of the Grand Remonstrance is printed in Gardiner, ed., *Constitutional Documents*, 202-32, esp. 206; Coates, *D'Ewes*, 185.

85 Larking, ed., *Proceedings in Kent*, 73. For an example of an historian with a profound respect for the persuasive power of a 'Puritan' sermon see Yule, *Puritans in Politics*, 75-82.

86 G.E. Aylmer has recently made a similar observation. 'If we emphasize the importance of religion, must we assume that the Civil War and what followed it occurred because some people were positively set on obtaining a new, and more radically Protestant, kind of Church settlement? May it not rather have been because many people were desperately afraid of a religious counter-revolution, seeing Archbishop Laud, Charles I, and the Arminians as the spearhead of a popish restoration?' 'Crisis and Regrouping in the Political Elites: England from the 1630's to the 1660's,' in J.G.A. Pocock, ed., *Three British Revolutions: 1641, 1688, 1776* (Princeton 1980), 140-1.

87 Coates, *D'Ewes*, 151; Gardiner, ed., *Documents*, 229-30

CHAPTER 5

1 For a stimulating discussion of late nineteenth-century German anti-Semitism, see Uriel Tal, *Christians and Jews in Germany: Religion, Politics and Ideology*

in the Second Reich, 1870-1914 (Cornell 1975); George L. Mosse, *The Crisis of German Ideology* (London 1966), esp. chap. 5. On American nativism see John Higham, *Strangers in the Land* (New Jersey 1955); Ray Allen Billington, *The Protestant Crusade* (New York 1938). See also Richard Hofstadter, *The Paranoid Style in American Politics* (New York 1964).

2 See J.R. Jones, *The First Whigs* (London 1961); J.R. Jones, *The Revolution of 1688 in England* (London 1972); J.R. Jones, ed., *The Restored Monarchy 1660-1688* (London 1979).

3 Jones, *Revolution*, 75; Jones, *First Whigs*, 10-12

4 J.R. Western, *Monarchy and Revolution* (London 1972), 2

5 John Miller, *Popery and Politics in England, 1660-1688* (Cambridge 1973), 82

6 Douglas R. Lacey, *Dissent and Parliamentary Politics in England, 1661-1689* (New Brunswick 1969), 30, 34-5

7 I.S. Wechsler, 'Some Remarks on the Psychology of Antisemitism,' in Koppel S. Pinson, ed., *Essays on Antisemitism* (New York 1946), 35, 38. See also Robert Gellately, 'Problems of Modern Anti-Semitism in Germany,' *Canadian Journal of History*, XII, 3, Feb. 1978, 383-8.

8 For an account of the transformation of nineteenth-century German anti-Semitism see Mosse, *The Crisis*, chap. 5; Tal, *Christians and Jews*, passim; Peter G. Pulzer, *The Rise of Political Anti-Semitism in Germany and Austria* (New York 1964).

9 J.G.A. Pocock, *The Ancient Constitution and the Feudal Law* (New York 1967), 195, chap. VIII, passim.

10 Anchitell Grey, *Debates of the House of Commons from the Year 1667 to the Year 1694* (10 vols., London 1769), VIII, 132

11 M.D., *Friendly Advice to Protestants* (London 1680), 3

12 Charles Blount, *An Appeal from the Country to the City* (London 1679), 7

13 Grey, *Debates*, VII, 149; Edward Pelling, *A Sermon preached on 30 January* (London 1679), 3; Edward Stillingfleet, *A Sermon preached ... 13 November* (London 1678), 2-3; Miller, *Popery*, 72-3. For an account of the growth of 17 November, Queen Elizabeth's accession day, as a day of public celebration see J.E. Neale, 'November 17th,' in his book *Essays in Elizabethan History* (London 1958).

14 Blount, *An Appeal*, 2

15 Gilbert Burnet, *A Letter, written upon the discovery* (London 1678), 1-2, 42-3

16 Gilbert Burnet, *A Sermon preached ... 30 January* (London 1681), 10-11, 16-17; Gilbert Burnet, *A Sermon preached ... 5 November* (London 1684), 27-8

17 Burnet, *Sermon*, 30 Jan. 1681, 13

18 Thomas Barlow, *Popery, or the Principles and Positions approved by the Church of Rome* (London 1679), 3, 72-3

19 Helen Stocks and W.H. Stevenson, eds., *Records of the Borough of Leicester, 1603-88* (Cambridge 1923), 549

20 Richard Baxter, *Reliquiae Baxterianae* (London 1696), 29. William M. Lamont notes that Baxter 'supported the Parliament in the Civil War because he thought that Irish Papists with the real (or forged) consent of Charles I were determined on the destruction of the Protestant Kingdom' (*Richard Baxter and the Millennium* [London 1979], 119).

21 William Cobbett, ed., *The Parliamentary History of England (1066-1803)* (36 vols., London 1806-20), IV, 1043; Grey, *Debates*, VII, 414

22 Gregory Hascard, *A Sermon preached upon the Fifth of November* (London 1678), 31; A Lover of his King and Country, *The Countries' Vindication* (London 1679), 1

23 M.D., *Friendly Advice*, 5

24 *Poems on Affairs of State*, ed. G. de F. Lord et al. (7 vols., New Haven 1963-75), II, 423

25 Roger L'Estrange, *A Seasonable Memorial in some Historical Notes upon the Liberties of the Press and Pulpit* (London 1680), 37; Roger L'Estrange, *A Memento Treating of the Rise, Progress and Remedies of Seditions* (London 1682), 18, 9, 13; Roger L'Estrange, *An Account of the Growth of Knavery* (London 1678); Roger L'Estrange, *An Answer to the Appeal from the Country* (London 1681), 23-6, 4, 17. See George Kitchin, *Sir Roger L'Estrange* (London 1913).

26 Roger L'Estrange, *A Compendious History of the Most Remarkable Passages of the Last Fourteen Years* (London 1680), 2-7

27 *The Protestants' Petition Against Popery* (London 1681)

28 John Nalson, *The Common Interest of King and People* (London 1677), 196-7, 208, 257

29 *The Cloak and its Colours* (London 1679), 9; Earl of Halifax, 'A Seasonable Address to both Houses of Parliament, 1681,' in *Somers Tracts* (13 vols., London 1809-15), VIII, 226

30 Edward Pelling, *A Sermon preached on the Thirtieth of January* (London 1679), 3; Anon, *An Impartial Survey of such as are not ... fitly qualified* (London 1679), 2; Henry Hesketh, *A Sermon preached ... 30 January* (London 1678), 37

31 William Dugdale, *A Short View of the Late Troubles in England* (London 1681), 36; Grey, *Debates*, VII, 411

32 *A Letter to the Earl of Shaftesbury* (London 1680), 2-3; Edmund Hickeringill, *Curse Ye Meroz* (London 1680), 23; Grey, *Debates*, VII, 385

33 The recent literature on sixteenth-century apocalyptic thought and seventeenth-century millenarianism includes William M. Lamont, *Godly Rule: Politics and Religion, 1603-60* (London 1969); Lamont, *Baxter*; Richard Bauckham, *Tudor*

Apocalypse (Abingdon 1978); Paul Christianson, *Reformers and Babylon: English Apocalyptic Visions from the Reformation to the Eve of the Civil War* (Toronto 1978); Katharine R. Firth, *The Apocalyptic Tradition in Reformation Britain, 1530–1645* (Oxford 1979); Christopher Hill, *Antichrist in Seventeenth Century England* (London 1971); Bryan W. Ball, *A Great Expectation: Eschatological Thought in English Protestantism to 1660* (Leiden 1975).

34 Bauckham, *Tudor Apocalypse*, esp. 13; Firth, *Apocalyptic Tradition*, 73ff

35 See Firth, *Apocalyptic Tradition*, passim; Bauckham, *Tudor Apocalypse*, esp. chap. 11 and 235–8; Lamont, *Godly Rule*, 8; see also K.Thomas, *Religion and the Decline of Magic* (London 1971), 169.

36 Lamont, *Godly Rule*, esp. chap. 4; Christianson, *Reformers*, 102, 129–30

37 Bauckham, *Tudor Apocalypse*, 12; Firth, *Apocalyptic Tradition*, 202; Lamont, *Godly Rule*, 33; W. Lamont, 'Richard Baxter, the Apocalypse and the Mad Major,' *Past and Present*, no 55, 1972, 71

38 Thomas, *Religion*, 171; see Hill, *Antichrist*, chap. 4, passim; Christianson, *Reformers*, 245; Lamont, *Godly Rule*, 20; Lamont, *Baxter*, 15; Miller, *Popery*, 88

39 Christianson, *Reformers*, 11

40 Edmund Bohun, 1645–1699, a vigorous opponent of both popery and dissent, wrote at great length through the 1680s in an attempt to win office. He was successful in becoming a licenser of the press but was dismissed in 1693. See *Dictionary of National Biography*. Gilbert Burnet, 1643–1715, effectively banished from England by both Charles II and James II, was probably the most influential churchman during and after the Revolution of 1688 as Bishop of Salisbury.

41 Grey, *Debates*, VIII, 145, 129; Halifax writes, 'knaves invent and fools believe, [Charles II] is now setting up for tyranny and popery ...' in *Somers Tracts*, VIII, 226; Edmund Bohun, *Diary and Autobiography*, ed. S. Wilton Rix (Beccles 1853), cited in K.H.D. Haley, *The First Earl of Shaftesbury* (Oxford 1968), 510. Bohun did not challenge the conventional identification of popery with arbitrary government. He did, however, question the intentions of the Whigs in 1678. In a comment on Marvell's 'Account of the Growth of Popery,' which he read in May 1678, Bohun wrote, 'The author is doubtless an honest puritan; his main design to teach the world the necessity and lawfulness of another rebellion; and, to that end, representing all the errors of government as intended enemies, and all the governors of the nation as a pack of fools and knaves; whereas, in truth, all the danger we lie under of popery or arbitrary government comes from the men of his faction.'

42 Blount, *An Appeal*, 1

43 Burnet, *Sermon*, 5 Nov. 1684, 10, 14, 17

44 *The Antichristian Principle* (London 1679), 27–31 (note pagination in British

Library edition is confusing. There are two sets of pages 17-30. This citation is for both sets). Grey, *Debates*, VII, 457, VIII, 129; W. Lloyd, *Sermon delivered at Funeral of Sir Edmund Bury Godfrey* (London 1678), 36. The contradiction between the violent paranoia apparent in the rhetoric of contemporaries when compared with the actual amity and toleration enjoyed by 'Papists of Quality' is acknowledged though not fully explained by those historians who have addressed themselves explicitly to the problem of seventeenth-century anti-Catholicism. See Robin Clifton, 'Fear of Popery,' in Conrad Russell, ed., *The Origins of the English Civil War* (London 1973), 164; Miller, *Popery*, 1, 16, 66; Conrad Russell, *Parliaments and English Politics, 1621-1628* (Oxford 1979), 120; J.P. Kenyon, *The Popish Plot* (London 1972), 25-6; K.H.D. Haley, ' "No Popery" in the Reign of Charles II,' *Britain and the Netherlands*, V, 1975, 106.

45 Gilbert Burnet, *A Sermon, 29 September* (London 1681), 29; Grey, *Debates*, VII, 51

46 Grey, *Debates*, VII, 149; Blount, *An Appeal*, 2

47 Grey, *Debates*, VII, 147, 256, *The Weekly Discovery of the Mystery of Iniquity*, no 1; M.D., *Friendly Advice*, 6; Blount, *An Appeal*, 8

48 Edward Pelling, *A Sermon preached on the Thirtieth of January* (London 1679), 3-4; see also Hill, *Antichrist*; Cobbett, *Parliamentary History*, IV, 1033; William Howell, *Medulla historiae anglicanae* (London 1679); Grey, *Debates*, VII, 147-8; *A Reply to the Second Return* (London 1682), 3. Philip Jenkins has recently described anti-popery as a 'long-standing British tradition, a national mythology, indeed the nearest thing in this period [the seventeenth century] to a popular ideology' ('Anti-popery on the Welsh Marches in the Seventeenth Century,' *Historical Journal*, XXIII, 2, 1980, 286).

49 In his account of anti-Catholicism in England on the eve of the Civil War, Robin Clifton considers the question of whether or not the fears were deliberately contrived and concludes that most of them were not. He writes that the frequency and the regularity of these outbreaks of fear suggest a 'very basic political attitude in the mass of the Protestant nation.' A similar argument can be made for the 1670s and 1680s ('The Popular Fear of Catholics during the English Revolution,' *Past and Present*, 52, 1971, 40-1).

50 George Elliott, ed., 'Autobiography and Anecdotes by William Taswell,' in *Camden Miscellany*, II, 1853, 11; Gilbert Burnet, *History of his own Time* (6 vols., Oxford 1833), I, 421-2; *Life of Edward, Earl of Clarendon* (3 vols., Oxford 1827), III, 84-96. *Calendar of State Papers, Domestic, Charles II, 1666-67*, ed. Mary A.E. Green (vol. VI, London 1864), 127. The author of this document, Ralph Hope, was testifying to the extent of the belief in popish responsibility for the fire, but he was not himself persuaded. He wrote: 'It is impossible to persuade the people into any other belief than that the Papists have a design to rise

and cut their throats and they impute the late sad conflagration solely to their continuance and propagation.' See also Walter G. Bell, *The Great Fire of London* (London 1920).

51 Taswell, 'Autobiography,' 11; *The Diary of Samuel Pepys*, ed. Robert Latham and William Matthews (10 vols., London 1970-6), VII, 356. See also Michael McKeon, *Politics and Poetry in Restoration England: the Case of Dryden's Annus Mirabilis* (Camb., Mass. 1975), 140ff.

52 Cited in McKeon, *Politics*, 140-1; Andrew Marvell, *An Account of the Growth of Popery* (Amsterdam 1677), 13

53 Cited in McKeon, *Politics*, 145; Pepys, *Diary*, VII, 407

54 For a fuller discussion of this point see Maurice Lee, *The Cabal* (Urbana, Ill. 1965), 186-8.

55 Burnet, *History*, I, 564-5. *Diary of Alexander Brodie*, ed. D. Laing (Aberdeen 1863), 327. *The Diary of John Evelyn*, ed. E.S. de Beer (6 vols., Oxford 1955), III, 608. Haley, *Shaftesbury*, 297-8. See also Lee, *Cabal*, 189-91.

56 *Journals of the House of Lords* (18 vols., 1767), XII, 524-5 [hereafter *LJ*]; Haley, *Shaftesbury*, 316 ff.

57 *LJ*, XII, 524-5

58 Grey, *Debates*, II, 11, 32, 78; *Journals of the House of Commons* (17 vols., 1803), IX, 250, 261 [hereafter *CJ*]. K.H.D. Haley, *William of Orange and the English Opposition, 1672-4* (Oxford 1953), 96. Maurice Lee makes essentially the same point: 'The Commons' firmness in regard to the Declaration was certainly due in part to their dislike of Charles' use of the prerogative virtually to nullify a statute. Far more important, however, was their fear of any concession to the Catholics' (*Cabal*, 197).

59 Basil Duke Henning, ed., *The Parliamentary Diary of Sir Edward Dering, 1670-73* (New Haven 1940), 128-9; Grey, *Debates*, II, 52; David Ogg, *England in the Reign of Charles II*, (2 vols., London 1956); Haley, *William*, 96

60 Stocks and Stevenson, eds., *Records of the Borough of Leicester*, 535, 546; *Victoria County History of Leicester* (5 vols., London 1907-64), IV, 112-13; *Return of the Names of Every Member Returned to Serve in Each Parliament* (3 vols., London 1878), I, 524

61 H.M. Margoliouth, ed., *Poems and Letters of Andrew Marvell* (3rd ed., 2 vols., Oxford 1971), II, 157-65. As in the 1620s, so during the reign of Charles II the anti-recusant legislation was honoured more in the breach than in the observance. No Catholics, clerical or lay, were executed between the Restoration and 1678 nor were the Catholic gentry severely mulcted. J.A. Williams has suggested that whereas the Convention Parliament had assumed, or pretended, that recusants would 'contribute' £18,600 per annum to the Exchequer, by 1672 their total fines amounted to £145 15s7d. The figure increases somewhat during the second

half of Charles II's reign but it never approaches the £32,000 collected in 1640. See J.A. Williams, *Recusancy in Wiltshire, 1660-1791* (London 1968), 17; J.A. Williams, 'English Catholicism under Charles II: the legal Position,' *Recusant History*, VII, 3, 1963, 138-9; J.A. Williams, 'Some Sidelights on Recusancy Fines under Charles II,' *Dublin Review*, no 481, 1959, 249-54; Richard Challoner, *Memoirs of Missionary Priests* (London 1924), 362; F.C. Dietz, 'The Receipts and Issues of the Exchequer during the Reigns of James I and Charles I,' *Smith College Studies in History*, XIII, 4, 1928, 151.

62 Marvell, *An Account*, 3. It is a moot point whether the 1670s saw an absolute increase in the number of Catholics in England. Philip Jenkins has recently suggested that 'the "growth of popery" much bemoaned in the 1670's was not entirely a myth,' whereas scholars such as John Bossy and Caroline Hibberd seem to be of the view that the Jacobean and early Caroline period saw the revival of English Catholicism at its peak. It is their opinion that the number of Catholics in England remained fairly static at around 60,000 for more than a century after 1640. Miller agrees with this estimate of the size of the Catholic population in the 1670s but suggests that there was a smaller number of priests – about 500 – which compares with about 725 in 1640. See Philip Jenkins, 'Antipopery on the Welsh Marches in the Seventeenth Century,' *Historical Journal*, XXIII, 2, 1980, 280. John Bossy, *The English Catholic Community, 1570-1850* (London 1975), 189; Miller, *Popery*, 40. See also chap. 4, n48.

63 Marvell, *An Account*, 5-7, 12-14

64 J.P. Kenyon, *The Popish Plot* (London 1972), 264-70

65 Grey, *Debates*, VI, 189, 204

66 Ibid., 126; *CJ*, IX, 524-30

67 Grey, *Debates*, V, 64-7. K.H.D. Haley has stressed the reasonableness of the fears of popery in the 1670s, pointing to the 'visibly increasing Catholic influences at Court,' the uncertainty concerning the number of Catholics, and the legitimate fear of the power that a Catholic monarch might exercise (' "No Popery," ' 113-17).

68 Grey, *Debates*, VII, 358-65; Haley, *Shaftesbury*, 554-5

69 Grey, *Debates*, 384-5

70 Ibid., VIII, 296

71 Ibid., 13, 35, 101, 105, 133

72 Ibid., 11, 132, 163-7

73 Baxter, *Reliquiae*, Part III, 181. *Memoirs of Sir John Reresby*, ed. Andrew Browning (Glasgow 1936), 152. Brodie, *Diary*, 404, 409. As W.L. Lamont's study of Baxter suggests, the great Nonconformist minister shared the common sixteenth- and seventeenth-century Protestant reading of the prophecies of Daniel and of Revelation fundamental to which, as we have seen, was a dialecti-

cal historicism, a continuous historical conflict between the Reformed forces of light and the popish forces of darkness. He appears to have believed in the reality of the popish conspirators in 1678 just as firmly as he had in 1641. See Lamont, *Baxter*, esp. 12, 119.

74 See J.R. Jones, 'The Green Ribbon Club,' *Durham University Journal*, XVIII, 1956, 17-19; Miller, *Popery*, 182-8. For accounts of the popular processions held on 17 November in the late 1670s see O.W. Furley, 'The Pope Burning Processions of the Late Seventeenth Century,' *History*, XLIV, 1959, 16-23; S. Williams, 'The Pope-Burning Processions of 1679, 1680 and 1681,' *Journal of the Warburg and Courtauld Institute*, XXI, 1, 1958, 103-12.

75 See, for example, Jones, *The Revolution of 1688*.

76 *State Tracts* (2 vols., London 1693), II, 435-6; Reresby, *Memoirs*, 528, 532-3

77 Evelyn, *Diary* IV, 596-600

78 Reresby, *Memoirs*, 537; *London Courant*, 12-14 Dec. 1688, cited in W.L. Sachse, 'The Mob and the Revolution of 1688,' *Journal of British Studies*, IV, 1964, 30, 40. See also Max Beloff, *Public Order and Popular Disturbances. 1660-1714* (Oxford 1938), 40-2.

79 The Diary of Samuel Newton, Alderman of Cambridge, in J.E. Foster, ed., *Publications of the Cambridge Antiquarian Society*, XXIII, 1890, 96

80 Robin Clifton anticipates this judgment when he writes: 'The emotions which, under Elizabeth, had unified and strengthened the nation against foreign attack were now turned inwards and helped to shatter it' ('Fear of Popery,' 167).

Index